Love and the Abyss

Love and the *Abyss*

An Essay on Finitude and Value

RALPH D. ELLIS

OPEN COURT
Chicago and La Salle, Illinois

To order books from Open Court, call toll-free 1-800-815-2280, or visit our website at www.opencourtbooks.com.

Open Court Publishing Company is a division of Carus Publishing Company.

Copyright © 2004 by Carus Publishing Company

First printing 2004

All rights reserved. No part of this publication may be reproduced, stored in a retrieval system, or transmitted, in any form or by any means, electronic, mechanical, photocopying, recording, or otherwise, without the prior written permission of the publisher, Open Court Publishing Company, 315 Fifth Street, P.O. Box 300, Peru, Illinois 61354-0300.

Printed and bound in the United States of America.

Library of Congress Cataloging-in-Publication Data

Ellis, Ralph D.
    Love and the abyss : an essay on finitude and value / Ralph D. Ellis.
       p.   cm.
  Includes bibliographical references and index.
    ISBN 0-8126-9457-0 (trade pbk. : alk. paper)
  1. Love. 2. Values. 3. Sex—Philosophy. 4. Interpersonal relations. I. Title.
  BD436.E46 2004
    128'.46—dc22
                                                      2004022651

Contents

Acknowledgments   vii

Introduction   1

1 Foundations for a Study of Interpersonal Value Experience   19
  1. Narcissism and the Circle of Egocentricity   19
  2. Can There Be Self-Understanding in the Wake of Postmodernism?   33
  3. Object Relations, Self Psychology, and Inspirational Effects of Transcendent Objects   50

2 Ways of Addressing the Finite Condition   63
  1. The Current Status of the Problem   63
  2. The Role of Symbolization in Primary Spiritual Partnership   85
  3. The Sense in Which the Experience of Spiritual Partnership Is an 'Experience of Positive Value'   95
  4. The Roles of Sexual Attraction and Sexual Polarity in Experiences of the Value of Being   100

3 Essential Dynamics of the Primary Transcendent Value Experience   117
  1. The Sexualization of Religious Experience in Relation to Transcendent Interpersonal Value   119

	2. A More Detailed Characterization of the Spiritual Partnership Effect	129
	3. Distinguishing Primary Spiritual Partnership from Other Interpersonal Value Experiences	137
4	**The Spreading-Out of Non-Egoistic and Nonhedonistic Valuation**	**165**
	1. Resistance against the Threat to Egocentricity	168
	2. The Spreading Effect as the Intensifying Edge of the Generalized Experience of Value	174
	3. Transferring Value Feelings to Derivative Objects and to Ideals that Organize the Self	182
	4. Nongraspingness and Gratitude	188
	5. From Spiritual Partnership to Generalized Agape	197
5	**The Interdependence of Courage and Compassion**	**201**
	1. The Problem of Evil and the Morality of Blame	206
	2. Fallacies in the Morality of Blame	213
	3. Toward a Constructive and Nonretributive Sense of Compassion	222
	Appendix: The Sexuality of Consciousness	**231**
	1. The Interdependence of Polarized Forms of Consciousness	239
	2. Critique of Jungian Formulations of Sexual Polarity	244
	3. Sexuality as a Catalyst for Self-Transcendence	250
	References	263
	Index	269

Acknowledgments

This book was twelve years in the making. Its initial inspiration and its long and slow metamorphoses through numerous drafts and versions are indebted to discussions and help from many kind friends and colleagues, whose thinking and careful criticisms kept the work on track even when I felt inadequate to the task, and also feared that in the end it would fall too far outside the specialized "problem areas" that tend to make up contemporary academic philosophy, psychology, and sociology. Perhaps as much as to me, the fundamental concepts of the book belong to Tracie Ravita, Gene Gendlin, and Randy Auxier, all of whom discussed the initial ideas with me before and during their formation and continuous reformulations, and contributed to their shape at a basic level. As in so much of my work, Gendlin's "focusing" method plays a crucial role. Several early and embarrassingly bad drafts of this manuscript were read and generously discussed with me by Shawn Beaty, Judith Bradford, Isaac Getz, Lloyd Gilden, Charlie Harvey, Joe Jones, Natika Newton, Robert Powell, Ed Ragsdale, Steve Rosen, and Jim Sauer. A target article (in press) overlapping with this book, in *The Pluralist*, includes commentaries by Harvey and by Jones, as well as by Gary Backhaus, Anthony Freeman, Robin Podolski, and Peter Zachar. A related target article in *Philosophy in the Contemporary World*, also in press, includes commentaries by Harvey, Jones, and Sauer, as well as by John Cogan, Bill Faw, and Ed Grippe. Still another target article in *Theoria* (in press) discusses the basic theory of emotion in which this book is grounded, and includes commentaries and/or related discussions by Cogan and Faw, as well as by Maria Adamos, Helena De Priester, and Louise Sundararajan. Moreover, my theory of emotion itself is partly derivative from that of Natika

Newton, my co-editor on the yearbook periodical *Consciousness & Emotion*, and it also owes a great deal to many of the contributors to *C&E*; I should especially single out Thomas Natsoulas and Jaak Panksepp as exerting crucial influences. Others too numerous to mention have generously commented on various aspects of the work during its genesis, especially at meetings of the Society for Phenomenology in the Human Sciences, the Society for Philosophy in the Contemporary World, the Society for Philosophy and Psychology, the Southern Society for Philosophy and Psychology, the Humanistic Psychology Division of the American Psychological Association, the Mid-South Philosophy Conference, the Society for Phenomenology and Existential Philosophy, and the Association for the Scientific Study of Consciousness. I hope that the book is now academically respectable as well as accessible to the lay reader. I really believe that this work is the product of a community of scholars, all of whose ideas are contained in it, and I hope that I have done justice to its expression. As always, I am also indebted to my wife Lynda for her kind encouragement and creative substantive contributions.

Introduction

A famous French chef recently learned that he was in danger of losing the widely coveted three-star Michelin rating that he shared with only twenty-four other chefs in all of France. Before receiving the news that the third star was not to be lost after all, he had already put a gun into his mouth and committed suicide. While these professional problems may only have triggered the suicide of an already clinically depressed man, he must have been clinging to his professional accomplishments as a very important source of meaning in life. By contrast, from the standpoint of the man's wife, the idea that a slight professional setback could have triggered this suicide was unthinkable.

Whether someone is clinically depressed or not, many serious problems, both philosophical and psychological, can result from confusion between merely instrumental values on the one hand, such as fame and career accomplishments whose purpose is to serve as means to other ends, and on the other hand real intrinsic values that can be valued for their own sake. The sophistication, social complexity, and cosmopolitanism of modern and contemporary cultures do not create this problem, but they do greatly exacerbate it, because modernity seems to bring with it an increased demand to contend with two interconnected problems: a tendency toward narcissistic overconcern with objectified self-imagery; and a heightened need to come to grips satisfactorily with the finitude of human existence—its finitude not only in time (as Heidegger and the classic existentialists emphasize), but also in power, significance, and experienced value. The attempt to substitute instrumental values for intrinsic ones and the failure to experience intrinsic values intensely enough to overshadow the negativity of our own finitude and limitations are particularly characteristic of modern and postmodern cultures, although not their exclusive domain. What I want to suggest in this book is that these problems also affect and are affected by the ability to love (as distinguished from the desire to be loved), and that the most intractable failures and misunderstandings of love stem from the two more fundamental problems just mentioned—narcissism and existential finitude—which need to be recognized as interconnected with the basic dynamics of the need to love.

If the dynamics of love, by their very nature, are intrinsically tied in with the problems of finitude—from which narcissistic disturbance is an attempted escape—then it would be predictable that cultures most afflicted with hubris and narcissism would also systematically fail to see these connections. They would misunderstand love by neglecting to consider that complete acceptance of the daunting facts of finitude is the first step to compassion, which in turn is the foundation of love, our consolation and inspiration in the face of adversity.

But how could such seemingly unrelated phenomena as love and finitude be intrinsically connected? Suppose for a moment that narcissism, as Christopher Lasch has claimed, is increasingly prevalent in modern and postmodern cultures where individuals are evaluated according to their instrumental rather than intrinsic value—their value in the eyes of others. It is possible to acknowledge such a condition without taking up all of Lasch's intellectual baggage, and I shall not attempt to take it up here. But if some such generally narcissistic condition exists, it would both create a heightened need for a positive value experience, to counterbalance the negativity of the unresolved finitude issues, and at the same time would render impossible a fully intensified experience of value. The reason for this last effect, to summarize preliminarily, is that narcissism fundamentally demands a denial or repression of finitude, in one way or another. The narcissist must hide her own ontological frailty from herself (not to say vulnerability to trivial, everyday concerns, which of course many narcissists, especially 'unsuccessful' ones, never tire of enumerating; everyday complaints can actually *mask* existential ones, in a variety of ways, as discussed further below—for example, by providing excuses for failure). In hiding the real extent of the basic existential threats from herself, the narcissist also must hide them from the other, and by projection she must also deny the essential vulnerability of the other's existential project—yet the sympathetic understanding of this existential vulnerability is a precondition for a full empathic appreciation of the other's basic existential condition, which in turn is a prerequisite for an emotionally intense and thus inspiring experience (familiar to many lovers, if only fleetingly) of the intrinsic value of being as instantiated in that person. Given the narcissistic escape from the significance of finitude, compassion for the other's finitude cannot sufficiently intensify admiration for her as a courageous but endangered conscious being embattled by the existential implications of this finitude—nor therefore the resulting feeling of inspiration needed to overcome the negativity of our own finitude. Instead, the other becomes a neglectful though omnipotent deity—a 'bad mother' who has wickedly withheld the promised perfect happiness so prominently advertised in popular romance novels, as Denis de Rougemont, Robert Johnson, and many other Jungians have amply observed.

I shall argue that this conflict between narcissism and the direct experience of intrinsic value is played out in the very structuring and traditional practices of what Lasch has called the 'narcissistic culture.' Contemporary attitudes toward human relationships are both direct and indirect results of the increasing narcissism of our culture. Direct effects include the influence of authors who theorize about love, such as (to name a few) Stendahl, Reich, Sartre, Marcuse, and the early Freud (prior to Freud's later rethinking of his own overly reductionistic assumptions). These thinkers fail to grasp the existential function of love relationships as intense, direct experiences of the intrinsic value of being as instantiated in the love object; instead, they interpret the value of relationships in terms of the desire of lovers to affirm their own value through the other's affirmation of them (thus reducing themselves in true narcissistic fashion to instrumental values). And the indirect effects of narcissism on attitudes toward human relationships are evident in the increasingly narcissistic self-imagery of the age, which reduces the individual to an instrumental value, thus leading to preoccupation with self-evaluations as if in the eyes of others. Under these conditions, even erotic love becomes an exchange between guarded and defensive individuals who are reluctant to allow visibility to each other's vulnerability, and must allow myths of extreme personal importance, merit, and admirability to eclipse the inspiring feeling of the value of being via intensified compassion. Even the increasingly prevalent self-image of dysfunctional victimhood serves (somewhat unsuccessfully) the same narcissistic escape from the problems of finitude, because it pretends that, if not for contingent and unjust disadvantages, the self would be irreproachable and free of any weakness. The mythology of the Victim persona excuses all possible shortcomings and failures. Urban-industrial hubris also plays a role here by threatening to relegate the individual to the status of a replaceable consumer-producer, thus contributing to the problems of narcissism and the trivialization of relationships. Leisure time becomes increasingly viewed as a mixture of frivolous entertainment and the daily drudge work of keeping life going.

Psychologists in recent decades have been increasingly interested in the problems of narcissism from a clinical perspective, as witnessed by the rise of object relations theory and self psychology discussed below, as well as the number of psychological publications on narcissism and related issues. It should be of interest that narcissism has a profound effect on the existential meaning of the experience of others. On my analysis, love, like any experience of intrinsic value (as opposed to instrumental value, including pretty appearances), requires experiencing the other's value with greater intensity than one could ever experience one's own, through both compassion for the other's existential vulnerability in the face of finitude (as in Levinas's *Totality and Infinity*) and an exaggerated admiration (as in Reich) for the other's courageous attempts to face up to these problems. What Levinas notices that is missed by Reich is that this experience of extreme admiration is felt more deeply when the compassion element just mentioned is in turn sharpened. We cannot make ourselves the object of such an intensified intrinsic value experience through an admiration quickened by compassion, with ourselves functioning as both subject and object of the same experience, because to do so would exacerbate both narcissism and the depressing feeling of self-pity.

A person whose primary interest is in affirming her own value through objectified self-imagery, and who is preoccupied with this issue as in narcissistic disturbance, will have trouble allowing the dynamics of admiration-through-compassion, as I shall attempt to understand it here, to work effectively. But when a person cannot love intensely, there is an effect on the person's general ability to experience the positive value of being per se, since this experienced intrinsic value (I shall argue) is most powerfully instantiated in a love object. Thus there are a number of different kinds of aberrations that result from the effects of narcissism. These include not only dysfunctional psychological phenomena (many of which are within the 'normal' range and not necessarily confined to clinical cases), but also dysfunctions of the culture as a whole. Individuals evaluated only instrumentally by their culture then learn to evaluate themselves and others in those terms; they thus create increasingly narcissistic forms of social interaction, which in turn feed back into the same process and exacerbate the spiraling dynamic further and further.

Christopher Lasch, Heinz Kohut, Alice Miller, and many other recent authors have criticized contemporary culture for a ubiquitous narcissistic disturbance—an overconcern with the projection of attractive, invulnerable, and 'superior' images or masks—which increasingly forces us into what Lasch characterizes as a Hobbesian 'war of all against all.' The demand to renounce the fundamental egocentrism of this narcissistic value system stems partly from the pragmatic dysfunctions of the narcissistic culture, with which we are all painfully familiar: Narcissistic preoccupation with proving one's own superiority (or noninferiority) can contribute to a breakdown of family and personal relationships, the social isolation and economic insecurity of self-absorbed individuals in advanced-capitalist, postindustrial social systems, exaggerated competitiveness, inability to cooperate in addressing collective problems such as environmental destruction and the abandonment of the 'underclass,' and so forth. The mere recognition that egocentricity exacerbates these social problems does not resolve them, but only traps individuals into a prisoner's dilemma in which each of us feels powerless to unilaterally abandon egocentricity lest we be trampled upon.

But there seems to be another dimension of human beings that demands the renunciation of the narcissistic value system for a more essential reason. The all-too-obscure phenomenon that I shall call 'transcendent value experience' arises from a human need that appears to be so pressing that its widespread neglect serves only to quicken its urgency. When this need does thrust itself into the awareness of contemporary people, it seems to do so with deceptive simplicity—as a relentless desire to sharply and directly experience the intrinsic positive value of life as instantiated in a conscious being other than ourselves—and to appreciate it in a more inspiring way, with stronger feelings, than we could ever appreciate our own value. Almost every fictional work since the beginning of the nineteenth century focuses in one way or another on the way the power of this need can uncontrollably hurl itself into a person's life. Either the protagonist is overwhelmed by mysterious, involuntary feelings toward a love object or, as in more existential literature (Sartre or Camus or Sinclair Lewis's *Babbit*, for example), the person suddenly feels the lack of such a transcendent value experience without which life is then experienced as deficient in value and meaning.

Many people are familiar with this effect only in sexual contexts, through the experience of being 'in love' or 'infatuated' with someone; but I want to suggest that the need served by this kind of experience is not essentially erotic, and that the effects of this kind of reverent feeling toward other conscious beings in principle is transferrable to nonsexual contexts, and ultimately to a person's abstract value system. Such an intensely positive value experience is required (I shall argue) to serve the essentially 'spiritual' need to either overcome or somehow find meaning within the dilemma of our own finitude—death, alienation, powerlessness, and relative insignificance in the ultimate scheme of things. To fulfill this need, we must do more than intellectually acknowledge the value of conscious beings; we must feel it through concrete emotions. The structure of human motivation requires not only that the melody of positive meaning in life be played, but that it be played loudly enough to subordinate the countermelodies of pestilence, famine, war (in all its forms), and death.

By 'transcendent value experience,' I mean the direct experience of the intrinsic value of an object that transcends the 'circle of egocentricity.' The meaning of transcendent value experience thus hinges on a definition of the circle of egocentricity. Within the circle of egocentricity, the value of an object can be experienced only as intensely as, ultimately, some *inner experience* arising from the object is valued for its own sake. For example, the value of an ice cream cone is experienced only as intensely as the *enjoyment* it facilitates is intense. In the same way, from the standpoint of the circle of egocentricity, the value of a spouse or lover is experienced only to the extent that the feelings of *happiness* or *fulfillment* she facilitates have value; thus people speak as though the value of love relationships were to make the lovers 'happy.' Within the circle of egocentricity, even the value of a deity is experienced only as intensely as the feelings of *existential security* or *meaningful existence* that the deity facilitates are valued intensely. The person experiences the value of religion insofar as it facilitates personal immortality or a feeling that life has meaning. In general, within the circle of egocentricity, the value of each object can be experienced only to the extent that the *experience* it facilitates is valued; strictly speaking, only the *extrinsic* or *instrumental* value of the object can be experienced in this case, because its value is experienced as dependent on the *intrinsic* value of the experience that it facilitates.

Since no *extrinsic or instrumental* value can exceed the *intrinsic* value that it facilitates, this circle of egocentricity automatically renders all other objects less valuable (experientially) than the self and its own experience, and there is no object whose value can be experienced in a more intensely positive way than the self can experience its *own* value. However, as I have already hinted, there are structural impediments to the *emotional intensification* of the experience of one's own value (compared, for example, to the intensity of value feelings toward a love object); thus the circle of egocentricity imposes severe limits on the intensity of *all* positive value experiences, yet does not impose any corresponding limits on the intensity of *negative* value experiences. The circle of egocentricity therefore leads ultimately either to a feeling of excessive meaninglessness, or to thinly veiled and fragile psychological defenses against this feeling. I am not claiming that a person who *intellectually acknowledges* his or her own value is caught in the circle of egocentricity. My claim is that the *emotional intensification* of this value experience requires a transcendent object for intrinsic valuation—that is, an object whose value transcends the circle of egocentricity.

The circle of egocentricity is not the same as ethical egoism. A person may have altruistic values and still be caught in it. What I mean by the circle of egocentricity is a condition in which, regardless of whether values are altruistic, the *intensity* with which their value can be experienced is still limited by one's own capacity to feel happiness or satisfaction. Thus the intensity with which one can positively experience the value of a charitable project, for example, is limited to the intensity with which one can experience the corresponding satisfaction if the project succeeds. Similarly, the negative experience of its value is limited only by the capacity for sadness, depression, frustration, and despair. Experientially, the satisfaction of the charitable impulse has become the limit of positive emotional intensity, and thus for practical purposes has become the measure of the experience of intrinsic value. From the subjective point of view, to experience something as intensely valuable is not the same thing as to intensely experience it as valuable. If the limit of the intensity of positive value experience is our own capacity for the corresponding feeling of satisfaction, then we are in the circle of egocentricity.

In today's philosophical climate, many people may think that the problem of the circle of egocentricity can be denied or ignored on the grounds that consciousness is born out of rather than into the world, in consummate reciprocity with its community and significant others from the very beginning. While this view is an advance over extreme individualistic atomism, the fact remains that, as soon as a two-year-old child learns to say 'no,' the child is already moving toward relative autonomy as a conscious being. Between the statement 'Jim has just finished a satisfying *boeuf au poivre*' and the statement 'John is starving,' there is no logical contradiction. While Jim may feel compassion for John, it is *Jim* who feels the compassion. The point for our purposes is that, if Jim's happiness on getting John fed is the limit of the *intensity* with which Jim can feel the value of John's being, then Jim's own happiness (which results from getting John fed) is still the most intensely positive way he can feel the value of this outcome, and if so he is still stuck in the circle of egocentricity in the sense meant here. The issue is not whether Jim can feel compassion, but that the *intensity* with which this compassion can be felt (and still remain a positive feeling) is limited by the location of the satisfaction or dissatisfaction of the altruistic motivation within Jim's own feelings of happiness and unhappiness.

In a transcendent value experience, by contrast, the intrinsic value of the object is experienced in a way more powerful than any value within the circle of egocentricity can be experienced. The reason, as Unamuno observes in *The Tragic Sense of Life*, is that the otherness of the other makes possible a feeling of compassion for the other's embattledness in the face of alienation, relative powerlessness, insignificance in the ultimate scheme of things, inevitable death, and radical finitude in the conditions needed to actualize the other's own project of being. This compassion intensifies our admiration for the other's courageous attempt at authenticity in the face of these ontological difficulties in a way that our own compassion for *ourselves* (i.e., self-pity) does *not* intensify admiration, but rather becomes a negative value experience. This possibility of feeling the other's value more intensely than we feel our own creates what Levinas in *Totality and Infinity* calls an "infinite curvature of intersubjective space." That is, there are types of relationships in which each person seems from the other's perspective to be elevated into a realm beyond the ordinary—a realm of transcendence or, in Levinas's terms, 'infinitude.' But, paradoxically, this infinitude of the other's value is accessible only through compassion for the person's vulnerability—that is, her ontological finitude. The psychology of this phenomenon becomes especially clear in Levinas's chapter on the 'Phenomenology of Eros,' which begins with the sentence, "Eros aims at the other in his frailty (*faiblesse*)" (1969, 256).

The question that Levinas himself ignores, however, is this: How can we really intensify compassion for a person's existential frailty if at bottom we do not *believe* in ontological finitude—namely, if we believe that God is infinite, all-powerful, and all-good, and thus is capable of solving all the problems of finitude, including the guarantee of personal immortality? We shall return to this question very shortly

The feeling of compassion is especially salient when fleshed out by a detailed grasp of the various respects in which even the love object's attempts to create conditions facilitative of *being who she is* tend to be thwarted and frustrated. Compassion for this aspect of finitude is an *ontological* compassion, not merely a pity for accidental misfortunes. By feeling concretely the radical finitude confronting a person's attempt to be who she is, we are overcome with an emotional appreciation for the extreme value of that existentially embattled being.

Erotic love relationships are not the only contexts in which this experience can be found. For example, it may be pulled in a quite intense and sustainable form by the ontological endangerment of a comrade-in-arms during the thick of warfare. To a lesser degree, or in a less sustainable way, it may also be felt between a younger scholar or artist and a 'mentor' figure. Or it may temporarily become very intense in a sudden life-threatening emergency, such as the bombing of the World Trade Center; suddenly the intrinsic value of the threatened being is emotionally felt with full intensity, even to an extent capable of inspiring complete self-sacrifice. What we are concerned with in this book is the phenomenon of a direct feeling of admiration-through-compassion that is both *intense* and *sustained* enough to persist until the sustaining of this very intensity accomplishes three outcomes: (1) The feeling spreads to a concrete experience of the value of many other conscious beings that is comparably moving; (2) this generalized feeling is pronounced *enough* that it realizes a continuing direct experience of the intrinsic value of being—as instantiated in many love objects—strong enough to counterbalance the ontological dilemma of radical finitude; and (3) it does so *without* the need for self-deceptive denials of the reality of this radical finitude (for example, a literalistic belief in the immortality of the individual soul, as occurs in religious fundamentalism). In sum, we are speaking not just of love experiences in general, but of a unique *kind* of love—an inspiring *and sustainable* admiration-through-compassion that can spread with comparable force to people generally and unify the self around an abstract value system rooted in this value feeling.

Because interpersonal experience cannot offer the possibility for the kind of overwhelming value experience envisioned here as long as we remain within the circle of egocentricity, a transcendent value experience as I have defined it requires a 'transcendent object'—that is, an object whose experienced value transcends any value it might have in relation to the egocentric motives of the subject. Obviously, such an object must be experienceable as having intrinsic and not merely extrinsic value. Thus the experience of transcendent objects as such requires an ability to empathize with the transcendent object, and transcendent objects therefore are always subjective or intersubjective kinds of beings—for example, human beings, deities, or works of art that express the collective experience of actual and/or possible subjectivities. Such artworks also 'symbolize' such subjective and intersubjective values in the sense that they provide a concrete, embodied matrix for their physical and emotional intensification, as I shall explain further below. Although there is a wide range of objects that are capable of becoming transcendent objects for someone, I shall argue here that only other intensely conscious beings (i.e., only other persons) are capable of adequately fulfilling the need for transcendent value experience on a permanent and sustainable basis. Although Tchaikovsky may have seemed on the surface to be a recluse living only for art, a cursory glance at his letters reveals intense interpersonal needs that actually played a major role in fueling his musical inspiration.

I shall speak of transcendent objects in both a primary and a derivative sense. Strictly speaking, a *primary* transcendent object is one who in principle would be capable of pulling me out of the circle of egocentricity in a sustained way without my previously having been pulled out of it by some prior transcendent value experience. This becomes possible, in my view, because of a mutually nonjudgmental and nondirective empathic structure, or 'space of empathy,' which allows defenses against vulnerability to be dropped. It facilitates such an extreme admiration and compassion that the circle of egocentricity as a whole seems trivial and insignificant compared with the positive value experience revealed through the direct experience (through empathy) of the other's intrinsic value. In more concrete terms, we must feel free to express ourselves independently of the other's narcissistic judgments if we are to be able to reveal ourselves openly enough to make it possible for the other to establish a real empathy with our own concern with the ontological vulnerabilities we face.

Mere empathy, then, does not constitute what I am calling a space of empathy. The space of empathy is a *way of interacting* that prevents strong empathic feelings from being somewhat quickly choked off. This way of interacting combines in a specific way two features whose coexistence is not frequently sustainable in human relationships: (1) It requires an unusual abstinence from any recriminations, blame, or judgmentalism of any kind, so that the other is allowed to reveal the most sensitive subjective conditions without fear of being judged. Additionally, (2) in the space of empathy, each person actively encourages such completely honest expressions and is intensely interested in them. This space of empathy therefore goes far beyond a mutual psychotherapeutic structure. In essence, it lacks the boundaries and constraints as well as the asymmetry of the psychotherapeutic relationship, so that each person is completely available to the other's empathy. On my analysis, this space of empathy is a prerequisite for the catalysis of the circular process in which compassion intensifies admiration, which in turn intensifies compassion, and so on indefinitely without short-circuiting.

Once such an experience has occurred, then it may be possible (if certain 'empathic skills' are developed) to transfer the way we feel toward a primary transcendent object to *other* persons (i.e., transcendent objects in the secondary or derivative sense), by reminding ourselves of the way we felt toward a primary transcendent object's intrinsic value, and by learning to focus on those aspects of others that make it possible to feel this way toward them, though usually with a lesser degree of intensity than with a primary transcendent object because the space of empathy with them is less complete, for a variety of reasons that will soon become obvious. Let me emphasize at the outset that this 'spreading effect' *does not require that those others have anything in common with the primary transcendent object*—only that they be similarly embattled by the ontological conditions that face all conscious beings, so that compassion for them can be pulled in the same way that we have earlier learned to feel it toward a primary transcendent object. Most 'mature adults'—those who to greater or lesser extents have moved beyond the circle of egocentricity (which sooner or later becomes self-defeating)—have experienced transcendent value in both the primary and the derivative senses, to a greater or lesser extent. To define the meaning of an entire life purely in terms of the transcendent value experience of one primary object is not possible.

The circle of egocentricity can exist to greater or lesser extents. If I abstractly acknowledge that intrinsic value is present in other conscious beings, but do not *intensely and positively feel* this value in an experience inspiring enough to counterbalance the angst connected with my own finitude—and do so without self-deceptive metaphysical fantasies—then the circle of egocentricity still exists to enough of an extent to constitute a problem that still demands a resolution. So it is important to realize that the need for a transcendent value experience is not merely brought about by a *complete* circle of egocentricity. It is brought about even if the circle of egocentricity exists to a *substantial extent*—substantial enough to leave unresolved the problem just mentioned.

Because it is important to speak in experiential as well as abstract terms, I shall also refer to primary transcendent objects as 'spiritual partners'—using 'spiritual' not in a conventionally religious sense, but in the sense of the French 'esprit.' A better expression might be the French 'comrades d'esprit,' which loses in English translation. The word 'spiritual' or 'd'esprit' is meant to emphasize the sense that the relationship centers primarily around the kinds of conscious, subjectively experienced, or intersubjective processes that can be revealed and further develop within the space of empathy. 'Partner' or 'comrade' suggests that a primary transcendent value experience requires mutuality, because it is facilitated by a mutual space of empathy in which people are able to reveal themselves somewhat defenselessly, so that each is able to directly and immediately empathize with (and not merely cognize) the other's most serious ontological vulnerabilities, facilitating strongly felt admiration and compassion for the other's ontological embattledness or endangerment.

Merely to 'love' other conscious beings does not accomplish this purpose by itself. To be pulled initially out of the circle of egocentricity requires a many-faceted process through which we first learn to intrinsically value a transcendent object with more emotional intensity than we can value ourselves (for reasons that will be explained more fully as we proceed). Thus, we value the transcendent object highly enough to genuinely overcome the circle of egocentricity to an extent adequate to sustain an inspiring enough transcendent value experience to render metaphysical denials of finitude superfluous. In this way, we achieve access to a direct experience of a conscious being's positive value structured in such a way that it can be felt more sharply and inspire us more enthusiastically than can the value of our own being—but only in conjunction with a threatening and disturbing abandonment of the fundamentally egocentric perspective.

This overcoming of egocentricity in itself is no mean accomplishment in a modern or postmodern 'culture of narcissism.' Once it has been accomplished, we must then face the fact that, if the sociocultural complexities of life are not to subvert the strength of this direct experience of the value of being, and at the same time if we are to avoid a clinging symbiosis (which also destroys the transcendent value experience), we must learn to *transfer* our ability to focus on a primary transcendent object's seemingly infinite intrinsic value by using the knowledge we have thus acquired to focus also on this same value as it exists in other people. In the process, one learns to abstract the valuational feeling involved so that it can serve as the basis for a set of motivating values felt strongly enough to unify the self toward the future. This unification restores the equilibrium that was lost when the need for transcendent value experience forcibly pulled us out of ourselves and dismantled the previous motivational unity of the self—that is, when that largely egocentric unity began to feel its inadequacy to counterbalance the dilemma of finitude. Once the new form of unity is achieved, through the ability to sustain a complete enough non-egocentric admiration-through-compassion for conscious beings as they bear up under the untamable harshness of the ontological dilemma of finite beings (with love for a past or present primary transcendent object serving as the paradigm for this feeling), then life is experienced as more than positively valuable enough to outweigh the negativity of its own unavoidable evils, and without the necessity for self-deceptively denying those evils through grand metaphysical theories. (This is not to deny, of course, the importance of metaphysics when done in a sober and non-self-deceptive way.)

By suggesting that, after this 'spreading effect' occurs, we then find adequate consolation for the negativity of the ontological predicament in an abstract value system, I do not mean to imply that the actual development of this value system must await the spreading effect. Many people develop well-grounded philosophical ideas about justice, beneficence, and so forth, quite early in life, often before there has even been any transcendent value experience through either a full spiritual partnership experience, or belief in traditional religion, or any other such inspirational effect. But, while very young people can easily hold well-grounded moral beliefs and act on them, the commitment to these moral beliefs, by itself, is not at that point able to bear the entire brunt of compensating for the negative aspects of the ontological predicament of radical finitude. Thus finitude is generally not completely faced up to during childhood and adolescence; while the young person may intellectually acknowledge death and limitation of power and importance, the situation is not really felt to be this radically finite. There remains some hope that we will turn out to be immortal or very powerful and important after all, perhaps by means of some as yet undiscovered metaphysical doctrine. Moreover, the circle of egocentricity remains intact at this point, unless eliminated by means of self-deceptive religious dogmas that deny the ultimate reality of finitude. Only after the occurrence of a transcendent value experience, of one kind or another, is the circle of egocentricity torn down. These points, however, must await chapter 4 for their justification.

When this 'spreading' and 'abstracting' process has been completed, the transcendent value experience is no longer merely a sentimental or starry-eyed obsession with a single love object, but rather a set of abstractions that are derivative from the concrete experience of intrinsic value that spiritual partnership has made possible. And the abstract ideals themselves are motivated by the emotional inspiration with which the now-generalized transcendent value experience is riddled through.

The need for inspiration is not a dispensable dimension of the human psyche. Psychologists and neuroscientists, after a century of attempting to treat living organisms as passive mechanisms reacting to external stimuli, are now finally coming around to the view that the emotional brain is a self-organizing system that must be inspired to energize and mobilize itself before other brain functions can be performed. An extreme example of the failure of this energizing function can be seen in the death of human infants from marasmus reported by Spitz, Wolf, and other clinicians. Even though the infants' consummatory needs are met, if they do not get enough cuddling and other signs of affection from their caretakers, they simply turn their faces to the wall and die. Spitz and Wolf, whose seminal study was conducted in an orphanage, learned to prevent the condition by recruiting women from a nearby prison to handle and nurture the infants. So, even in infancy, meeting consummatory needs is not enough; there must be a feeling of inspiration to motivate the organism to care enough to mobilize its other functions.

This basic need for inspiration is by no means derivative through learning or socialization from other needs. Neurophysiologists such as Damasio and Panksepp now show that the deepest parts of the emotional brain—midbrain and brain stem areas—must activate the higher parts of the brain to do their jobs, by acting as a self-organizing dynamical system. In adults, the failure of inspiration leads people to commit suicide, become alcoholics, embrace fundamentalist religions, follow Fuhrers, destroy marriages with philandering, and engage in a plethora of other destructive and self-destructive activities. An anonymous poem written ostensibly by a monkey, after enumerating dysfunctional human behaviors to which no self-respecting monkey would stoop, concludes as follows: "Yes, man descended, the ornery cuss, but brother he didn't descend from us!"

When the need for a feeling of inspiration is understood as primary, we can begin to understand the psychology of religion in other dimensions than simply self-deceptive wish fulfillment. At that point, I shall argue that there are two fundamentally different approaches to spiritual experience, whose essence is that it serves the need for inspiration, which is heightened in humans: we can either work to fulfill this need, or we can repress and deny the existential conditions that exacerbate it.

Why is this need exaggerated to such a degree in humans, so that it can even take priority over other fundamental needs? On my view, the reason the striving for inspiration becomes so pressing and problematic in humans is that sophisticated conscious and emotional beings are intelligent enough to realize that their hopes and dreams are seriously threatened by fundamental conditions of finitude. The span of our existence is short, and our power to accomplish goals is fragile and limited, as are our abilities to establish needed social and personal relations and to make much of a valuational difference in the grand scheme of things. This awareness of our overall existential condition heightens the human need for inspiration beyond that of other animals, while at the same time threatening its realization by crowding imagery of past, future, and hypothetically possible evils into the mind.

At this point, the problem of exaggerated narcissism enters the picture by rebelling against these conditions of finitude. If narcissistic disturbance interferes with the full experience of the intrinsic value of being in the way I suggested above, it would then create a deficiency of inspiration. Given the seriousness of this problem, it is no wonder that the narcissistic denial of the reality of one's own finitude, if such a denial ironically then precludes an intense enough experience of the value of being through a selfless enough feeling of compassion, would exacerbate the very problems for which it is meant as an escape, and lead to hopelessness, despair, and sometimes even suicide and the other destructive and self-destructive activities to which no self-respecting monkey would think of stooping.

The aim of this book is to understand this need for an intense experience of the intrinsic value of being, along with the way in which it is accessible through a certain kind of human relationship that facilitates transcending the circle of egocentricity, by allowing compassion to intensify admiration and thus the feeling of inspiration and the direct and powerful experience of the intrinsic value of being as instantiated in conscious beings other than ourselves. At the same time, we will be able to explore the ways in which escapes from the experience of finitude, through exaggerated narcissism and fundamentalist forms of religion, block this transcendent value experience and therefore ironically exacerbate the deficiency of inspiration.

1

Foundations for a Study of Interpersonal Value Experience

The first section of this chapter will briefly summarize my reasons for believing not only that human love can serve the spiritual need for the kind of transcendent value experience just outlined, but also that people historically have increasingly tried to use various forms of love for this purpose. Especially in recent times, as traditional religions serve the purpose less and less adequately, many people have turned more and more to romantic or sexual love for this function. But, for the same reason, mere sexuality is increasingly confused with other forms of compassionate love as vehicles for transcendent value experience. Because people therefore remain so confused about what it is they are trying to do, the attempt often tends to fail, and does not lead to the spreading effect or to the ability to be inspired by abstract moral commitments discussed above.

Section 2 will explain the method of approach I intend to use in studying this problem—essentially, a disciplined method for introspectively clarifying the nature of subjective value experiences, with frank recognition of the dangers of prejudice, unreflected category systems, and self-deception, and with a little added help from hermeneutic phenomenology. Section 3 will then discuss some theoretical work in psychology that will help to shed light on our discussion at several key points. The thinking of certain psychologists on the issue of narcissism will become especially relevant.

1. Narcissism and the Circle of Egocentricity

The idea that a strong enough love for one's fellow human beings might serve a spiritual or religious need without the help of metaphysical or supernatural doctrines is not new. John Dewey, for example, proposes just such a notion in *A Common Faith*, beginning with the following characterization of 'religious experience':

> There are . . . changes in ourselves in relation to the world in which we live that are . . . inclusive and deep seated. . . . Because of their scope, this modification of ourselves is enduring. . . . There is a composing and harmonizing of the various elements of our being such that, in spite of changes in the special conditions that surround us, these conditions are also arranged, settled, in relation to us. This attitude includes a note of submission. But . . . it is something more than a mere Stoical resolution to endure unperturbed throughout the buffetings of fortune. (1934, 16–17)

For Dewey, religion is that which provides a sustainable sense that life itself (as opposed to specific goals attained *in* life) has more than enough ultimate meaning or value to counterbalance its pains and failures, however serious and numerous they might be. From this definition of religious experience, Dewey argues that "when the ends of moral conviction arouse emotions that are not only intense but are actuated and supported by ends so inclusive that they unify the self" (22), then "the sense of the dignity of human nature is as religious as is the sense of awe and reverence" (25). Thus, "Human relations are charged with values that are religious in function" (72).

Ludwig Feuerbach, too, insists that the legitimate objects of religious feeling should be human beings. But, according to Feuerbach, we are too alienated from ourselves and from each other to enact such a love completely enough to be felt as a religious awe—that is, as an intensely positive experience of the extreme value of conscious beings. We therefore feel impelled, in effect, to imaginatively imbue a deity with the properties of consciousness and personality. By projecting onto the deity what is good in ourselves (i.e., in conscious beings), we avail ourselves of a love object devoid of any evil that might interfere with our ability to love the being. As Robert Tucker insightfully points out, this is why Marx, who studied Feuerbach very seriously, thought that the sociopolitical overcoming of human alienation would eliminate the need for the 'opium' of traditional religions.

The idea that human love can serve a religious need becomes more plausible if we define the 'religious need' in question in the way that Dewey, Ernst Cassirer, Otto Rank, and many anthropologists have defined it: as a need to address the problem of our own finitude in the face of the ontological predicament of finite beings—that is, our own inevitable death, powerlessness, alienation, and relative insignificance in the ultimate scheme of things. Some people may object to the use of the word 'religious' to describe this need. The reason I choose this word is that all religions of the world seem to try in one way or another to meet such a need. Indeed, the attempt to address the ontological predicament of the individual's radical finitude might well be the *only* thing all religions have in common with each other.

I shall use the term 'fundamentalism' to refer to religious beliefs that deal with the problems of finitude by literally denying their existence. This usage is consistent with the usual sense of 'fundamentalism' as 'literal interpretation,' but the aspects of fundamentalism that concern us here are the ones that directly bear on issues of human finitude. In times of desperation, such as loss of a loved one, people often console themselves that the deceased has literally survived death and that this individual's soul literally exists somewhere else—for example, in a heaven conceived of as a new location in which the same individual can continue to exist. But to the extent that fundamentalism simply denies the tragic dimension, it also interferes with another important function of religion—the 'mythic' dimension—which is to provide an inspirational value experience strong enough to *compensate* for the inevitably tragic facts of finitude. Fundamentalism interferes with this type of experience not only by eliminating the *need* for it, but also by rendering the emotional life in general inauthentic. This trade-off and tension within traditional religions between fundamentalism and the consolatory effect of inspirational experience in the face of frankly acknowledged finitude will be discussed further as we proceed.

'Fundamentalism' in this sense must be clearly distinguished from *fanaticism*. The gunslinging abolitionist John Brown was a religious fanatic, in the sense that his actions were both extreme and enthusiastic. But he was not a *fundamentalist*—someone who uses absolute belief in a completely literalistic *ontological scheme* to deny the facts of finitude.

Almost any sophisticated theologian, from Ibn Rusd (Averroes) to Paul Tillich to Joseph Campbell, will admit that the metaphysical 'truths' of religion must be interpreted mythically rather than literally. But even the most sophisticated still face the temptation to lapse into fundamentalist literal denials of the facts of ontological finitude, because those facts simply are so disturbing. Thus Aquinas speaks as if the 'first cause' were to be understood in terms of continuous creation, as an immanentist would have it (clearly, the first cause for Aquinas was not first in the order of time, as literal interpretation of the creation myth would imply); but then Aquinas argues that God is transcendent rather than immanent, because an immanent God would seem too natural, and could not act miraculously on the physical world from without. In general, there is always the temptation to allow mythological intuition or an abstract 'God of the philosophers' (whether that of Aquinas or of Whitehead) to morph into the all-powerful benevolent Creator who will literally solve all unsolvable problems, rectify injustice, ensure personal immortality, and guarantee the meaning of life.

But if theology is allowed to remain sophisticated, and does not lapse into these self-deceptive temptations, then religious experience will emphasize myth, ritual, and direct experience of intrinsic value rather than fundamentalist dogma. Even traditional religions, when not indulging in fundamentalist denials, have attempted to create a positive value experience powerful enough to counterbalance the harshness of our finite predicament rather than merely self-deceptively denying it; and to create such an inspiring value experience, in concrete terms, seems to require a feeling of love, because to keenly and directly experience the positive value of a being other than ourselves, through awe-stricken appreciation for the uniqueness and irreplaceability of that being, means to love the being. Traditional religions try to make possible such a love by projecting onto a metaphysical principle or force (for example, the Logos, the Unmoved Mover), or onto a totemized animal, or onto a mythologized sun or moon, the properties of personality and consciousness, so that the believer can concretely feel the emotion of love toward that being. Most religions speak in terms of the believer's 'loving' the deity. But if this love is to refer to a concrete feeling, then it must have something in common with the above observations about the way love in general is emotionally intensified—namely, through some sort of space of empathy that can allow admiration and compassion to intensify each other.

One might wonder initially how love for a *deity* could involve *compassion* for the courageous authenticity of a conscious being in the face of its embattlement and opposition. But a typical feature of virtually all religions (Judaism and Christianity are obvious examples) is that lower representatives of the all-powerful and infinite deity are needed—prophets, saints, angels, the Madonna, Jesus, and ordinary human religious leaders—to provide a finite love object capable of inspiring intense compassion for their suffering, sacrifice, and often frustrated good intentions. Such an intermediary often may serve as a more effective object of concrete feelings of love than the all-too-powerful deity may. In other cases, the deity's frustrated good intentions toward the waywardness of humanity pulls the feeling of compassion, which then emotionally intensifies the believer's admiration.

The reason we cannot very intensely love ourselves in this sense is not so much, as Feuerbach thought, because we are too alienated from ourselves (although it is true that we are self-alienated); rather, it is essentially because an intense focus on our own embattled authenticity in the face of the ontological predicament—our own finitude—is much less a positive than a negative experience. The very thing that is most valuable in our existence—that we are irreplaceable centers of conscious sensitivity— is precisely what most arouses our existential anxiety. To focus on our irreplaceability and essential sensitivity (hence vulnerability), and the inevitable ontological obstacles to even actualizing the forms of being that we project for ourselves, would require focusing too pointedly on our finitude. Ideally, the projection of consciousness and personality onto a deity should make possible such a love for a being *other* than ourselves, hence a *positive* value experience capable of overriding the negativity of the finite dilemma.

But there is an increasing problem with the inspiring transcendent value experience offered by traditional religions. It seems that the rational element in the contemporary mind is no longer as willing as it once was to be pushed aside to make room for the needed anthropomorphizing of a deity, be it an abstract principle or a metaphysical or physical 'force.' A science fiction film that popularizes the motto 'The force be with you!' is one of the few socially important American films in recent years to require only 'parental guidance' for children under 13; it is not considered to corrupt the moral or religious thinking of the youth, even though it reduces the deity to just such an impersonal 'force.' The contemporary mind increasingly demands this depersonalization of the deity, because we are unable to take fanciful anthropomorphisms seriously enough to inspire the real feelings that are needed to overcome the bleakness of the ontological predicament. An egocentric and self-deceptive belief in personal immortality through some sort of magical operation of physics (or some nebulous 'merging' with the physical universe) is thus retained, while love for a deity becomes increasingly incomprehensible. And, because the remaining belief in immortality is so thoroughly self-deceptive, it only further complicates our dilemma rather than solving it.

The point is that religion, either in its popular fundamentalist or in its 'scientific' forms, therefore becomes less and less able to address the finite predicament, and the result—as René Muller argues in *The Marginal Self*—is increasing anxiety, neurosis, suicide, drug use, automaton-like conformism, authoritarianism, and various other methods to temporarily distract ourselves from the harshness of the predicament without really reconciling ourselves to it or coming to terms with it. What, then, of the possibility of coming to terms with it by means of admiration as enhanced by compassion for the consciousness of other human beings? Why can't the combination of extreme compassion with extreme admiration for a conscious being who is the *object* of our experience result in a powerful direct feeling of the value of being, which we are then able to activate through empathy? We have seen already how, when such feelings are potent enough, they might have the power to pull us out of the circle of egocentricity to directly experience the value of another being more fully than we can experience any positive valuation from the egocentric perspective (because, again, we cannot very positively appreciate our own finitude and irreplaceability). Why, then, can we not in this way create a positive value experience so pronounced, which so permeates our entire value system, that it overrides the negativity of the ontological predicament? And if so, then perhaps this positive valuation could spread to incorporate other people and experiences, so that they too are experienced from a less egocentric perspective; thus our attitude toward them would also be permeated with the intensity of Unamuno's 'tragic sense of life,' but with a feeling of positive, quasi-aesthetic awe resulting from having undergone the psychological process of spiritual partnership, the beginning of which is that the other's value is experienced as superseding our own.

Without prematurely abandoning hope for traditional religions, let's consider this other alternative for a moment. (For, in the end, we shall find that it has a great deal in common with traditional religions on their mythic as opposed to fundamentalist interpretations, provided that the seductive temptations of the latter are avoided.) It might seem initially implausible that human relationships could seriously rival traditional religions in their ability to pull us out of the circle of egocentricity so that such a powerful value experience could occur that it would lead to adequate compensation for the full brutality of the finite predicament without the help of metaphysical denials of the predicament. If such an experience commonly occurs in human relationships, then why are so many of us still disturbed by the predicament, and why do we still need to find such devious and far-flung methods of deceiving ourselves about it or numbing ourselves to it? But on the other hand, if such relationships are very rare, then with whom might such a relationship occur, and under what conditions?

The answer to this question is very complex, and it varies individually, culturally, and historically. While it may be possible that many kinds of relationship, under certain personal and historical circumstances, would fulfill the function of creating a transcendent value experience capable of breaking the circle of egocentricity, a key question is whether the parties to the relationship understand the concepts necessary to *use* this opportunity wisely, or whether they misconstrue it in terms of inappropriate categories. For example, I shall try to show that the reduction of such an opportunity to a case of mere 'sexual attraction' or 'romantic infatuation' is a common type of misconstrual in our own time, because people who have opposite sexual polarity and/or are sexually attracted to each other are especially well-suited to serve the primary spiritual partnership function for each other. On my view, this is one of the main reasons why the relationship between the sexes has always been such a tumultuous battleground, and why even the most nonsexual relationships between opposite-sexed individuals have been so anxiously and elaborately tabooed. It is not merely sex that is tabooed: Sex and spiritual partnership have a strong tendency to be linked because, even though sexual attraction and sexual polarization are not essential ingredients of the transcendent value experience of spiritual partnership per se, they nonetheless may often serve as catalysts for the development of the experience. It is this crucial emotional relationship, not mere sexual activity, that is regarded as so earthshakingly important.

A wild variable throughout history is the extent to which sexual relationships can also double as spiritual partnerships on a sustained basis, or whether the social contextualization of sexual relations undermines the space of empathy. And since sexuality is only a catalyst for spiritual partnership, the latter will be found in other types of relationships in some social contexts. It is true that, in some periods of history, romantic relationships seem fairly easily to lend themselves to the possibility of a certain amount of spiritual partnership, in which people can serve as transcendent objects for transcendent value experiences, provided that the romantic partners succeed in playing their cards right. But, of course, even during those periods, people all too often do not play their cards right. And during other historical periods (like the present one), the effects of violent social upheaval, extremely conflict-prone social and economic relations between the sexes, and other factors somewhat systematically cause romantic partners to feel defensive and mistrustful toward each other—a necessary precaution against the cataclysmic pain that a bad or frustrating romance or marriage can inflict if we make ourselves too vulnerable to it. The increasing narcissism of contemporary culture also contributes to this problem, as we shall see. During still other periods, women are trapped in isolation and in such subordinate roles that meaningful spiritual interaction between romantic partners becomes virtually impossible (a problem that is the central focus in the writings of Kate Chopin, for example). At such times, spiritual partnership—in the sense needed to facilitate transcendent value experience—is often found outside the context of the romantic or erotic sphere. For instance, judging from the *Symposium*, it seems likely that the henpecked husband Socrates found spiritual partnership with the erudite hetaira woman, Diotima—as well as with young men (considering certain remarks in the *Phaedrus*, the *Parmenides*, and other dialogues; note also that Socrates always seems 'immune to seduction' in these contexts, and is always interested in the spiritual side of such relationships rather than the physical side.) As another example, judging from certain biographies of Sir Thomas More, it appears that the relationship between More and his daughter tended strongly toward spiritual partnership, as did the initial nonsexualized relationship between John Stuart Mill and Harriet Taylor. Indeed, one can think of numerous instances in which men and women not engaged in sexual relationships nonetheless are heavily invested in selfless loyalty and devotion, as in the tradition of chivalry among Medieval Catharists. Some of these examples will be discussed as we proceed.

Jung and his followers—for example, Robert Johnson and Denis de Rougemont—suggest that a common element in such overwhelming and involuntary feelings toward an opposite-sexed person, whether the feelings are sexual or not, is a need for self-transcendence. According to these theorists, the two people interact in such a way that each learns from the other to empathically enact a vast realm of spirituality (or pattern of consciousness) that is readily accessible in the other but largely suppressed in oneself. This Jungian approach is enticingly consistent with the fact that, in modern and postmodern cultures, the spiritual partnership experience is increasingly linked to sexuality and romantic love: Typically, in the Jungian type of analysis, a predominantly 'masculine' subject and a predominantly 'feminine' subject (terms whose meaning certainly must be rethought after the past half-century of feminism and sexual revolution) interact so that each learns through empathy to vicariously enact the intensely admired differentness of the other's style of being. Even when the culture has successfully minimized these differences—which enhances opportunities for empathic interaction—the differences still exist.

However, in the context of our present discussion, it is not necessary to defend Jung's postulate that the ultimate purpose sought by these impulses is a kind of personality growth achievable only by filling in the 'missing half' of the self, characterizable along gender-based lines. Unlike in Jung's analysis, the important point for our purposes is not whether or not this learning to enact the style of each other's different forms of being has great value for its own sake; the point is rather that, in the process, each learns the dramatic effect of the principle that another conscious being's value can be experienced in a more intensely positive way than one's own, provided that certain conditions for a complete space of empathy are present. I have already suggested that such a relationship is not a static condition that endures unchanging, but rather a dynamic process that unfolds through a series of different stages or movements, and which results, if followed all the way through these various stages, in the spreading effect and the ability to be inspired by the abstraction of the value system rooted in the transcendent value experience.

In fact, one problem that some readers may have to guard against in following this presentation is that, in essence, they *already may have lived through* a transcendent value experience in the crucial respects, including all or many of the spiritual changes that it is capable of engendering. In this case, they may have trouble remembering what it is like to experience the dilemma of finitude as an anxiety-provoking and sometimes even suffocating threat to the ultimate value of being; correlatively, some readers may already have met, to greater or lesser extents, their 'religious needs' in the sense I am using. The story I am narrating here should be taken as hypothetical in the same way that the social contract stories of Kant and Rawls are hypothetical. The story begins at the point when the ontological dilemma of the individual's radical finitude has been fully, non-self-deceptively acknowledged and felt, so as to create the need for an intense enough value experience to overshadow this negativity. As I have already suggested, this can have occurred in a variety of different ways. And we shall find later that the spiritual partnership effect may actually have been pieced together by means of a series of various kinds of relationships each of which moved us a little further toward the ultimate 'spreading effect.' There will certainly be many individual differences in this regard. But, in each case, the question is whether the problem of finitude continues to be dealt with through denial, or whether there has been a transitional phase in which the problem of finitude is taken seriously rather than merely denied, so as to necessitate the inspirational effect offered by spiritual partnership. What I believe is really in need of being explored, though, is the series of changes that may flow *out of* such a spiritual partnership experience, because it is these changes—not the spiritual partnership experience by itself—which are capable of resolving the finite dilemma in a positive, constructive, and permanent way. As many young lovers know, but many older ones tend to forget, spiritual partnership can catapult us into an entire 'realm of the sublime,' where all valuational commitments and relations with others can take on the inspirational glow that has spread to them from an initial primary relationship. This 'spreading effect,' along with the conditions that facilitate or thwart it, will be a central focus of this book.

I shall try to show that, during the contemporary period, people often fancy themselves as 'falling in love' when what is really happening has only a superficial connection (or perhaps even no connection at all) with eroticism, but rather is primarily the pull of the need for transcendent value experience, which becomes more pronounced at certain times of life. In other cases, 'falling in love' itself results from an intensification of feelings toward a potential spiritual partner by *symbolizing* purely spiritual needs sexually—that is, by means of allowing one's entire being to be permeated with sexual feelings (in the ways I discussed more extensively in *Eros in a Narcissistic Culture*). Ironically, precisely because sexual feelings and behavior can be enlisted for the purpose of symbolizing and intensifying the spiritual partnership experience, these sexual feelings and behavior themselves are allowed to replace the spiritual partnership effect per se. In this case, the tendency is to fail even to see the potentiality for the transcendent value experience made possible by spiritual partnership in either its romanticized or its nonromantic forms.

This tendency to misinterpret our own experience in terms of mere physical sexuality (perhaps combined with ordinary friendship toward the sex object) results from a largely hedonistic and egocentric worldview, which now is especially promoted by the unlucky combination of consummatory-drive reductionism in the social sciences and advanced-capitalist consumerism in the popular media. Such influences make us feel that the essential motivation of human beings should be to obtain benefits for themselves and to project attractive (and essentially invulnerable) images. (This is the now widely discussed 'narcissistic' value system, which in my view is by no means limited to modern Western cultures, but only tends to be exacerbated in them). We thus find ourselves unable to see spiritual partnership as a kind of relationship that, purely by virtue of the emotional magnification of the feelings of compassion and admiration, can lead beyond the circle of egocentricity precisely because both people's authentic *ontological vulnerabilities* are revealed for each other's empathy. Instead of seeing the possibility of spiritual partnership in these terms, we tend to categorize the experience as a mere sexual attraction or romantic infatuation and, by substituting sexuality and romance for the transcendent value experience, destroy its spiritual implications.

Thus frustrated in the need for transcendent value experience through an adequate space of empathy with a primary transcendent object, we then feel guilty for our dissatisfaction, and therefore become still more defensive and constricted in our relations to others. This self-contradiction and resulting internal conflict arise from a mistrust of our own motives caused by a distorted view of the nature of human consciousness, especially in its motivational dimension. Having assumed that motivation is egocentric and entirely driven by consummatory drives such as the physical need for sex, we then erect a taboo, in effect, which virtually designates any significant personal interactions between men and women as sexual overtures and scripts them into preconceived, conventionally 'romantic' patterns. This rigidified fear of the opposite sex then 'protects' us from just the kind of interaction that could teach us how to revere the spirituality in human beings with the extremely positive feelings that the intrinsic value of an intensely conscious being can render possible.

Such reverent admiration mixed with compassion can occur fully and on a sustained basis only when admiration is multiplied by compassion rather than dulled by contempt for shortcomings, and at the same time when defenses against this possible contempt do not block the space of empathy. Both these conditions are facilitated when each person is able to nondirectively and nonjudgmentally empathize with the other's authentic states of consciousness in spite of and in part even *because of* her foibles and imperfections, thus providing a mutual space of empathy in which each stream of consciousness is able to unfold in genuinely motivated directions. In this way, each person's authentic consciousness is for the most part defenselessly exposed to the other without pretense, and at the same time both can feel that they are allowed to be fully and unpretentiously who they are. This rare combination of intense consciousness and exposed vulnerability then allows each to deeply admire and take compassion for the other's courageous attempt at authenticity in the face of both social and ontological conditions that threaten and endanger the self-actualization of authentic consciousness at the needed level of intensity.

By 'authenticity' in this context, I simply mean being honest with ourselves about the content and meaning of our own consciousness. This is of course a matter of degree, and there is not necessarily anything 'inauthentic' about having had our consciousness shaped or influenced by history or environment, provided that we do not pretend (to ourselves) to think or feel differently from the way we really think or feel. Granted, this is not a sharp distinction. When I write a budget proposal, arguing that I need more money than I really need because I know the granting authorities will provide less than is requested, I may in the process convince myself that I really need the additional amount. To some extent, I may now genuinely believe that I need the additional amount, but to some extent I know on some level that some of the arguments were trumped up and that I really do not need as much money as I pretend (to myself) to believe. To this extent, the belief is inauthentic. Authenticity is an important concept with regard to the workings of the spiritual partnership phenomenon, because I shall suggest that there is a strong need to relate to someone on an authentic level in order to experience one's own consciousness, as well as to experience the other's being and value in a full way; yet fully authentic relationships are rare and difficult to establish. (I am fully aware of the objections many of my postmodernist colleagues will raise against the use of this notion of 'authenticity,' and will take up the epistemological problem involved here in the next section.)

The complete letting down of psychological defenses necessary for the trust, nondirectiveness, and nonjudgmentalism that facilitate the space of empathy required by spiritual partnership obviously does not occur routinely in human relationships. These factors do not result from any passing whim, but from an investment of energy and concerted effort toward the goal of in-depth communication of subjective processes. No one would want to engage in more than a few such relationships in a lifetime, and the nature of the requirements just listed almost inevitably entails, if successful, a long-term commitment. It cannot be entered lightly, or taken lightly once begun. Thus it is natural and reasonable to be fearful of letting down our defenses to this extent at all. To do so is to set into motion a chain reaction that tears down the self-interested and egocentric orientation even more than we could ever originally intend or want, because we depend on this egocentricity for survival and effective functioning in the practical arena.

It is for this reason that the process of spiritual partnership, if carried through to its natural conclusion (and not aborted through narcissism and the danger of clinging dependence and deficiency-motivated symbiosis, which will be discussed later), catapults us whether we like it or not (and most of us initially do not like it) into humility, gratitude, and generalized agape. Our focus on the spiritual partner's finitude (i.e., the person's uniqueness, fleetingness, and irreplaceability) in a sense tricks us into a non-egocentric perspective in which we appreciate the other's value more sharply than we can our own (again, because we cannot focus this intensely on our own finitude in a positive way). We then learn to experience the uniqueness, fleetingness, and irreplaceability of all people and events, but in a decidedly positive way (not in chronic anxiety, despair, or depression) because of the inspiring effect of the intensely positive valuation of a primary transcendent object.

What, then, is spiritual partnership? How does such a phenomenon come about and function? How does it facilitate the spiritual transformation that I have claimed is capable of resolving the finite dilemma without self-deceptive denials of finitude? Why does it seem to orient itself so much more spontaneously around relationships between people of opposite sexual polarity? And most curiously of all, why does it so often fail, so that recourse to self-deceptive denials of finitude end up replacing the ability to experience the value of being intensely enough to counterbalance a frank acknowledgment of the facts about finitude? This book will attempt to address these perplexing questions, which until now have remained largely outside the domain of philosophical discourse, although their urgency for our time becomes increasingly obvious.

The first step in addressing these questions must be to lay a careful methodological groundwork for studying such issues. This methodological groundwork is especially difficult in the context of a study of transcendent value experience, because here we are in a realm where direct experience is crucial, yet temptations to self-deception are ubiquitous. The next section will take up this problem.

2. Can There Be Self-Understanding in the Wake of Postmodernism?

The subject matter of this study involves emotionally charged issues about the meaning of life and the ways in which this meaning is affected by anxiety-arousing or otherwise potentially disturbing aspects of the ontological condition—our own impending nonbeing, our estrangement from others with whom we need authentic and empathic relationships in order to sustain our conscious being in its motivated patterns, and our own vulnerability and relative insignificance in the scheme of things. These are the kinds of issues toward which the problem of working out an adequate epistemological approach is especially difficult. To apply a logical-empiricist approach, for example, would be virtually impossible, because empirical observation alone can too easily miss the subjective meanings of experiences (see Ellis 1983, 1986). Moreover, the circularity between the ways we see reality and the prereflective, self-deceptive, and value-laden categories that distort what we see is especially troublesome when the subject matter itself includes the constitution of our emotional orientation toward the value of life and thus the very self-deceptive process that threatens to undermine the inquiry.

In more straightforward terms, the epistemological problem of the relationship between consciousness and its subject matter is more difficult when consciousness itself is the subject matter. Without getting too bogged down in technicalities that I have discussed in a more detailed way elsewhere (Ellis 1983, 1986, 1992a, 1995), I find it advantageous in this kind of context to apply a modified introspectionist approach—modified, that is, somewhat in the direction of 'poststructuralist hermeneutics'—a dangerously ambiguous label that I shall attempt to define clearly enough to serve our purposes here.

An introspectionist approach, if workable, is especially useful when analyzing the nature and processes of consciousness. Introspection, if we can devise methods to keep it careful and disciplined, can allow us to reflect in a rigorous way on the 'experiential' dimension of consciousness per se, rather than approaching it from the standpoint of some abstract theory constructed on the basis of empirical-scientific research that is already contaminated by a selective-attention process motivated by value-laden categories (as philosophers of science such as Thomas Kuhn and Larry Laudan have amply shown). For example, Freud directed his attention to observations relevant to certain neurotic phenomena in the attempt to help patients with certain types of disturbances; the resulting theory, as Maslow has pointed out, was skewed toward a view of human motivation that not only is essentially neurotic, but in fact is characteristic of certain *types* of neuroses. Indeed, Karen Horney has suggested in *The Neurotic Personality of Our Time* (1950/1991, 71) that the Oedipal conflict probably does not even occur in relatively normal development, where neurotic psychodynamics on the part of parents have not already set the stage for such high-pitched jealousy reactions. Kohut and recent object relations theorists tend to endorse this criticism of Freud's thinking. As Giorgi emphasizes, any abstract theory about subjective experiences that is ultimately derivable from research operating within such selective biases is in principle further removed from reality than direct, introspective experiencing of the subjective processes themselves.

As another example of the selective-attention process in empirically based theory, the motivational theories of behaviorists emphasize those aspects of functioning that most readily lend themselves to precise measurement in the behavior of rats and other such laboratory animals. Here again, the understanding of conscious beings is bound to be skewed in certain directions, depending on which phenomena are most accessible to the research paradigms that are most conveniently accessible (and for which grant monies are most available).

Perhaps more important, empirically observable phenomena per se (for example, 'behavior') can be correlated with conscious processes only if we already understand *what* the conscious processes are, so that we can determine whether they correlate with the observed behavior in question. But *what* the conscious processes are can be understood, if at all, only introspectively. No amount of empirical study of the brain can reveal to a neurologist what a headache feels like if the neurologist has never experienced anything like a headache. Moreover, a psychologist is not likely to understand what forms of consciousness a patient is attempting to communicate if the psychologist cannot empathize by vicariously imagining what it would be like to subjectively experience those forms of consciousness. As Kohut says, "empathy is the mode by which one gathers psychological data about other people and, when they say what they think or feel, imagines their inner experience even though it is not open to direct observation" (1985, 115). Kohut regards such empathic data as the fundamental starting point from which Freud and later psychoanalysts have elaborated their theories, and suggests that psychology "move from a preoccupation with the elaboration and refinement of the established theories to one of renewed emphasis on the gathering of primary data, a return to the empathic observation of inner experience" (73).

Of course, the obvious objection to introspectionism (and the vicarious introspection of empathy) is that our interpretations of the meaning of directly experienced conscious processes (our own as well as others') are notoriously distorted by tacit prejudices, preconceptions, and overly simplistic category structures of which we remain largely unaware. For example, I may think that I am morally repulsed by a terrorist act because it targets innocent civilians in order to achieve a political objective, without any war's having been declared. But at the same time, I may fully approve of Nixon's bombing of innocent civilians in Cambodia and Vietnam without any war's having been declared, in order to achieve a political objective; or of Reagan's bombing of Mumar Qadaffi's family (innocent civilians), which killed Qadaffi's daughter, without any war's having been declared, in order to achieve a political objective. Or I may approve of Truman's bombing of German and Japanese civilians, where a war had been declared, but not of the bombings in Vietnam where no war was declared, yet the lack of a declaration of war may be incidental to my disapproval. The ultimate upshot is that, although I believe myself to disapprove of something by virtue of its being an instance of killing innocent civilians to achieve a political objective with no war's having been declared, the reality is that what I feel repugnance toward is something other than simply the killing of innocent civilians, or of killing to achieve a political objective, or killing without declaring war, or even any combination of these factors. That is, I still feel the repugnance even when each of these factors is imaginatively removed from the experience of the phenomenon, yet it may seem at first as if some or all of these factors constitute the essence of that toward which I feel the repugnance. Thus the content of consciousness is not self-transparent—as Merleau-Ponty shows well in his *Phenomenology of Perception*.

Thomas Frank, in his book *What's the Matter with Kansas*, admits that, as a young man, he fell into the popular habit of railing against the "liberal elites" who supposedly were destroying America. Later, he realized that the term 'liberal' in these railings had no coherent meaning, although he had fully thought it did at the time. The meaning of his own thoughts was opaque even to himself.

The same thing happens in physics. I may think that I understand what I mean by saying that time and space are homogeneous and that they cannot be distorted as a result of distributions of mass and the relative velocities of reference systems. But when I finally have understood the basic principles of the theory of relativity, I realize that formerly I *did not* know what I meant by the homogeneity of time and space, though I thought I did (see Ellis 1992c). It turns out that what I thought I thought, and felt that I felt, I did not really think and feel; and what I thought I meant was not what I meant. Consciousness is therefore 'opaque,' not self-transparent in a simple reflection.

But what many of the critics of introspective methods do not fully appreciate (sometimes because so many of them have not read extensively the works of Husserl, Heidegger, Merleau-Ponty, and other classic phenomenologists) is that phenomenology tries to offer a careful and rigorous methodology to get beyond the distorting effects of these prereflective prejudices, presuppositions, and category systems. While the limitations of this method are now widely acknowledged, I would like to argue that we should first understand the method and then try to improve on it, rather than simply throwing out the baby with the bathwater. The method, familiar to all students of phenomenology as 'phenomenological reduction,' is a way to 'bracket out,' 'suspend,' or 'put temporarily out of commission' all assumptions *about* a given object of experience that had already been accepted as assumptions *before* the specific experience took place. This reveals not what the experience would look like without any presuppositions, or from no particular vantage point, but rather it reveals the *ways in which* our prereflective presuppositions and the nature of our vantage point contribute to the appearance of the object, whether it is an object of thought, emotion, perception, or theoretical-scientific investigation.

The most tangible way to apply this 'bracketing' technique is the way Husserl describes in his *Lectures on Phenomenological Psychology* under the label of 'imaginative variation.' The way this method is supposed to work is that we vary in our imagination every aspect of an experience—one by one, and then in combination—reflecting in each case on how this particular variation would alter our impression of the original phenomenon. In the case of the moral feeling toward the terrorist act mentioned above, for example, we might imagine how we would have felt if the terrorist had been a U.S. president rather than a nameless Arab from some country that no longer exists, or if the victims had been Arab civilians hit by an Israeli bombing retaliation, noting in each case how each of these imagined variations in the perceived situation might have altered the way we felt. After a number of such variations, we usually realize that what we felt and what the feeling was 'about' were really substantially different from what we initially supposed. What is left after excluding contaminating elements from our experience in this way is called the 'phenomenological residuum,' which is a more pure description of the way the experience actually presents itself, as divorced from the preconceived category structures that have been eliminated through the imaginative variation process. We therefore learn to come closer to the truth about the meaning of our consciousness and what the consciousness is 'about' in the objective realm.

Even granted the ability to identify some of our hidden presuppositions in this way, the problem remains that the 'phenomenological residuum' that seems to be left intact after the process is complete may *still* be shot through with prereflective category structures, of which we are still unaware. The limitations of our category structures may determine the limitation of our imagination in just such a way that, when we perform the imaginative variations, we forget or fail to vary just those aspects of our impression of the phenomenon that led to a distorted view of it in the first place. For example, strict Freudians or behaviorists may think that they are *unable* to imagine a motivation that is not essentially hedonistic and drive-reductive; such a thing may seem *unimaginable* to someone with certain habits of thought, just as the notion of a nonhomogeneous space or time was unimaginable to most nineteenth-century physicists. This point is clearly illustrated by the following riddle: Why is it that a racist cannot recognize that he is a racist? The answer: because he is a racist.

This problem is especially pronounced when the phenomenon in question is an emotion-laden one such as love, one of the main topics of the present study. Romantic love, for example, seems to us in the present period of history to present itself as manifesting certain essential forms of feeling, whereas the truth may be that these forms have been created and purveyed through history as the result of a mythology that a certain culture built up around the love of the sexes for certain historical or religious reasons of which we are no longer even aware (as de Rougemont has suggested). In fact, I shall rely heavily here on an analysis somewhat similar to this of our culture's mythology of romantic love, without, however, endorsing the historical specifics of de Rougemont's explanation. This kind of prereflective inheritance of culturally sedimented preconceptions is the reason why, to a certain extent in my view, phenomenology must be supplemented (not simply replaced) by a kind of 'poststructuralist hermeneutics.'

Poststructuralist philosophies emphasize that the meanings of experiences are interpreted in terms of the implicit category structures purveyed by the language, mythology, value-laden rituals, and patterns of personal interaction prevalent in a given culture as inherited from its historical development during a given period. They recognize, however, that none of us can stand outside of our category structure in order to inspect the categories themselves from an objective or neutral perspective, since our perception of the categories themselves will be shaped and interpreted in terms of the category structures that we bring with us to any experience. It is therefore impossible to clearly identify the categories as such. And if we cannot identify them, then we cannot submit them to a critical scrutiny capable of determining whether they facilitate 'true' or 'authentic' interpretations of experience, or on the contrary distorted and inaccurate interpretations. Since epistemology depends on separating the truth from misinterpretation, many poststructuralists conclude that there is never any objective criterion for separating truth from falsehood on any issue whatever.

This extreme version of this view is more prevalent among theorists of literary criticism than among philosophers. My essential reason for rejecting an extreme relativization of truth on this basis is that doing so presupposes that there are *no* structures or features *whatever* that characterize conscious beings (at a certain level of complexity and intensity—human beings, for example) simply by virtue of being conscious beings (at that level of complexity and intensity), and not merely by virtue of being members of a specific culture, historical epoch, or set of circumstances. The appropriate limitation of the relativization of truth is thus defined by the extent to which certain things are true for conscious beings per se once they have arrived at a certain level of intensity and complexity (i.e., once they have arrived at the level of intensity and complexity applicable for the most part to human beings). For example, one cannot be a conscious being without enacting a certain amount of change and self-transformation, because without a certain amount of change and transformation a being lapses into a *stasis* and thus does not exist as a conscious being, but rather as some other kind of being—a stone or a piece of dead wood.

Extremely relativistic poststructuralists, such as Rorty and Foucault, would counter this argument by insisting that, if our categories are shaped by our culture and history, and if we cannot step outside this category structure in order to criticize it, then there is still no way to determine which categories are universal in the sense just described, and which ones are culturally and historically specific. But this argument begs the question. If we were to assume *a priori* that finite conscious beings have nothing in common with each other under different historical or cultural contexts, then of course we would have no universal epistemological standards by which to evaluate those standards that *are* historically or culturally relative. On the other hand, if conscious beings *do* use *any* epistemological standards that are *not* culturally or historically relative, then these standards would allow for a nonrelative assessment of the extent to which those standards that *are* culturally or historically relative tend to distort our interpretation of our experience. But the fact is that finite conscious beings per se do have something in common with each other: They are all attached to bodies of some sort, and thus require concretely embodied symbolization in order to actualize their existence as conscious beings. The *forms* of symbolization may vary widely, as may the *ways in which* people relate to their bodies. But the *fact* that conscious beings need embodied symbolization in order to be *qua* conscious beings is inescapable. I have argued this point more extensively elsewhere (especially in *An Ontology of Consciousness* and in *Questioning Consciousness*) and will further pursue these arguments here.

If it were true that all conscious beings have *no* fundamental features in common with each other, simply by being conscious beings, then the argument for an absolute relativism might work. But if conscious beings do have *anything* in common with each other, then there is no reason to presuppose that *all* epistemological standards are the arbitrary product of some particular culture or historical situation. And if some epistemological standards are culture-independent in this sense, then they would provide a vantage point from which those standards that *are* culture-specific can be viewed as such. What is necessary, however, if a standard is to be considered reliable for this purpose, is not merely that the standard be employed in all cultures; it must be one whose employment is not the result of any specific cultural prejudices, whether these happen to be universal, or whether they happen to be shared by only a few cultures. Such a standard would apply to all *possible* communities of authentic conscious beings to the extent that they are conscious. It would derive from features that conscious beings share *because they are conscious beings*, not because their circumstances accidentally happen to be similar. And it would derive from the *authentic* features of conscious existence (not self-deceptive ones), because our consciousness is present to us as what it really is only to the extent that it is authentic—as we shall see, and as I have discussed more fully in other contexts where epistemology was the central focus.

The extreme relativization of epistemology can thus be traced to the notion that there is nothing that all conscious beings share in common with each other by virtue of being conscious beings. The impetus for the notion that human beings have nothing in common with each other originates from two main sources. First, from anthropologists, who throughout the twentieth century tended to overemphasize the differences between peoples, especially their value systems. As I have explained in more detail elsewhere (1992b), anthropologists reached these overgeneralized conclusions because they did not clearly understand the philosophical distinctions between intrinsic and extrinsic values, and between prima facie values and values in an absolute sense. An 'extrinsic' value means one that is considered valuable only because it promotes or facilitates the achievement of some other end beyond itself, and would not be considered valuable in the first place if it did *not* seem to promote those other ends. For example, by this definition, money is only an extrinsic value, no matter how obsessively someone may be committed to it. 'Intrinsic' value, by contrast, refers to things that would have been valued even if they had not seemed to promote some end beyond themselves. The preservation of human life, for example, is generally felt to be an intrinsic value, at least prima facie. By prima facie, most philosophers mean 'unless some other value takes priority over it.' For instance, the Hottentots used to put their parents to death at age 60 in order (as they put it) to "relieve them of their suffering and misery" (Duncker 1939). Yet, when this value (the relief of suffering and misery) is *not* in opposition to the preservation of human life, they are just as committed to the latter value as anyone else. Thus both the relief of suffering and misery and the preservation of human life are valued prima facie by the Hottentots, but these two values sometimes compete with each other, and choices must be made. The Hottentots' values thus are not so different from ours as the example at first seems to suggest.

In more general terms, the anthropologist Ralph Linton pointed out many years ago that cultures more often differ with respect to *extrinsic* values (i.e., the *methods* of promoting intrinsic values) than with respect to the intrinsic values themselves. And, though they may differ with respect to the comparative importance of prima facie values, they tend to converge with respect to the kinds of things that are considered to have intrinsic value. So the early-twentieth-century anthropologists' notion that people from the various cultures they were studying did not share any common conscious structures or contents really stemmed from a failure to apply rigorous philosophical analysis to the consciousness of the people in those cultures—for example, the failure to distinguish intrinsic from extrinsic value, or to distinguish prima facie value from that which is valued 'all things considered.'

The other main source of extreme relativism in this regard is the view expressed by many existentialists that, as Ortega puts it in *History as a System*, "man has no nature." But here again, this is based on the notion that humans must choose what we want to be, rather than having it pregiven or predefined for us. The reasons *why* humans must choose our own being thus become the 'essential features' of 'human nature,' so that Ortega, in reaching so many conclusions about the nature of human beings per se, seems to contradict his own position. This contradiction is ameliorated when we realize that, when Ortega says 'the essence of man is that he has no essence' (which sounds self-contradictory), what he really means is that 'man has no essence *except* for those features of human beings that describe the process of choosing our own essence.' But the features of people that describe the process of choosing our own essence are themselves subject matter enough for a rich ontology of what it means to be a human being, provided that we do not confuse these 'ontological' features of being human with the sometimes-tacit interpretations that derive from a specific culture's category system.

For example, to many European settlers in America, Native Americans did not qualify as human beings. Yet it is obvious that Europeans and Native Americans shared certain features in common by virtue of the fact that both are examples of conscious beings whose consciousness is complex enough and intense enough that existential issues become a problem for them—whether they self-consciously reflect on these issues or not. Both feel dread in the face of the threat of nonbeing (with greater or lesser degrees of courage, and with more or less self-deceptive mythologies that help ease the dread); both seek intensification, change, and self-transformation in their consciousness rather than the mere stasis, stagnation, and lethargic complacence of a simplistic, consummatory drive-reductive hedonism (see Neihardt's *Black Elk Speaks* for exploration of these issues in Sioux culture, for example); both need somewhat authentic relationships with other people in order to find adequate opportunities to express and concretely symbolize their thoughts and feelings so that the stream of consciousness can unfold with the desired degree of intensity and change; both feel the need to resolve in some way the problem of the individual's relative powerlessness and insignificance in the ultimate scheme of things;

and both feel the conflicting pulls, toward greater authenticity on the one hand (in order to enhance the intensity of consciousness), and on the other hand toward complacent self-deception (in order to be falsely reassured against the threats to one's being pressed by these existential conditions).

It is these most general features of the conditions necessary for the actualization of conscious being that will concern us in this study. In developing an effective epistemological approach for these kinds of issues, we must consider the techniques phenomenologists have offered for clarifying subjective introspection, but we must also consider the poststructuralist and hermeneutic criticisms that emphasize the limitations of these methods. We must maintain both phenomenological reflection and a careful critique of the limitations of our interpretations of experience, in continual dialogue with each other. Above all, we must avoid the error that would be considered hopelessly naive from either the phenomenological or the poststructuralist perspective—of thinking that we can simply 'read off' the 'data' of our subjective experiencing without seeing that the way we interpret the meaning of our own experience has always already been colored by a prereflective category system, attributable largely to sedimented cultural legacies, and that this category system both influences the content of experience and distorts it in the interest of selective inattention and self-deception.

A recent philosopher who discusses this balancing act between introspection and hermeneutics in a helpful way is Eugene Gendlin (see especially his *Experiencing and the Creation of Meaning*, as well as the two papers he published in 1992). According to Gendlin, we can learn a great deal that is epistemologically useful from the Heideggerian notion that the human body is not just a receiver of perceptual information from the world, but is also a real being *in* the world. As such, it is already in interaction with its environment prior to any conscious perception or thought. The body therefore contains preconceptual and preperceptual 'information' about its environment, just as a plant's body contains 'information' about the direction of light and the mineral balance of the soil. If we can find an effective way to 'listen' to our bodies, they can therefore tell us something about their preconceptual orientation to their environment. Gendlin puts it this way:

> To begin philosophy by considering perception makes it seem that living things can contact reality only through perception. But plants *are* in contact with reality. They *are* interactions, quite without perception. Our own living bodies also *are* interactions with their environments, and that is not lost just because ours also have perception. . . . Our bodies . . . interact as bodies, not just through what comes with the five senses. . . .
>
> Merleau-Ponty . . . meant perception to include (latently and implicitly) also our bodily interactional being-in-the-world, all of our life in situations. . . . The body senses the whole situation, and it urges, it implicitly shapes our next action. It senses itself living-in its whole context—the situation. . . .
>
> From one ancient bone one can reconstruct not only the whole animal, but from its body also the kind of environment in which it lived. . . . The body even as a dead structure still contains all that implicit information about its environment. . . .
>
> My warmth or hostility will affect your ongoing bodily being whether you perceive it or not. You may find it there, if you sense how your body has the situation. (1992a, 344–50)

The hermeneutic question about this, of course, is: How can we listen to this bodily information without allowing our cultural, historical, and linguistic categories to distort or misrepresent or just plainly not see it? Let me reformulate this question in a more positive way: How do we know when we have adequately identified what a 'bodily felt sense' of a situation is telling us about the situation? How do we know what a state of consciousness is 'about' in relation to the 'bodily sensed' environment?

To use a very simple example, consider Gendlin's description of the "odd feeling of knowing you have forgotten something but not knowing what it is":

> You are troubled by the *felt sense* of some unresolved situation, something left undone, something left behind. Notice that you don't have factual data. *Your body knows but you don't.* . . . You find a possibility. "Helen's party! I forgot to tell Helen I can't come to her party!"
>
> This idea doesn't satisfy the feeling. It is perfectly true that you forgot to tell Helen you would miss her party, but your body knows it isn't this that has been nagging you. . . . Your body knows you have forgotten something else, and it knows what that something is. That is how you can tell it isn't Helen's party. (Gendlin 1981, 38–39)

When we try to answer any question, we refer to the felt quality of the question itself in order to decide whether a proposed answer satisfies the question. The felt quality of the question is given in the act of asking the question, and this bodily-sensed given serves as a constraint on the acceptability of proposed answers. I may be unsure whether the name I forgot is Bill or Tom, but not *just any* name will feel even remotely familiar. Similarly, the problems of quantum mechanics raise questions about relativity theory, and there might be many equally plausible perspectives from which to propose answers, but what is manifestly clear is that a reversion to Newtonian physics will *not* work—will *not* satisfy our questions. Only by un-asking questions that we have already asked could we now be satisfied by Newtonian physics. So the answers we accept or reject to a given question are not completely arbitrary. Although many answers may work, not all answers work equally well.

The reason we know that a given answer will not work is that it does not satisfy the felt quality of the question. Thus, 'I forgot to tell Helen I can't come to her party,' though true, fails to elicit any 'bodily shift' from the felt quality of the question as to what it is I am trying to remember. Ultimately, the fact that I have a body anchors me in reality, because the being of my body (in relation to other beings) *is* a reality.

But, even if some proposed answers will not satisfy a question at all (so that an absolute relativism can be avoided), we must still deal with the obvious problem that many proposed answers *seem* to work (or not to work) only because our sedimented preconceptions and categories *prevent us from asking the questions about them* that, if asked, would reveal that the proposed answer does not really work the way we thought it did after all. An example is the narcissistically disturbed person's failure to realize that his discontent does not arise from the failure of his son to take out the garbage, or from any specific triggering incident, but rather from the narcissist's general failure to simulate an impossibly grandiose ego ideal while simultaneously enjoying everyone's acclaim and approval. This fundamental frustration will lead him to seek out opportunities to express contempt for others as misdirected symbolizations of a rage that has no remedy as long as the narcissistic disturbance persists. Yet the narcissist's motivated category system will keep him from seeing these aspects of himself by preventing him from asking the right questions in the right contexts.

On the other hand, we all know from past experience what it feels like to have struggled to maintain a comprehension of a situation within a certain category system, and then to give up the old category system and comprehend the situation from a new category system. A visual Gestalt shift is an example of this feeling. Another example is the realization that we have been taken in by a dishonest salesman who played on our own self-deceptive desire to avoid the trouble of investigating more thoroughly. In the instant of this realization, we know that our former conceptualization of the situation was all wrong, and a 'Gestalt shift' occurs. So, barring continuing purposeful self-deception, we know how to recognize this 'bodily shift' when it occurs.

This bodily felt shift can be combined with Husserl's idea of imaginative variation to move us closer to a way of looking at situations that satisfies our questions more adequately—in a more coherent way. The more we rule out inappropriate presuppositions that have affected the way we see a situation, the closer we come to a view of the situation that is at least self-honest and comprehensive. The way we do this is to imagine the way we would react to the situation if one or another of our presuppositions were removed from our interpretation of it.

In the context of understanding the differences in the meanings of various forms of love—their intentionality, or what they are really about—we can use imaginative variation to ask ourselves, for example in the case of erotic love: Could I be sexually attracted to someone, and at the same time like them personally, without having this feeling that announces itself with so much emotional intensity and obsessiveness? Even if there have been no real-life experiences from which to draw an answer, using Gendlin's 'focusing' method can enable us to answer such a question. There is a distinct bodily shift, like a Gestalt shift, at the point when I imagine that alternative scenario, telling me that neither sexual attraction nor personal liking for someone, nor even a combination of the two, would necessarily produce this particular felt quality. And this means that the feeling is about something other than either sex or friendship.

Imaginative variation allows us better to understand the extent to which the way an experience made us feel or react is specific to a peculiar situation, a particular cultural context, or a particular scenario in our own personal lives, as compared to the extent to which we would have felt and reacted similarly even if these kinds of circumstances had been different. A good example of the use of imaginative variation in the present work is the attempt to understand the extreme admiration that people with opposite sexual polarization often feel toward each other, and how this relates to spiritual partnership. At first (having come under the sway of some Jungian ideas) I thought that opposite polarization was a necessary element in spiritual partnership, because my own experience, as well as literary works I had read (not only Western, but also non-Western works such as *Black Elk Speaks*, *Sidhartha*, and Ibn Hazm's *The Ring of the Dove*) seemed to suggest that there was always some connection between opposite sexual polarity and love experiences of the particular kind I was considering. But at length, I began to question this, and finally asked myself to imagine what would happen in a culture where everyone had developed both their 'masculine' and their 'feminine' polarities exactly equally (supposing for the moment that this would be possible). I then realized that the need for spiritual partnership would still be just as pronounced in such people as it is for us, because they would still need to address the dilemma of finitude—including the problems of death, alienation from needed others, and relative powerlessness and insignificance in the ultimate scheme of things. But, lacking oppositely polarized people to pull the spiritual partnership experience, they would be limited to the use of other ways to symbolize the intense 'admiration-through-compassion' that characterizes spiritual partnership, so as to intensify it in some other way than through quasi-aesthetic appreciation for the oppositely polarized forms of consciousness posited by Jung. For example, they would use as a symbolization vehicle their feelings of simple sexual attraction (even without sexual polarization in the consciousness of the other person) to intensify their more spiritual feelings toward each other. I then saw immediately that the Jungian notion of *anima-animus* interactions (which I will critique later in this text) is not an essential part of the meaning of spiritual partnership, but only an accidental catalyst for it that happens to be prevalent in modern Western culture (and, perhaps to a lesser extent, in many other cultures as well). Feelings toward the opposite sexual polarity, like bodily feelings of sexual attraction, are only ways to give concrete symbolization to the experience so that it can be felt more intensely, developed more fully, and carried forward in other possible directions. Without imaginative variation, I would never have noticed this, and would have ended up with a theory of sexual polarization resembling Jung's *anima-animus* notion.

One way of stimulating imaginative variation is to compare one's understanding of one's own experiences with those of others. For example, in the case of the issue of sexual polarization, one of the spurs to further imaginative variation on my part was that too many people with whom I spoke did not feel that their consciousness had ever included much more of one polarity than the other, yet they did seem able to relate to the spiritual partnership experience roughly in the way I was describing it—usually in contexts where they had, in fact, been sexually attracted to the person or engaged in a sexual love relationship. One way to get past the limitations of one's own categories, then, is to see how the same phenomenon might look from someone else's category system—not in order to unreflectively accept those other categories, but to stimulate imaginative variation with respect to one's own.

I have spoken with a good number of people about their somewhat similar (and somewhat different) experiences—including people of different age, nationality, gender, racial and ethnic groups, and social class, and including psychotherapists, people with psychological disturbances, and simply normal people—in order to further spur questioning about how much of what I have experienced is simply autobiographical information about myself, and how much of it seems to apply to people generally. The point here is not to reach inductive generalizations based on this small and unscientific sample, but to facilitate imaginative variation. Many people with whom I have spoken have experienced phenomena very much like 'spiritual partnership,' sometimes only in a few respects, sometimes in every important respect. Others could not even understand what I was talking about, or thought that I was referring to some other readily categorizable kind of human relationship. Yet even the information gleaned from this latter group highlights striking differences between the experience of those other categories and the spiritual partnership effect.

Another aspect of the poststructuralist hermeneutic modification of this (neo-) phenomenological method must consist in the attempt to understand what there is about modern and postmodern culture that, on the one hand, leads us to feel more and more pressed to try to fulfill what I have called our 'ontological' needs by means of love relationships (especially romantic ones), yet on the other hand find that the structures of interaction in our form of culture are less and less compatible with the 'space of empathy' that is needed if such relationships are to serve these needs on an adequate and sustained basis.

Although I use the following word cautiously, it will be necessary in a sense to 'deconstruct' certain assumptions that have permeated human worldviews since around the time our species initially evolved. These assumptions result from the difficulty of coming to terms with various aspects of our own finitude in such a way as to preserve the feeling that to be a conscious being has a significant amount of positive value. The main ones of these assumptions for our purposes are: the immortality of the individual soul; a 'free will' that avoids being the product of its early psychological environment, genetic inheritance, and sociopolitical context; the existence of all-powerful deities who can solve all unsolvable problems; and a morality of blame and guilt that despises and purposely inflicts suffering on the victims of psychological disturbances rather than showing compassion for them and trying to remove the ultimate causes of such problems. All these ways of confronting (or avoiding confronting) our ontological dilemma have been prevalent since human beings first became intelligent enough to worry about the problems of finitude, and all of them, as I shall argue, are more or less dysfunctional because they lead to self-deceptive defense systems.

At the same time that these ostrichlike assumptions were being used to simply deny or ignore the reality and implications of finitude, it seems that a more authentic and ultimately more effective method of coming to terms with these problems was also in the process of evolving. This other method, I believe, was the use of spiritual partnership to strongly affirm the value of being a conscious being, in spite of and in part because of the reality of finitude, through appreciation of this value as directly experienced in the person of another conscious being, whether a deity or a human love object.

In connection with this last point, the next section will look at some psychological groundwork that has already been laid for us.

3. Object Relations, Self Psychology, and Inspirational Effects of Transcendent Objects

'Self psychology,' as developed by Heinz Kohut, is generally regarded as an offshoot of, or as falling under the broader heading of 'object relations theory,' as exemplified by Melanie Klein, Jacques Lacan, Alice Miller, Christopher Bollas, Peter Zachar, and others. Although I am aware that some followers of Kohut (for example, Ornstein) choose to emphasize the differences between object relations theory and Kohut's self psychology—and thus to insist on separating the two—the differences are not very relevant to our discussion here. I shall therefore speak of self psychology as falling under the broader heading of object relations theory (as Alice Miller does, for example), since the points of interest for our purposes are issues on which Kohut and his followers completely agree with the earlier object relations theorists (and in fact with most 'ego psychologists').

Object relations theory and self psychology focus centrally on the ways in which we use our emotional relationships to certain selected 'objects' in our environment ('selfobjects,' in Kohut's terminology)—especially significant other people—to facilitate the development of the self and its continued cohesion through the various developmental stages of childhood and adulthood. Since this kind of approach attributes great importance to the dynamics through which we enact idealizing feelings of love, 'awe' (Kohut 1985, 104), a 'longing' to 'merge' with the idealized object (80), and even 'addictive' fixations (114–15), it seems natural to assume that this area of psychological research is especially relevant to the phenomenon of 'spiritual partnership' as I shall be describing it here.

The most basic assumptions of object relations theory (and self psychology) are essentially derivable from the central assumption discussed in the previous section—that conscious beings require a concrete matrix of embodied symbolization in order to facilitate the enactment of their conscious potential. It is necessary only to add to this assumption two others: First, that embodied symbolization requires interaction with other conscious beings; and secondly, that one of the most important kinds of consciousness that needs to be actualized in this process is the experience of the *value* of being. The opening section of this book began to introduce the argument that the need to affirm the value of being requires that we experience this value as instantiated in other conscious beings, through empathy. This leads to a need for 'idealization' of a transcendent object to facilitate a transcendent value experience.

Object relations theories rely on very similar reasoning. The 'idealized object imago,' according to object relations theory (and self psychology), is supposed to be a person whose image or presence is made to carry the ideals of the self during any time of weak or weakened self-concept. Such times include not only early infancy and neurotic regressions to infantile states, but also any period of self-doubt, self-restructuring, or radical soul-searching, as during the germinating phase of intense creative work (Kohut 1985, 192–93). According to Theodor Reik, a similar period of weakened self-concept is often the precursor to falling in love. (In *Eros in a Narcissistic Culture*, I qualified Reik's view to include cases where, even though all is going well in our egocentric life projects, we experience this worldly success as radically inadequate to provide a sense that life has enough 'ultimate meaning' or 'significance.' The precursor to love in this case is still essentially similar to the kind of soul-searching and self-questioning that Reik posits.) Since personal growth and self-actualization comprise a kind of creativity that demands radical soul-searching and restructuring in a more obvious way than any other kind of creativity (as in Rollo May's *The Courage to Create*), this view would also imply that the idealization of significant others plays an important role in the normal process of self-actualization, as many theorists of love have suggested (see May's *Love and Will*, Ethel Person, Nathaniel Branden, the Jungian Robert Johnson, Maslow, Kohut, and Miller, just to name a few). God also is interpreted in this approach as an idealized other with whom strong longings for merger (through empathy) are felt. Saints, martyrs, ancestors, or any other worshiped religious love object could be viewed in the same way.

All the psychologists within this tradition emphasize that we often need to find another person in whom we can envision our highest ideals embodied, because we cannot fully enough make ourselves into an object for such appreciation. While object relations psychologists recognize this phenomenological fact, because they perceive it through empathy and introspection, they are less clear as to *why* it should be the case. Kohut seems to assume that it is difficult for the same being to play the role of both subject and object of the same experience. Thus consciousness, in order to actualize itself, needs to become 'intentional' consciousness in the phenomenological sense—needs to be conscious in relation to some object. For Kohut, as for many phenomenologists, 'consciousness is always consciousness *of something*' (for example, see Lauer's discussion of this point); furthermore, this *something* which constitutes the object of consciousness is usually construed as something *outside of* or *over against* the experiencing subject (for example, see Sartre's *Transcendence of the Ego*).

I shall suggest below that the subject-object relation is more complicated than this, and that, as David Carr has shown very well, the object need not always stand over against the subject; there may be nonintentional experiences, as Husserl grants in *Ideas*. But, generally speaking, a state of 'intentional' consciousness does not take just that state itself as its object: Anger is anger *about* something; jealousy is jealousy *of* someone. It is important to note, however, that we often take the intentional objects of feelings to be more specific and immediate than they really are, by confusing mere triggers with the real issues at stake, which inevitably include more general areas of concern. When a motorist cuts in front of me in traffic, I may think for a moment that the motorist is the reason I am so angry, but a moment's reflection will reveal that the motorist is only a trigger—too trivial an incident to be the real issue *about* which I feel such violent emotions. I then realize that the motorist is only being used as a symbol for more important events and issues in my life, and that it is these more complex matters that the feeling is about. In many instances we may be confused as to what our feelings are 'about' in this sense, and we are often motivated to misconstrue their meaning or hide it from ourselves, but there is still *something* about which we feel what we feel.

I also suggested in *An Ontology of Consciousness* that, in many cases, we take something as the 'object' of a feeling, not because it is what 'caused' us to feel that way, or because it is the essential 'subject matter' of the feeling, but rather because that particular object serves as a *symbol* or *symbolization matrix* in relation to which the feeling can be enacted more fully—as when an otherwise indifferent piece of music is used to call up the fullness of feelings toward a love object. The music is not the primary reason why we feel what we feel; it only serves as an 'object' in the sense that it helps us to symbolize and thus make more concrete the way we feel. Gendlin, whose introspective method was discussed in the last section, has oriented an entire cognitive theory and psychotherapy around this point. By giving an adequate concrete symbolic expression to a cognitive or emotional state, we bring further implicit aspects of it from a preconscious to a conscious status, thus intensifying it as consciousness and allowing it to unfold. This also seems to be the reason for Bollas's point that "the subject selects and uses objects in order to materialize elements latent to his personality" (1989, 2). And again, "True self use of an analyst is the force of idiom finding itself through experiences of the object. . . . the analysand's aim is not [at such times] to communicate a child-parent paradigm script, but to find experiences to establish true self in life" (16–17).

Because the kind of symbolization process that is relevant here depends on *concrete embodiedness*, object relations theorists are also correct in stressing that not only must consciousness actualize itself in relation to an object; it is also easier to make a *concrete* object than an abstraction serve as the bearer of idealized feelings—especially very early in life, before the ego has developed far enough to allow for embodiment of such abstractions (in the form of an 'ego ideal' component of the superego). This is often one of the reasons for the idealizing 'transference' to another person, such as a psychotherapist (in which the latter appears 'larger than life' and is made to serve as the object either of the patient's need for narcissistic gratification, or of the need for an ego ideal); according to Kohut, the transference occurs as part of a regression to a more disorganized period of development because the self concept is in the process of being questioned and reconstructed. Since the patient has trouble focusing on the guiding ideals of his or her own superego (which is in transition and disarray), the person either takes the analyst as an ideal in their place, or tries to get the analyst to affirm the weakened narcissistic ego. But we must remember that such idealization of another person does not occur only in regressive or neurotic conditions. It occurs when people fall in love, or idealize a 'mentor' figure (as, according to Jones, Freud did in relation to the admired image of Fliess), or use a fellow artist or scientist as an 'alter ego' (as, according to Gedo, Picasso did in relation to Braque). In Kohut's view, this idealization occurs frequently as a natural part of the creative process. As the artist or scientist wrestles with the radical deconstruction of her own previous worldview, resulting in chaos and a disintegration of the feeling of stability, direction, and competence of the self (and thus her identity as a person), she finds another person in whom to invest the now unavailable ideals (Kohut 1985, 193–94).

The main reason for all the transformations of idealization from the abstractions of the ego ideal to the concreteness of another person or to an artistic or scientific product is, in my view, traceable ultimately to Gendlin's point about the need to symbolize feelings in a concrete way in order to allow them to be fully felt—as for example feelings of depression can be intensified, focused, and worked through if we find the right piece of music to listen to in order to facilitate the process, or as talking to someone about our frustrations enables us to feel them more fully and more accurately. The role of this kind of symbolization will be explored much further as we proceed.

In the case of adults, the main reason we so frequently take a *conscious* being as the idealized imago seems to be that (as argued more fully in my *Coherence and Verification in Ethics*) conscious beings comprise the one type of being in the universe that most obviously and most strongly has intrinsic and irreducible value. This is why it is difficult to imagine any moral value in a universe completely devoid of any conscious beings whatever. But, as I have already suggested, it is possible to *directly experience* the value of a being *other than ourselves* in a much more intense and positive way than we can directly experience the value of our own being.

The reason for this last point goes beyond the abstract philosophical assumption that the same experience cannot be both subject and object for itself. As adults, we obviously are able to have quite intense feelings about ourselves—for example, self-pity, pride, self-hatred, anxiety about the meaning of our being, and at times depression about its seeming meaninglessness. When we speak of relatively normal adults (not severely schizophrenic, autistic, or mentally retarded ones), we are speaking of beings who have learned not only to make themselves the object of certain feelings, but also more or less to make a distinction between feelings toward the self-as-experiential-process and feelings toward the self-as-object-for-others. For example, we may feel depressed because the self-as-experiential-process cannot find the right opportunities to express itself or meet its needs adequately; or on the other hand we may feel depressed because the self-as-object-for-others is negatively evaluated by important others. We thus know how to make some sort of distinction between the self as experiential process and the self as object (although we may sometimes confuse the two), and we often feel emotions toward ourselves in both these senses.

Even so, the fact remains that adults tend to feel their idealization of others more intensely than they can feel their idealization of themselves. To understand why this is the case, we must explore the feeling of love not as the outcome of an abstract philosophical principle of intentionality, but in a concrete way. In this exploration, we see that love, in the sense of a deeply inspiring feeling, entails both admiration (positive valuation) and compassion for an intrinsically valuable conscious being in the face of its ontological endangeredness. One of the main ways in which love is intensified is to focus on this endangeredness of the conscious being in its finitude. But to focus on our own finitude is to enter the realm in which we must remain stubborn, stoic, and militant in our fight *against* the forces and conditions that make us finite. To give up this rugged attitude of strong-mindedness would be to lay down our arms, give up the struggle, and wallow in self-pity. Not only is this a luxury we cannot afford, but it would also become an intensely *negative* rather than positive feeling. Thus, paradoxically, to focus on the existential embattledness of another being emotionally magnifies our love and thus our admiration and the floating, euphoric feelings that go with love— the direct feeling of the positive value of life which inspires us; whereas on the other hand to focus on our *own* embattledness has a strong tendency to depress and discourage us.

The feelings of *admiration* in love also tend to be more strongly positive when the love object is someone other than ourselves. One way of seeing this point is to reflect on the stagnation that results from too much self-admiration. Another way to see it is to notice that admiration tends to be intensified when the forms of consciousness in the other person are of a kind that we would like to actualize in ourselves, but cannot or have not been able to do so. We therefore intensely crave the other person's presence, so that we can vicariously experience the admired form of consciousness, and at the same time we fear the person because our lack of control over this urgent need in ourselves gives the love object so much power over us. The urgency of the craving and the fear of having it frustrated greatly intensify the felt quality of the feeling of admiration for the other person. As a clear example, consider how much more frequently we tend to completely intensify admiration toward persons of opposite sexual polarization (and/or those toward whom sexual symbolization of the feelings is possible), often to the point of distraction and 'divine madness'—and sometimes madness that is not so divine.

To suggest that infants have not yet learned to feel both admiration and compassion in the same emotion is entirely consistent with this approach. If the infant admires the omnipotent other, such admiration is more likely to stem from this object's power to meet the infant's needs than from the object's vulnerability or sensitivity. And if the infant can feel compassion toward itself in some sense, this compassion is more likely to be a negative experience (the 'depressive position') than a form of admiration. When the omnipotent object fails to meet an infant's needs, the appropriate response is anger or even denial that the failing object is even the same entity as the omnipotent one (i.e., the 'good mother' and the 'bad mother' are dissociated from each other). And when the infant succeeds in admiring itself, such admiration is more likely to result from its supposed power to meet its own needs and win the admiration of others, not from the sensitivity toward which one feels compassion. Thus it is unlikely that infants can feel 'love' in the adult sense (which combines both admiration and compassion) that is the primary concern of this book.

Nonetheless, for their own reasons and in their own ways, infants need to relate to admired others through patterns that are emotionally significant not only because they serve to meet the infant's needs for homeostatic drive reduction, but also because the interactions serve to facilitate the infant's ability to actualize its own patterns of consciousness as they unfold toward increasing complexity. And intense feelings toward the significant other seem to play a part in many of the interactions needed to serve this 'symbolizing' function. Here again, the relation of infant to significant other is analogous in this respect to the relation of a listener toward a piece of music that enables the listener to work through certain emotional processes by 'symbolizing' and 'concretizing' them in relation to the music. Without the availability of significant others, this symbolizing function would be thwarted, and consciousness could not sustain the desired level of intensity and complexity. This much seems to be as true for infants as for adults.

Object relations theory's approach to interpreting the meaning of religious experience is clearly more sympathetic to the possibility of a legitimate and healthy role for such experiences in the normal psyche than earlier psychoanalytic approaches, such as those of Freud and Rank. Freud and Rank seem to view religion essentially as a form of self-deception as defense against the too-painful reality of our own death. While I agree with Freud and Rank that religion occurs in response to a human need to come to terms with the problem of our own finitude (not only death, but also the powerlessness, alienation, and relative insignificance of the individual), the idea of spiritual partnership is also in agreement with the object relations theorists' contention that self-deceptive forms and functions of religion are only one way of dealing with this problem. Other forms and functions of religion attempt to deal with it, not by denying the harsh reality of finitude, but by providing a positive value experience intense enough to counterbalance the harshness of our dilemma, so that we can fully appreciate and directly experience the positive value of life in spite of the reality of such evils. Spiritual partnership is in effect a way to experience this value through non-egocentric feelings of positive valuation toward other conscious beings—an experience we learn to have by means of a certain sequence of phases that must be undergone at the point when we have entered into a relationship that embodies an especially good space of empathy and thus an unusually strong proportion of spiritual partnership. On this interpretation, Jesus, Mohammed, and God serve the function of heavily invested 'selfobjects,' in the same way that a relationship to a primary spiritual partner functions.

Although some psychoanalysts might interpret the phenomenon of spiritual partnership as a narcissistic transference in the interest of regression to an infantile condition as a result of unresolved 'mirroring' needs (i.e., phase-appropriate gratification of narcissistic needs that should have been met by the infant's caretakers), such an interpretation begs the question. It deflects to an earlier period of life the question as to why conscious beings need to invest feelings of idealization in other conscious beings than themselves. To explain such needs entirely in terms of an infant's strategies to get its homeostatic drives reduced is to resort to a complete homeostatic drive reductionism that Freud originally championed but then rejected in *Beyond the Pleasure Principle*, and for good reason. If the only aim of living organisms were to reduce their homeostatic drives, the easiest way to accomplish this result would be suicide. For this reason Freud recognized that not only do we want to reduce our consummatory drives, but we also want to remain *conscious* while doing so, and we want to maintain this consciousness with a certain degree of intensity and complexity. Recent neurophysiologists who study the emotional brain underscore this point. Of Panksepp's seven emotional brain systems, only one is driven by consummatory needs. Exploration, play, curiosity, and even nurturance are types of activities that are valued because they enhance self-organizational complexity rather than leading to consummatory satiation. I have argued elsewhere (1986, 1995a, 1995b, forthcoming a, b) and will further argue here that the earlier Freud was wrong, and the later Freud was right on this point. If so, then the demand to maintain a certain level of conscious existence motivates a realm of needs that cannot be explained simply as methods of attaining homeostatic drive reduction. To deny such explanations is neither to affirm dualism nor to deny psychological determinism (which I shall take up later), but only to insist that certain needs can be understood only in terms of self-organizational tendencies in biological organisms, where the form of organization seeks to appropriate needed microconstituents rather than merely being determined by the activities of these microconstituents (as recently discussed, for example, by Kauffman and by Monod). 'Existential' needs are geared not toward reduction of the drives of our microconstituents, but toward experiencing ourselves as fully alive, as conscious in an interesting and meaningful way. In order to actualize conscious potential in this way, we need to engage in certain kinds of significant relationships with other people.

Bollas even suggests that the neonate is already possessed of such needs, that it already has a drive toward actualizing certain potential forms of being that will lead to more and more complex forms of consciousness until a complex and self-actualizing self finally eventuates. If so, then the neonate would be merely one among many instances of a conscious being who has existential as well as homeostatic needs and faces the problems inherent in the finite condition (alienation from needed others, powerlessness, etc.). True, the neonate confronts this condition in a more painful and cataclysmic way, at least in some respects. But this does not mean that only the neonate confronts it. Some psychologists, notably Adler and Horney, have elevated the infant's difficulty in dealing with its relative powerlessness and alienation to the leading concept in the etiology of neurosis. But, of course, all adults, whether neurotic or not, must continue to confront and deal with these same basic existential problems.

This is why I say that to explain all human needs for intense positive value experiences through love, idealization, and so on, as regressions to an infantile stage of development is to avoid the real question. Such an explanation would trivialize the question as to why conscious beings have such needs in the first place. At the same time, we can profit immensely from the insights about idealizing love relationships that theories of object relations (and self psychology) now offer us. And the understanding of object relations obviously can help us to see better why certain kinds of love toward a deity, or toward a human being, can serve the need to come to terms satisfactorily with the problems of our own finitude. Kohut, for one, insists strongly that the need for idealizing feelings toward others persists throughout the life cycle, and is not 'resolved' in infancy.

It would therefore seem that we can summarize the relationship between universal ontological problems of the human condition and the particular neurotic dysfunctions of individuals and cultures in something like the following way:

1. Certain inevitable anxiety-arousing conflicts are unavoidable for conscious beings per se, regardless of their circumstances. Among these are relative powerlessness, death, insignificance,

and the threat of alienation from others whom one needs for the experience of value and the actualization of one's own potential.

2. Different people may experience these conflicts with greater or lesser intensity, depending on their physiological constitution and previous experiences.

3. Infants tend to experience them in a more cataclysmic way than others because of their extreme powerlessness.

4. Some people's interpersonal environment (especially during childhood) is such that these inevitable conflicts are even more severe than they need to be.

5. If a person is constitutionally oversensitive, or if the conflicts are exaggerated by a dysfunctional environment (especially during childhood), the probability of a neurotic solution is increased. On the other hand, if a person is constitutionally undersensitive or environmentally understimulated, the conflicts may be simply ignored rather than resolved. In this case too the result may be neurosis. But, in principle, the basic conflicts are ones that all conscious beings must confront and try to work out, whether normal, neurotic, adult, or infant.

6. It follows that the difference between 'normal' and 'neurotic' people is not whether they must deal with the anxieties stemming from these ontologically necessary conflicts. The difference arises from the *way in which* we deal with them. It is therefore a mistake merely to write off a philosophical or religious attempt to deal with them as an essentially neurotic project for which there would be no need if it were not for certain underlying neurotic conflicts. The conflicts themselves are universal, although those who deal with them in inadequate ways may of course experience them more cataclysmically, and therefore become immobilized as far as any realistic facing up to them is concerned. But these are the very people who are most likely in one way or another to *deny* the ultimate realities of their own death, vulnerability, threat of alienation, and relative insignificance in the cosmic scheme. To deny or ignore these problems therefore is by no means a sign of psychic health, and to worry about them is not necessarily a sign of

neurosis. The real question is not *whether* we worry about them, but rather the adequacy and honesty of the *methods* we employ in coming to terms with them.

These kinds of psychological considerations will become particularly helpful when the time comes (in chapter 4) to understand how the idealization of a spiritual partner must eventually become the basis for an abstract set of guiding ideals felt strongly enough to unify the direction of the self toward the active promotion of intensely cherished motivating values based on the powerful and concretely symbolized appreciation of the intrinsic value of conscious beings per se. In effect, the love for a primary spiritual partner becomes transferrable to other people who share with the spiritual partner the essential condition of all conscious beings as they face the ontological predicament. This 'spreading effect' enables us in a sense to 'abstract' the Valuable from our experience of the spiritual partner without depriving it of its emotional power. At this point we can therefore incorporate the love for the spiritual partner into a comparably powerful love for the values that guide the self, thus becoming relatively autonomous rather than utterly dependent on an idealized object. This newfound independence, however, is derivative from the sense of awe and reverence we feel for a past or present spiritual partner, and is indebted to this sense for the strength of the feeling that the values that guide us are important enough to overshadow the all-pervasive hardness of the ontological predicament.

2

Ways of Addressing the Finite Condition

1. The Current Status of the Problem

Emanuel Levinas in *Totality and Infinity* defines erotic love in terms of a strongly felt appreciation of the other person's conscious being as "foreign to the world too coarse and too offensive" (1969, 256). In this sense, it might not be overly dramatic to say that all conscious beings are too good for the world in which we must struggle for our tenuous existence. Whether the vulnerability of a sensitive and half-ethereal being presents itself as threatened by death, alienation, powerlessness, or an inability to find opportunities to express and actualize itself, all these instances of finitude are essentially constitutive of what I have been calling the 'ontological dilemma' of consciousness—that is, the various problems that stem from our inevitably finite condition, including death, alienation from needed others, and our relative powerlessness and insignificance in the scheme of things. The ontological dilemma is primarily just this: Conscious beings depend on the physical realm and on other conscious beings to enact the meaning of our existence (as Adler, Horney, Heidegger, Camus, and others emphasize). Furthermore, the very notion of meaning for conscious beings involves unfolding in time and thus projection into the future (Heidegger, Rank, Binswanger, May). All of these needs entail that the incongruity and unsupportiveness of the hostile realm in which consciousness must struggle to maintain a sense of meaning precipitates such a fundamental problem—such a difficulty in accepting what Hemingway in *A Farewell to Arms* calls the 'dirty trick' of finitude—that only a very strong and sustainable experience of positive value can compensate for it.

This characterization of the individual as finite, and therefore relatively powerless and insignificant in the face of the *Sturm und Drang* of the cosmic scheme, is not equivalent to what Marcel calls the 'despairing worldview' of the person who has lost hope, does not expect good things to happen, or cannot enjoy them when they do. Rather, it is a frank recognition that, as Karen Horney puts it in *The Neurotic Personality of Our Time*, "Factually all of us are helpless toward forces more powerful than ourselves, such as death, illness, old age, catastrophes of nature, political events, accidents. This anxiety of the *Kreatur* [existential anxiety] has in common with the basic anxiety [of the neurotic] the element of the helplessness toward greater powers. . ." (1950/1991, 81). But it does not embody, she adds, the various distinguishing features of neurosis, which might be summed up with Horney's phrase, "The neurotic . . . stands in *his own* way" (21, italics added). Thus recognition of the finite condition, along with the anxiety it precipitates, is not inseparable from despair or neurosis. It becomes despair or neurosis when we attempt to deny or flee from our own finitude, and therefore develop dysfunctional orientations toward it. In fact, Horney, like Adler, Rank, Alice Miller, and the object relations theorists, attributes neurosis in general to a lifelong attempt to deny the reality of our own finitude, resulting in an essentially narcissistic disturbance that she regards as the most basic building block of the irresolvable conflicts that underlie more specific neurotic symptoms. The narcissist attempts to overcome feelings of powerlessness, alienation, and insignificance by constructing a 'grandiose idealized self,' leading to self-contempt and defensive maneuvers when the real self fails to measure up to the impossible standard of superiority and invulnerability.

Does the prospect of radical finitude, when taken seriously, really warrant such a negative emotional reaction as to precipitate existential anxiety? I think it is safe to assume that, for most people, finitude is *experienced* as a negative enough prospect to present a strong temptation to trump up fanciful metaphysical doctrines whose main purpose is to deny the reality of finitude. Is it simply a logical or philosophical *mistake* to think that the fact of radical finitude affects the meaning and value of life to this extent?

Many philosophers nowadays forget that Heidegger in *Being and Time* did not merely *assume* that death, for example, is anxiety provoking. He presented an argument as to why it should be anxiety provoking. Heidegger's observations about the way subjective consciousness unfolds in time imply that each present moment has meaning only insofar as it occurs in an overall context in which consciousness is motivated to unfold into its future potentialities. Without such a projection into the future, consciousness would collapse into a zombieistic stasis, and in effect become less conscious. As Merleau-Ponty and other phenomenologists have emphasized, consciousness is a pattern of change, and cannot exist as stasis. It must project itself into the future. If there were to be no next moment in time, then the act of running for political election, or driving to the voting place to vote, or even swerving my car to avoid hitting a pedestrian would have no meaning.

A simple thought experiment can illustrate the main reason for believing that consciousness is a process of change. Suppose as I am listening to my favorite symphony, all the atoms in my brain are gradually replaced, one by one, while the patterns of their activity remain the same, just as an old automobile's parts might be replaced. There is no point in this process at which I or my consciousness would be disrupted. As long as the patterns of activity continue, consciousness continues across the replacement of the microcomponents that subserve the activity. Besides being intuitively compelling, this conclusion is also consistent with many neurophysiological studies (see my *Questioning Consciousness*, or Newton's *Foundations of Understanding*, for example). But it also follows from this point that, if all the material components were still present, but not engaging in any activity, my consciousness of the symphony would cease (which is consistent also with the actual experience of neurological patients with even partial disruptions of certain brain processes). So consciousness is not equivalent with any bundle of physical stuff, but requires a pattern of change *in* the physical stuff if it is to occur.

If consciousness is a process of change, and cannot exist as stasis, then the meaning of each moment in consciousness is connected with the meaning of other moments, as Husserl shows in *The Phenomenology of Internal Time Consciousness*. One of these interconnections is that each moment is experienced in terms of its projections toward future moments (see Ellis and Newton 2000). In the example of listening to the symphony, each note has a meaning only in its context with the other notes. A dominant seventh is heard a certain way because, in a certain context, we would expect it to resolve to the tonic. Good composers will often surprise and play with this expectation, but if there were no expectation, the surprising element itself would have no meaning. In the case of valuational experience, running for political office or swerving to avoid hitting a pedestrian have meaning only because we anticipate that the political policies we could execute if elected, or the survival of the pedestrian, in turn will have some meaning.

Heidegger's argument is that if the meaning of the present moment is largely contingent on the meaning of some future moment—say, tomorrow—and the meaning of that future time is contingent on a still further future—the next day—then ultimately the meaning of the present is contingent on the meaning of a still more distant future, which inevitably at some point threatens to destroy all meaning if there is to be a point when no one will any longer exist. The longer we can expect to exist, the more hope for meaning there is, but with literally *no* future there would seem to be no meaning, and with a very short future, the possibility for meaning seems very limited.

It is true, as Heidegger freely grants, that if I know that I will die tomorrow, this actually may enhance my feeling that the present moment has value. If, just as I am about to take a drink of beer, I see that my train car is irretrievably tumbling over a cliff to destruction, the drink of beer may take on magnified meaning for that moment. But obviously, if given the choice between that drink of beer, even with its magnified meaning, and living the remainder of my seventy or so years, I would choose the remainder of my life. This seems to show how little meaning a single drink of beer, given no future beyond itself, would actually have compared with a full lifetime. Correlatively, it also seems to show that the shortening of a life is a terrible thing, and that death itself is terrible, compared with the alternative of living longer—unless we are already in such misery that death is welcomed. In short, if the meaning of the present is largely contingent on the meaning of the future, then the fact that there soon will be no future—that at some point the future itself may have no meaning—seems to present a serious problem in relation to the meaning of the present. Heidegger is not arguing, of course, that this problem of finitude cannot be addressed in some way, but merely that it *is* a problem, and thus needs to be addressed.

Nor will it help to suggest that others' memories of us will give the future meaning. Geologists predict that, within the next 5 billion years, the earth will be destroyed by a large meteor. A slumbering student on hearing this news awoke in alarm because he thought the professor had said 5 million years; reassured that the number had been 5 billion, he calmly resumed his nap. But in existential terms, it makes little difference in general principle whether the number is 5 million or 5 billion or 5 years. If the meaning of each present is contingent on the meaning of some future, then the meaninglessness of any future, no matter how remote, seems to affect the meaning of the present. On the other hand, it would also do no good to try to escape this problem of the 'ever-receding future,' as Alan Watts calls it, simply by living in the present moment without reference to the future. To lock ourselves into a static present which is not projected into the future is to stagnate, to cease changing in meaningful directions, and thus lapse into either semiconscious complacence or stifling depression.

Some Buddhists speak as if the assumption that things like death are problems is *itself* the problem. The problem is that we have assumed that there must be some grand value and meaning in life. If only we could realize that the fact that nothing matters itself does not matter, then we could give up this demand for meaning and value, and existential anxiety about such issues would then naturally fall away. We would no longer desire that things have any more value than they do have.

The main problem with this way of escaping from the problems of finitude is that Buddhism itself must make room for an ethical component in the religion, if it is not simply to disintegrate into a cynical nihilism in which people do whatever they wish to do at each moment without regard to consequences either for themselves or for others. But as soon as the ethical component is allowed into the religion, then in practical terms it *does* matter what we do, and we are again interested in the value and meaning of our actions. At this point, we have inserted ourselves back into the Heideggerian time-stream, where the meaning of the present is related to projections into the future, and we again risk allowing these projections to lead to an ever-receding future, which now threatens the meaning and value of each present moment. We cannot project instrumental ethical values unless there are intrinsic values from which the instrumental values derive their significance. And these intrinsic values must be valuable *enough* to justify the amount of hardship, suffering, and work required to maintain them.

In a paper called "Toward a Phenomenology and a Metaphysic of Hope," Marcel characterizes Heidegger's ideas about death and finitude as a 'despairing worldview,' because, according to Marcel, it makes no difference how probable or improbable our impending death or immortality might be, as long as there is *any* hope for immortality whatever. The reason is that the 'elasticity of hope' remains independent of all probability assessments, since the intensity of hope correlates not with the probability of fruition of the hoped-for outcome, but rather with the intensity of emotional commitment to the valuational importance of that outcome. By an 'elastic' hope, Marcel means one in which it is always possible to find other grounds for hoping if the initial grounds are swept away. For example, if a mother's son who had been missing in action is reported dead, then the grounds of hope for his survival shift to the metaphysical realm of the immortality of the soul; if it is then shown that personal immortality is a logical impossibility, then she hopes that some nonpersonal form of immortality, perhaps as yet undiscovered by philosophers, will turn out to be possible, or that some as yet undiscovered fallacy will later be found in the reasoning of those whose arguments refuted personal immortality. The one thing she will not do is to pin her hope in her son's continued existence on some finite set of assumptions that could be definitively refuted beyond all possibility of further hope. Thus the intensity of the hope can never be daunted by any conceivable assessment of reality, and the person therefore never lapses into despair no matter how bleak things may appear.

But by insisting that we must pin our hopes on one specific outcome—the immortality of the soul—Marcel defeats his own purpose by rendering it impossible for the hope to remain 'elastic' enough while at the same time remaining compatible with an authentic worldview. Simply to ignore falsifying evidence encourages an inauthentic, dishonest attitude toward the realities of our condition. To maintain a certain viewpoint despite all contrary evidence is the most classic kind of self-deception. To base the meaning of life on hope for a ridiculously improbable outcome would be as inauthentic as if, at my current middle age, I were to base all my hopes on the possibility that I still might become one of the world's greatest professional soccer players, despite the fact that I have never played soccer in my life, except once in a high school gym class when I succeeded only in injuring the ankles of several of my own teammates. At the deeper level, I know that there is little hope for this ridiculous dream, and therefore cannot feel very hopeful about the prospect, while at the superficial level I pretend to feel hopeful and convince myself that this is how I feel. To maintain such a blatant and thoroughgoing denial of reality, I must distort my entire thinking with convolutions of logic, ridiculous *ad hoc* hypotheses, neurotic defenses, avoidance mechanisms, and ultimately an inability to relate meaningfully to a real world toward which it would be possible to feel authentic emotions. I shut out reality, reduce my consciousness, and convert my real emotional life to a constricted and semiconscious status. Losing so much of my consciousness in this way leads to a constriction of the meaning of being. A consciousness that cannot unfold authentically is shut off from its potential and thus reduced to a stasis and to a placid, lifeless somnambulism.

For Marcel, it is enough that, through hook or crook, one is able to maintain the belief that there is just an outside chance that one's cherished long shot will come through. It does not matter how improbable this outcome might be, because the strength of the feeling of hope arises from the strength of the value commitment that gives rise to it, not the likelihood that it will achieve fruition. The strength of this hope then allows us to live each moment as if we assumed that the hoped-for outcome were quite likely to come about. Despite all contrary evidence, the condemned man may live as if confident of being reprieved just in the nick of time, or of living on in the afterlife.

To live simply as if things were different from the way they obviously or probably are is to riddle the entire structure of consciousness with denial mechanisms that lead to misinterpretation and even unfeeling of our own emotions, and generally a blocking out of awareness of important elements of our conscious life, without which we are not fully conscious. Since consciousness desires to be (i.e., to be fully conscious), this reduces the meaning of life, so that even if we protest that our lives are infinitely meaningful, on a deeper level we know that our lives are based on lies, distortions, and unrealistic fantasies. Moreover, once we have taken the step of believing that whatever we wish to be true is true, we lose all epistemological bearings and no longer can apply any criteria to the decision to believe or disbelieve anything about anything. Everything becomes arbitrary, and nothing seems real. But a life in which nothing seems real also is not experienced meaningfully. A person who has abandoned all epistemic criteria cannot really be said to believe anything. It is the old problem of the congruence of absolute skepticism with absolute dogmatism, familiar to any introductory philosophy teacher.

To say, with Kierkegaard, 'I believe *because* it is absurd' fails to get us out of this difficulty. To see this, we must examine a little more carefully the phenomenology of beliefs as they affect emotions. There are two aspects to the question: First, what does it mean to say 'I believe that all the evidence points against proposition X, yet I believe that X is true'? As Marcel himself points out, to say 'I don't believe the evidence points to X' is already essentially equivalent to saying 'I believe that X is probably false.' The second question is therefore the more crucial one: Granted that there is uncertainty as to an outcome, how does the degree of probability of the outcome affect the positivity or negativity of my emotional orientation? Marcel's position is that the positivity of hope need not correlate with the degree of probability of the hoped-for outcome, as long as there is even an outside chance of fruition. There is much to be learned by scrutinizing this position.

Suppose my favorite baseball team is in last place, so far down in the standings that its chances of winning the championship have been almost mathematically eliminated by midseason. If I pin my hopes on the possibility that they may win the season anyway, I cannot really enjoy the remaining games, because I have merely deceived myself. Each day that the team falls still further behind is only a further confirmation of the underlying despair which—given the unitary goal that I have used to define my motivation—can only deepen and become more inconsolate. The extent to which I can authentically feel happy because the team still might win becomes negligible in proportion as the chances of winning become negligible, while the despair at probable defeat becomes deeper as the chances of defeat approach inevitability. In sum, if my hope is staked on a specific outcome, the probability of that outcome does affect my ability to maintain a positive feeling of hope toward it.

On the other hand, suppose I grant that the team probably will not win the pennant, but also refrain from pinning all my hopes on this specific outcome. Then suddenly I regain the ability to enjoy the games. In this case, I orient my expectations toward other possible hopes. The team's best hitter may still win the league batting title; or its best home run hitter may break a record; the leading pitcher might lead the league in strikeouts; or someone may lead in stolen bases for the month of September; or the team may defeat its archrival in one particular game. Paradoxically, as soon as I am willing to give up hope that the team will win the season, and authentically come to terms with this fact, it is precisely at this point that I regain the ability to hope. I now allow the elasticity of hope to be determined by the breadth of the range of possible good things that might happen, rather than by the ability to ignore evidence against one particular hoped-for outcome. It is the indefiniteness of the range of outcomes that qualify as good outcomes that makes the hope elastic with respect to a broad range of evidence that might challenge any one good outcome. A 9-0 score in the first inning does not preclude the possibility that someone will set a stolen-base record, or make an awe-inspiringly miraculous defensive play.

Flexibility with regard to hoped-for outcomes also contributes to the elasticity of hope in another way. Suppose no hoped-for outcome comes to fruition. As long as the range of possible objects of hope remains indefinite, there is still the possibility that even my own subjective constitution may change in such a way that I will find myself able to experience appreciation for objects that I do not now know how to appreciate and do not anticipate being able to appreciate. Of course, this is just what any trained psychologist will suggest that a potential suicide victim should think about. Thus, even in the worst-case scenario—if I am certain that nothing that I would now consider good will ever come to pass—this still would not require abandoning hope, because it is always possible that the range of outcomes that I experience as good may change. For example, if I fail to win the woman of my dreams, I may later find myself in love with some other woman. Or, with reference to the problem of death, if I fail to attain immortality of the soul, I may later find myself able to appreciate the value of some experience in such a positive way that it more than adequately compensates me. Even if I cannot at present imagine such an experience, this is no reason to close off the possibility that I may later learn to experience it.

But does the contingency of the meaning of the present moment on the future, together with the probability that the earth will be destroyed by a large meteor, not refute the very logical possibility of such an intensely positive experience? I think not. The reason is that the meaning of the present moment, strictly speaking, does not depend on the assumption that the future times toward which it is directed will have meaning infinitely into the future; it only depends on the assumption that the present moment is directed toward some future moment *simpliciter*, and that this simple projection is extensive *enough* to provide a sense that this finite segment of time has enough intrinsic value to compensate for the amount of travail and misery associated with the task of living through it and suffering under the yoke of the necessary labors and travails.

So the problems of death and all the other instances of radical finitude do matter, but they do not automatically trump all possible meaning in the present. Yet if experience means projection in time, we must always be concerned with whether we will have power enough, and will survive long enough, to feel that there is a *strong enough* positive value to achieve this purpose, and these limitations will always be sources of serious concern. In my view, the limitations in power, longevity, and personal significance are serious enough threats to this project that most of us are at least tempted to find a way out, through self-deceptive metaphysical fantasies, even though we may resist the temptation. Thus existential anxiety is not neurotic or silly, but is a realistic response to a realistic set of ontological problems—not to say, however, that existential anxiety cannot be successfully dealt with in an authentic way.

Ever since the first apes became vaguely aware of the phenomenon of death, they were unable to reconcile themselves to it, and therefore exhibited existential anxiety in a primitive form. A mother ape carries around her dead infant for days or weeks, unwilling to admit that it is dead (*Nature*, 1989). Confronted with the death of one of their own, apes invariably display their usual symptoms of anxiety and distress. Once rid of the dead body as reminder of the reality of death, they again enjoy the tranquillity of the present moment, just as do lower animals who are too unintelligent to appreciate death's existential implications even in a rudimentary form. But when the apes' intelligence evolves further still, they will find themselves less and less able to forget or ignore the harshness of the finite condition which increasingly dawns on them (if only unconsciously, since it is too painful for full awareness).

It is at this point—roughly the dawn of human intelligence—that the idea of religion presents itself. Whatever their particular dogmatic content—theism, animism, ancestor worship, and so forth—religions address the problems of finitude (death, powerlessness, alienation), and they do so in two main ways. The first way, to which I referred earlier as the way of mythic experience, does not deny the harsh realities we confront, but attempts to create an experience of positive value so pronounced that it compensates us for the cosmic insult of our dilemma—or, what amounts essentially to the same strategy, to create a frame of mind in which the terrible facts of ultimate reality (i.e., the inevitable problems of finitude) can be accepted without self-deception.

The second way, on the other hand, the way of fundamentalism, addresses the problem simply by denying its existence, very much in the manner of an animal in combat at the moment of capitulation: The animal pretends that the adversary does not exist, thus repressing out of awareness the terrible reality that faces it. It gazes distractedly into the distance, scratches itself, and even preens itself just as the predator prepares to deliver the deathblow. In this way it numbs itself to inevitable destruction, while hoping that the adversary will miraculously take pity and decide to spare it. This seems to be the way primitive conscious beings naturally orient themselves toward overwhelmingly insurmountable threats to survival. In the same way, the fundamentalist kind of religion—unfortunately, the kind most popular in the modern world, at least when it comes to finitude issues—self-deceptively assumes that an all-good and omnipotent deity has it within his power to solve all unsolvable problems. It thus 'solves' the ontological dilemma by pretending that such things as death, evil, unredressed injustice, or insurmountable personal problems (other than those created by one's own moral faults through 'free will') simply do not exist, or are somehow nullified in the ultimate scheme of things.

But in order to shut itself off from reality in such a thoroughgoing way, consciousness must riddle itself with such convoluted defenses that the ability to consciously experience the positive value of life is reduced to a fraction of its former self (because the experience of reality itself is reduced to a sham), and the same defenses lead to increasingly pervasive self-deception, irrationality, conflict, alienation, incompetence, and even violence. Again, we can find detailed discussion of these self-deceptive and essentially 'neurotic' consequences of the attempt to deny the reality of finitude in Horney's *Neurosis and Human Growth* and, at the wider cultural level, in *The Neurotic Personality of Our Time*. Although Horney seldom mentions religion in this regard, it is clear that the *second type* of religion, the kind that assumes the fundamentalist stance toward finitude issues, because of its self-deceptiveness, will often contribute to similar consequences. The extreme example is presented by the al Qaeda terrorists who bombed the World Trade Center, having literally convinced themselves that nothing here on earth matters since an infinite number of virgins await them in the afterlife. But less extreme examples occur whenever we tell ourselves that any instance of finitude (finitude in time, power, or significance) will conveniently be nullified for us through religious means—that the deceased is literally smiling down at us from Heaven, that God will punish our enemies, that if we pray with enough faith, our child's cancer will be cured. In effect, it becomes necessary to revise beliefs about almost every aspect of reality to buttress the sugarcoated metaphysical system, and each new denial of reality makes authentic experience still more tenuous. All of these dysfunctional consequences severely worsen and complicate the very crisis of meaning that the denial of harsh realities was meant to 'solve' in the first place.

We need not be detained here by the argument that faith increases the odds of recovering from severe diseases. The question is whether there are ways to have hope and a strong enough sense of the value of being without self-deceptive fantasies—in short, the central question of this book. A mythic religious orientation, or even no religion but in the presence of a different sort of transcendent value experience, can serve the purpose at least as well as a fundamentalist belief system.

Someone might object that we have committed ourselves here to the view that all primitive peoples are neurotic, since they believe in very far-fetched metaphysical scenarios. I do not believe the above remarks imply that primitives are any more narcissistically disturbed or self-deceptive than moderns, or even that they are more fundamentalist. Primitive religions serve the value-affirming as well as the self-deceptive function of religion, and ontological beliefs that would require a great deal of self-deception in an age of highly developed science do not require nearly as much self-deception in a primitive time when fewer scientific theories and observations are available to challenge the going system of metaphysics. Every age has its own healthy as well as unhealthy ways of contending with the finite condition, as I shall further argue below.

The two very different functions of religion—the authentically value-affirming mythic experience, and the self-deceptive function associated with fundamentalist dogma—usually commingle with each other in a virtually inseparable way. If the goal is to create an intense positive-value experience, religion must present its adherent with the image of a conscious being in whom this positive value can be appreciated, since conscious beings are the only beings that manifestly, unquestionably, and by their very nature have extreme and absolute intrinsic value (and not merely instrumental value). For reasons which I have further elaborated in *Eros in a Narcissistic Culture*, it is practically impossible for a conscious being to directly experience its own positive value in an intense enough way to accomplish this purpose (i.e., to compensate adequately for the brutality of our dilemma). A person may *intellectually* acknowledge his or her own extreme positive value, and may intensely *experience* the positive value of *objects* of consciousness—other people, music, or awe-inspiring landscapes; one may also very intensely experience the *negative* value associated with one's own being (through depression or anxiety). But we cannot *very intensely* experience our own *positive* value in the way we do the positive value of another being. To *very intensely* experience the positive value of a being means to focus on the finitude of that being, to take compassion on the courageous authenticity of the finite being in its irreplaceability and uniqueness in the universe, which also means to *admire* the being in its uniqueness and irreplaceability. In sum, it means to love the being—to concretely experience the 'tragic' significance of the being in the sense spoken of by Unamuno, who emphasizes that love focuses on the value of a being by focusing on its uniqueness and irreplaceability, which arise precisely from its finitude.

In the case of an omnipotent God in the traditional Judeo-Christian-Muslim sense, one empathizes with His finitude in the sense that He creates other beings who are independent of Him, enters into various kinds of relationships with them, and suffers when His creation goes awry. One also empathizes with the finitude of God's representatives—saints, martyrs, prophets, Christ on the cross, and so on. It is most of all in this finitude that one can concretely *feel* love toward an omnipotent God, or toward His representatives, as toward a vulnerable human being. But the important point for now is simply that we cannot love *ourselves* in this intense and positive way, because to do so would require that we intensely take compassion on our own finitude, which would mean to wallow in self-pity. To wallow in self-pity is to experience life in an intensely negative way, not an intensely positive way. At the same time, such emphasis on self-love would demand a form of self-idealization so inflated as to lead to narcissistic disturbance in the ways described by Kohut, Horney, and others.

The objection might be raised that these points are not applicable to a religion like Buddhism, since Buddhism does not necessarily posit a deity and encourages people simply to realize that the demand for some Grand Meaning in life is itself misguided. One might even characterize the ideal of nirvana as a realization that the demand for such a Grand Meaning is simply an illusion. However, anyone who practices organized Buddhism is quickly exposed to a vast realm of dogma analogous to other religions. I remember watching a recitation by Buddhist youngsters who had been taught by their monk to proclaim joyously that death does not really exist, and thus that when people appear to die, they do not really die. But it is also in the ethical component of Buddhism that we find the emphasis on a positive value experience analogous to what I am calling a transcendent value experience, and this experience is made available primarily through feelings of empathy and compassion that intensify our love for finite beings.

Since we cannot love ourselves in an intense enough direct experience of our own tragic significance to appreciate the value of being in a positive enough way to compensate for the harshness of the ontological dilemma, we must find another conscious being on whom to project this experience. But to invest this extreme positive-value experience in another finite human being is inherently risky. Finite human beings are all too prone to cut off the kind of empathy needed to fully experience them (i.e., to vicariously experience their subjectivity through empathy). The most minimal requirement for the availability of this reverent kind of empathy is that there must be a 'space of empathy' as defined above. The crucial point is that the space of empathy facilitates dropping the defenses that protect us from admitting the true extent of our ontological limitations, so that both our ontological vulnerability (finitude in time, power, and value) and our defenses against it can be experienced by ourselves and vicariously experienced by the other. Thus we must feel that we are not judged and measured to determine whether we are inadequate or inferior in terms of standards that treat us as if our value were to be assessed instrumentally, from the other's perspective. In this sense, we are absolved and forgiven for all limitations and shortcomings. This space of empathy occurs when we feel that the other person simultaneously both admires and takes compassion on *our own* embattled authenticity, whether the other in question is a human being or a deity or the representative of a deity.

The case where the space of empathy occurs with a living human being, rather than with a saint or deity, is actually the clearer and simpler case. Both people must be willing to allow each other's consciousness to flow in a way unobstructed by judgmentalism, directiveness, defensiveness, or mistrust; yet at the same time they must be interested enough in discovering each other's most intricate thoughts and feelings to encourage the difficult task of expressing, explicating, and further clarifying them—which also causes consciousness to unfold, intensify, and change. In this way, both people are able to be fully who they are in relation to each other, so that the richness of each other's being becomes visible to each other. When human beings are involved, the transcendent value experience requires that the relationship be reciprocal, because the undeflected flowing of one person's authentic consciousness contributes to the liberated, euphoric feelings in the other, and vice versa. A space of empathy must be created in which both people feel free to fully exist their authentic thoughts and feelings in relation to each other, to unfold in directions and patterns of consciousness that only each other's presence facilitates, and thus to make available a full and clear perception of the other's conscious being in all its frailty and existential embattledness, which then is admired with all the intensity of this heightened consciousness of it.

But to engage in such mutual spiritual nakedness with another human being presents certain problems. Not only are human beings reluctant to open themselves up to such a complete space of empathy because of their own psychological insecurities, self-deceptions, defenses, and insensitivities; the space of empathy may also be destroyed by one person's legitimate fear and mistrust of the other's 'undependability,' which drives the former to avoid 'dependence' on the latter.

One of the most obvious candidates for such an intense mutual experience of positive value through a space of empathy of this kind naturally presents itself in the phenomenon of erotic or romantic love. However, the attempt to meet the need for an idealizing relationship by means of romance presents three main difficulties. First, a relationship to one individual cannot supply the entire meaning of life on a sustained basis. If asked to do so, it becomes a stifling symbiosis whose effect (as we shall see) is to destroy rather than facilitate spiritual partnership. Secondly, the need for the other to be sexually attracted to us in romantic love is apt to force narcissistic issues to the forefront. Concern with whether the other perceives us positively enough thus tends to compromise our willingness to drop defenses for a full space of empathy. The third main problem is that, as Simone de Beauvoir and others have suggested, the sexual need and the reproductive function lead couples who are in erotic love to become a socially defined 'couple,' set up housekeeping, and thus try to make their relationship double as a social institution—an economic and utilitarian arrangement that creates moral and cultural tensions and conflicts, questions of guilt and blame, and so forth. And this social institutionalization, for a variety of reasons that I discussed in *Eros in a Narcissistic Culture*, can severely dampen or even completely destroy the space of empathy, and thus diminish the feeling of awe-stricken admiration through compassion that could provide an extreme yet sustainable experience of positive value and thus override the negativity of the ontological dilemma. To the extent that these three conflicts remain unresolved, erotic relationships lose their ability to fulfill the need for the kind of sustainable experience of value that we have been discussing here.

On the other hand, *non*-erotic relationships do not often allow for as intense and concrete an experience of the other's value. The reason is that erotic feelings provide an intense *physical-symbolization* vehicle for the experience of love, in which one's whole being can be enlisted in a fully actualized, concrete feeling process (as can be introspectively observed in erotic love). There is an important sense in which physical symbolization through some embodied activity (language, gesture, imagery, music, etc.) is crucial for the intensification of any state of consciousness. Most people cannot easily imagine how a nonerotic friendship could provide a matrix of physically embodied activities that could serve as a concrete enough symbolization, and thus intensification and extreme actualization, of the feelings in question. This comparative calmness of nonerotic forms of love seems obvious from the fact that romantic feelings, at least in their initial phases (and at certain key times throughout a good romantic relationship), are felt in a way more intense and overpowering than the sedate, level-headed liking and concern for a friend or family member. Not only is the possibility of physical expression through sexual behavior unavailable, but also all the other physical embodiments of the feeling of being in love are absent—shortness of breath, continual adrenaline which causes sleeplessness, the cramped feeling of 'restlessness' in the chest, obsessive and involuntary mental imagery, and other physical symptoms with which lovers are familiar, whether the love is 'consummated' or not.

In theory, religion offers the ideal alternative to the limitations of either erotic or nonerotic human relationships. On the one hand, it allows us to intensely enough experience the positive value of being to compensate for the harshness of our ontological predicament. The personalities of deities, ancestors, martyrs, and saints offer the believer an image of a conscious being in whom this value can be directly experienced by loving the being in a way that does not necessitate power struggles and conflicts *with* that being, nor cut into the perfection of the space of empathy because of mistrust, social role-playing, or need for self-aggrandizement and avoidance of blame for real or imagined shortcomings—problems that are almost universal in permanent erotic-love relationships.

Yet, at the same time that the relationship to the deity, ancestor, martyr, or saint avoids the problems of erotic relationships, it also preserves the essential advantage that erotic relationships have over nonerotic ones: the use of physical, concrete symbolization of the feelings involved through the phenomenon of dramatic ritual and all-consuming artistic expression—music, architecture, eulogies to the dead, verbalization of prayers, kneeling, genuflecting, lighting candles, wearing special jewelry and clothing, and so forth. Other emotionally significant events—for example, puberty, marriage, and death—are also converted to use for religious ritualization. All these religious rituals thus provide physical symbolization for the love of the deity.

Moreover, priests allow indirect empathic communication with the deity; thus reciprocation of the love is assured. Nor does the deity harbor any psychological shortcomings of its own which might destroy the feeling of empathy. As for the danger that our own defensiveness might destroy empathy, all of our own faults are forgiven or absolved, so that in theory it should be possible to avoid the inauthentic defensiveness on our part that otherwise would constrict consciousness and destroy the space of empathy.

The problem with this kind of positive value experience as a solution to the finite dilemma, however, is that there is a strong tendency to think that the ideal conscious being (i.e., the deity) can effectively serve this purpose only to the extent that the ideal being literally exists as a personal and conscious being. But the process of convincing ourselves that this ideal being (which we would like to believe exists) actually does exist, simply *because* we would like for it to exist, sets up a psychodynamic that already threatens to catapult us into an almost irresistible self-deception. As soon as we begin believing that things are true simply because we would like them to be true, we are already dangerously close to the realm of irreality. In this case, there is no longer any reason to try to avoid the self-deceptions inherent in the *fundamentalist* type of religion, in which we simply 'deal with' the finite dilemma by denying the truth that it exists—with all the consciousness-destructive consequences mentioned above. One pretends that people do not really die when they die, that there is no injustice or evil in the ultimate scheme of things, and that the only purpose of enduring our harsh and perilous existence 'here below' is to wait for death to deliver us to the rich pleasures of 'heaven' or the 'nonphysical realm.'

But to make these kinds of beliefs credible, the believer increasingly feels the need to adopt and defend a whole host of untenable and socially harmful philosophical theories: In the case of any occurrence that seems inconsistent with the ontological trappings of this rigid and literalistic kind of religious belief system—such as the suffering and death of innocent children or the destruction of entire cities by tidal waves—the natural tendency is to trump up some *ad hoc* hypothesis, such as the notion that the child was destroyed in order to teach the parents a lesson, or that the entire city was sinful. A whole philosophical worldview is then constructed that systematically denies any facts inconsistent with any of these *ad hoc* hypotheses. To resolve the problem of evil, we must suppose that humans have 'free will,' and thus people must be blamed and punished for their psychological faults and aberrations rather than prevented from acquiring them through constructive social institutions. We then feel constrained to assume a dualism of mind and body rather than a harmonious reciprocity between them, so that the psychological motivation of human beings must be viewed in terms of conflicting 'physical' and 'spiritual' driving forces, leading to inability to understand ourselves. The tendency then is to enhance the congruence of the belief system with moral principles by supposing that poverty and other social disadvantages are fitting punishments for laziness and sloth (which result from free will); thus beneficial social programs must be viewed as infringements of the 'freedom and responsibility' of the individual, and the entire system of moral values must be distorted to make room for the importance of such 'just retribution' and 'individual responsibility.' The victims of social problems and other misfortunes must be held accountable for their own difficulties (on pain of undermining belief in free will, which is needed to solve the problem of evil); thus they must be required to 'pull themselves up by their bootstraps,' and morally blamed if they do not. The correlations between 'religiosity' (in a fundamentalist sense), political conservatism, and authoritarianism documented by Adorno and others are therefore not mere coincidences. For many believers, it evolves quite systematically from such a belief system that patriotism and military heroism are among the most important of all virtues, since neither soldiers nor civilians really 'die,' and since war against evil adversaries is necessary to reinforce the belief system, as Durkheim and others have suggested. Perhaps most important, the credibility of the whole edifice is reinforced by assuming that any person or thing that threatens to challenge this delicate patchwork of *ad hoc* hypotheses is wrong and evil and thus must be destroyed, suppressed, or ostracized.

Once the belief system has become this bizarre and convoluted, the believer must riddle his or her entire thought process with such systematic distortions of logical thinking that the defense mechanisms of denial, repression, and self-deception become habitual, and thus the same illogic that characterizes this sort of religious belief also permeates the perception of reality. Inauthenticity becomes pervasive and therefore reduces the capacity for genuinely intense experiences of positive value—as indeed the intensity of consciousness generally is eroded because of the extent to which experience is simply shut out of awareness. One becomes a placid, cud-chewing creature, or, in T. S. Eliot's phrase, a 'hollow man.'

We seem to have reached the point in human history when these kinds of fundamentalist belief systems no longer serve their purpose very effectively. To be sure, the attempt is still made, but without much success in alleviating the anxieties it is meant to address. One may speculate as to the reasons for this erosion of dogmatic theocentricity in modern life, but the event itself seems undeniable. Accurate proof of the unequivocal existence of evil and injustice is now too readily available. The cosmic scheme of fundamentalist or literalistically interpreted religion is too much in conflict with science and technology (and thus with the demands of utility and survival) to motivate literal ontological belief in a transphysical being who can eliminate our ontological dilemma for us; yet a merely symbolic or mythological deity still seems too fanciful to inspire the kind of deeply felt love required to give life the needed meaning. And the complexity of social life makes alienation, competitiveness, and mutual hostility such all-pervasive and inescapable realities that the authoritarian and philosophically ungrounded morality of dogmatic religions come to seem at best more and more irrelevant, at worst a cause of repressed resentment and frustration in the psyche of the believer, who supposedly must practice a morality that seems to unilaterally undermine one's competitive position in the struggle for survival in an urban-industrial form of culture.

Moreover, the pervasiveness of self-serving propaganda on the part of authority figures makes modern people rightfully skeptical of authoritarian pronouncements—pronouncements which in religious matters increasingly oppose themselves to readily available factual information about the nature of reality (for example, that the earth is not the center of the universe; that humans evolved through natural selection; that the human characteristics of fetuses come into being gradually rather than instantaneously at a clean-cut point in time; that population control is necessary to avert environmental destruction; or that the personalities of evil people result from developmental dysfunctions that are largely fostered by unhealthy or impoverished environments and predisposed by brain chemistry). But, for whatever reasons, the inability of literalistic religious beliefs to resolve the finite dilemma for modern people seems to be a given fact. We might look back nostalgically to the time when praying and genuflecting were adequate to quell these ontological concerns, but to actually return to such times seems as unlikely as that the world economy will return to a predominantly agrarian rather than urban-industrial basis. The facts with which religious belief must be reconciled, and the logic needed to reconcile them, preclude the possibility that a magical and superstitious form of religion can any longer be taken very seriously by clear-thinking people.

Against this background, modernity's increasing tendency toward investment of religious meaning into romantic relationships, with all its obvious foibles and inadequacies, is understandable as addressing an urgent need for a different approach to religious experience—one that perhaps would not depend on pie-in-the-sky self-deceptions or absurd metaphysical fantasies. This tendency is an attempt to reorient the experience of the numinous toward a finite rather than infinite love object—a conscious being who physically exists and with whom one can concretely relate. But such an attempt falls short of serving religious ends adequately if it is done in such a way that fully authentic communication within a free space of empathy would be destroyed by the complications of narcissistic sexual concerns, the social institution of marriage with its built-in roles and moral conflicts, and the vast matrix of empathy-destructive demands that sexual partners in our form of culture seem almost inevitably to place on each other, at least to a considerable extent, whether in or out of 'wedlock.'

As just one preliminary example, consider the bitter battles so prevalent in erotic relationships over 'who is to blame' for any given problem—battles that are virtually nonexistent in nonerotic friendships, where they would normally be considered silly or even neurotic.

But we should not dismiss the possibility too quickly that, if we are to be able to fulfill the function of a transcendent value experience in such a radically finitized way, that is, if we are to have a positive value experience capable of compensating for the negative realities stemming from the finite dilemma, there may be a better way to facilitate religious reverence for the value of being as instantiated by other conscious beings—a dimension of human relationships for which we have not developed adequate names or categories. This dimension must be experienced fully enough to make possible a kind of love for a concretely existing conscious being that is not based either on the trappings of romance or on sexual activity as a symbolization process (at least not primarily those); yet at the same time it must provide a more elaborate matrix for the physical symbolization of emotion than is normally available in ordinary nonerotic friendships or relationships with family members or work colleagues.

In light of the above considerations, it seems likely that people have been unconsciously groping toward such a religious alternative for at least ten centuries now (and probably longer) through the increasing sexualization of spirituality, in which a relationship to a 'romantic' love object becomes the spiritual center, the meaning-giving element, and the balm for all injury in so many people's most basic hopes and dreams, if not in reality.

The problem is that this sexualization brings with it a new set of neuroses and malfunctions indicating that something is fundamentally wrong in the basic assumptions we have made about the use of eros for this purpose. Instead of facilitating spiritual partnership, romantic symbolization seems largely to conflict with, inhibit, and divert attention from the kinds of symbolization processes needed to allow the process of spiritual transformation (beyond narcissism, egocentricity, and the dread of finitude) to reach its needed outcomes. But to recommend that people should simply eschew this tendency toward the humanization of religious objects as a dead end and a bad idea would be like telling people who are breathing contaminated air that they should simply stop breathing. People grope toward psychological solutions as a plant gropes toward light. What we must do now is to analyze what we have been doing for all these many centuries, and why we are doing it. Only then can we perhaps improve on it.

2. The Role of Symbolization in Primary Spiritual Partnership

If spiritual partnership is to facilitate the process of transcendent value experience, it obviously must include forms of concrete symbolization for purposes of intensification that are different from the romantic and sexual ones with which everyone in our culture now has been inundated. To see what form this symbolization must take, we can begin with the observation that, since the object of the kind of admiration-through-compassion I have been describing must reciprocate in order for a space of empathy to be established, a relationship of primary spiritual partnership must be mutual. We cannot relate to someone as a spiritual partner in the primary sense unless that person also relates to us in this way. If we were to choose as a spiritual partner someone who did not choose us in this way, we would only be fantasizing the relationship, not really enacting it—very much as self-deceptive forms of religion merely fantasize spiritual relationships and therefore reject the principle of self-truthfulness in principle, thus ultimately blocking consciousness out of awareness by denying whatever it suits one's fancy to deny.

The reason primary spiritual partnership must be mutual and reciprocal is that it entails a relatively complete space of empathy in which each person allows the other to express authentic consciousness without fear of evaluative condemnation, directiveness, opportunistic taking-advantage, and so on. Such complete acceptance and even encouragement of the baring of souls, without masks or camouflage, can occur in a real-life context, and on a secure and sustained basis, only if each person reciprocates the other's strong feelings in order to motivate such an attitude. These kinds of feelings make possible the odd combination of a nondirective and nonjudgmental, yet at the same time encouraging and intensely interested, attitude toward the other's expressions. Each person's admiration-through-compassion encourages the other's authentic exposure of precisely the ontological vulnerabilities that are available to intensify admiration. Thus the space of empathy must be mutual, and therefore must be a really existing situation, not a mere fantasy.

Part of the reason for the importance of the space of empathy is that, in order to lend physical embodiment to states of consciousness, it is necessary to concretely 'symbolize' them; only in this way can they occur with much if any intensity. By 'symbolization,' I mean the relationship that obtains between a piece of music, for example, and the feelings and other conscious states that we enable ourselves to feel or entertain by listening to or playing that particular piece. The piece intensifies or brings to full concrete awareness the experience of those feelings by symbolizing them in a concrete, physical way. Many of the most important feelings enabled by the music are not actually 'about' the music, but are only facilitated and symbolized by it. In a similar fashion, talking to another person who listens in the right way can enable us to explicate feelings and ideas that we could not or would not have explicated if we had not had the opportunity to symbolize them. Feelings are felt more fully the more fully they are symbolized; and, as Merleau-Ponty says in the *Phenomenology of Perception*, "thought crawls along speech" (1962, 182). If we fail to find physical ways to symbolize feelings, the feelings tend to die out or remain latent possibilities that are never really actualized—a point emphasized by Gendlin in his 'focusing' approach to psychotherapy, by Suzanne Langer in her theory of emotions, by Carl Rogers in his 'client centered therapy,' and by Kohut and Bollas in the notion that 'object use' (for example, the use of the therapist) enables prereflective experiencing to be explicated—to become more conscious and thus to unfold, move forward, and be felt more fully.

The all-important problem that must be solved in order to explicate transcendent value feelings toward a spiritual partner so that they at least initially serve a religious or inspirational need (i.e., the need for intense enough positivity to override the negativity of the finite dilemma) is this: How can admiration mixed with compassion for the existentially embattled conscious being of a spiritual partner be adequately symbolized through a *physically embodied* process capable of serving as physical substratum for the feeling, so that it remains a living feeling and not merely an idea to which one pays lip service? The feeling of love is not merely a state of belief, as when one firmly believes that the other person is good, superior, worthwhile, admirable, or heroic. To know from reliable sources that *Death of a Salesman* is a moving tragedy is not the same as to directly experience this moving quality by actually seeing the play. Love is a matter of directly experiencing the other's value, not abstractly affirming or cognizing it. And the intensification of the direct experience of the other's value, through focusing on the person's uniqueness and irreplaceability and thus also the person's finitude and fleetingness, requires a correspondingly special kind of symbolization activity.

Most people in our culture know of only four forms of symbolization that can facilitate such an intense focus on the other's transcendent value in a genuine and sustained way, and all four of these ways tend to fall short of the full and permanent spiritual intensification they are meant to facilitate. Most obvious is the experience of romantic love. This experience makes us feel that life is infinitely valuable and worthwhile in spite of the ontological predicament of finitude and the brutal conditions of material strife. We are able to sustain the intense appreciation of the other's positive value because these feelings are physically symbolized by means of bodily globalization of sexual feelings mixed with many other bodily sensations—shortness of breath, continual adrenaline that leads to sleeplessness, loss of appetite, a cramped feeling of 'restlessness' in the chest, and many other physical embodiments and symbolization activities (for example, sexual caresses), as I discuss in *Eros in a Narcissistic Culture.* In the context of this feeling of romantic love (not just friendship plus sexual attraction), sexual acts are felt as quasi-religious rituals of worship for the other's value (of which one is in quasi-aesthetic awe) rather than as a merely consummatory, pleasure-giving activity like eating or drinking. Erotic feelings differ from merely consummatory ones, for example, in that the pleasure of eating an apple, unlike the pleasure of *eros*, is in no way enhanced if the apple is aware that I am eating it, or if it enjoys being eaten. The important point is that the experiences involved in romantic love facilitate heightened spirituality and positive value feelings only because there is a way to symbolize the experiences concretely. Nonetheless, we have seen that romantic relationships also entail a morass of interpersonal and sociocultural problems that tend to erode the space of empathy to greater or lesser extents. I shall return to this problem in the next chapter.

The second common form of symbolization for an intense appreciation of the value of another conscious being is through religious ritual, as discussed earlier. One of the elements of this symbolization is the finitization and humanization of the deity. The love for a deity could not be concretely experienced and intensified if not projected onto finite and tragic beings—saints, martyrs, Christ himself on the cross, and the 'god-spirit' in one's fellow humans through agape. A god who does not become finite and suffer cannot be loved concretely, although one may be in awe of him as one is in awe of Xeno's paradoxes or of a view of the heavens through a telescope—impersonal forces like the 'god of the philosophers.' A god who is to be loved must experience intense feeling, and this entails suffering and embattledness. One must be able to empathically appreciate the deity's uniqueness and irreplaceability, thus its finitude. Even if the god is believed to be omnipotent, we still must imagine some power outside of the deity, some dark force of evil or recalcitrant element in creation that challenges or opposes Him in some way. This finitization of the deity is part of the symbolization function of the physical incarnation of the deity, the Trinity, and the Passion. In effect, one imagines God (or his representative) as challenged by the ontological predicament in order to love him—otherwise the feeling is not one of empathic love for the being *qua* conscious being. This is precisely why physically embodied ritual is needed for symbolization of the feeling. The abstract contemplation of intellectual dogma alone cannot inspire love. In any event, we have already discussed some of the reasons why, for increasing numbers of people, dogmatic religions, even with their symbolic rituals, no longer very effectively counteract the finite dilemma in our time.

A third way to symbolize intense appreciation of the value of another consciousness is through certain kinds of artwork. For example, *Death of a Salesman*, if approached in the right frame of mind, evokes powerful feelings of compassion for its protagonist's finitude, and we also admire his courage, despite its Quixotism, as an instance of 'man, slighted but enduring.' Epic poetry also makes us intensely appreciate heroic figures—especially at the moment of their stoic self-denial or their death, moments that pull both admiration and compassion simultaneously for the embattled authenticity and tragic finitude of the conscious being. In the case of music, we empathize with the subjective condition of a composer who makes himself into a representative of the plight of all conscious beings (not to imply, of course, that this is the only significant aspect of the musical experience).

The problem with these aesthetic experiences, however, is that they are usually too few and far between to provide a *lastingly* intense appreciation for the consciousness of their characters or authors that would be positive enough to override the negativity of the finite dilemma. What is needed, if we are to experience a feeling of positive valuation of another being in such a way as to override the negativity of the ontological dilemma, is a real person with whom one can really interrelate within a space of empathy and on a sustained basis. There may be a few rare individuals who can resolve the ontological dilemma through art alone, but even the great composers, poets, and artists whom one might suppose to fall into this category show through their life histories a pressing need for still some further resolution of it, usually through either love or religion, or both.

A fourth kind of symbolization for love is the enactment of feelings for friends and family members, especially one's own children, by means of altruistic behavior toward them. A child comes closer than any other family member to eliciting the kind of intense valuational feeling that a primary spiritual partner does, because not only do altruistic behaviors serve to concretely symbolize the feeling; the child's vulnerability and rapid change also pull our compassion and our focus on the child's finitude, hence its uniqueness and irreplaceability.

But the fact is that such relationships very rarely seem to serve the purposes of primary spiritual partnership. Why this is the case will be discussed in a later context, but as a preliminary example, consider the parent-child relation. Its asymmetry seems to prevent a complete space of empathy from flowing in both directions: The parent cannot bare his soul to the child, even if the child can do so to the parent to a great extent; the space of empathy thus short-circuits and cannot be a complete one. Once past the brief period of sentimental baby talk and selfish pride of the parent at having procreated, the child must largely sever this overenthusiastic empathy in order to avoid being smothered by it. As Rank and others have emphasized, the child must define herself by contrast against her surroundings in order to become an autonomous entity. Beyond the period when the child's favorite word becomes 'no,' the child wisely resists being used too much for the parent's attempts at meeting the parent's own emotional needs. Correlatively, it is a commonplace of family counseling that parents who define the purpose of their life in terms of benefitting their children, or living vicariously through them, or investing heavy emotional needs of whatever kind in a child, are placing unfair burdens on the child, stunting the child's growth toward autonomy and freedom, and failing to set their child the example of adults whose own lives are meaningful without the need to usurp someone else's autonomy. By thus harming the child, they cut off empathy and destroy the positiveness of the feeling of love, so that the relationship becomes an emotional tug of war rather than an intensely positive appreciation of each other's value in the sense of quasi-aesthetic awe. The child is used as a crutch, to the spiritual detriment of both parent and child. The asymmetry of the situation dictates that the love of a parent is inevitably a unilateral love and must be willing to 'let go' and avoid a harmful dependency on the child.

The list just enumerated does not exhaust the possible attempts to intensify the experience of another being's positive value strongly enough to create a positive value experience adequate to overpower the harshness of the ontological predicament. Relationships between comrades in arms, between fellow artists and scholars, and between mentors and their charges also exhibit some of these features. With the possible exception of a few rare and unique individuals—an occasional Buddhist monk, for example—everyone seems to exhibit a need to experience the value of being through relation to others in some such ways as the ones I have described. But, in each case, the symbolization method for the feelings involved is either too weak, too occasional, or too impermanent to accomplish its objective very well, and for very long, without some additional help from some form of symbolization especially equipped to facilitate spiritual partnership per se, and not to be confused with the symbolization methods just discussed, which really owe their development and character to forms of relationship *other* than spiritual partnership. In the classic example of the romantic relationship, the mere fact that couples have sexual arrangements, set up housekeeping, and raise children does not necessarily equip them to communicate in the ways required by a sustained transcendent value experience.

The problem, then, is how to concretely symbolize the transcendent value experience of a spiritual partner through some concretely embodied means other than sexualization, art, self-deceptive mythologies, or the autonomy-inhibiting 'nurturance' that a parent's existential dependence on a child would require. Such a purpose can be accomplished only through a kind of altruism that seeks to come to the person's assistance not primarily in terms of solving the practical problems of life (since that would be the 'nurturing,' 'mothering' attitude toward a helpless child or sniveling emotional weakling), but rather in terms of facing the finite human dilemma (in the broad sense defined above) that all conscious beings must face to the extent that they are conscious, and therefore in terms of facilitating the person's full conscious existence as it can be actualized only in relation to a spiritual partner. In concrete terms, this entails among other things that (1) we empathize with feelings in the other that cannot effectually be entertained except in relation to us; and (2) we help the person to *express* feelings in ways that could not be expressed except through relationship with us.

Jung's characterization of the initial phase of romantic love might illustrate this point, although I have already hinted that in my view Jung misconstrues the ultimate purpose of this kind of interaction. In his view, the main purpose is to facilitate one's own spiritual growth by incorporating the opposite polarity. In my view, the goal is simply to intensely experience the intrinsic value of being as instantiated in the other. But the differences in polarity still may be helpful not only in 'pulling' this process, but also in providing a matrix for concrete symbolization. In Jung's analysis, a 'masculinized' form of consciousness may express love for a 'feminized' subject by helping give voice to her 'masculine' conscious potential, just as she provides expression for the masculine partner's feminine forms of consciousness and therefore helps him to enact this conscious potential in himself. By fully empathizing with forms of consciousness in the other that are different from those we have found in ourselves, and by enacting the symbolic ritual of trying to give concretely embodied expression to those, we feel pulled out of ourselves toward an intense reverence for the value of the other's form of conscious being. This is why opposite polarization tends to motivate a space of empathy, except that this motivation conflicts with self-protective, egoistic motives. This tension will be explored in a later chapter.

But, although the fact that *I* exist more fully in this interaction may be what initially pulls me into such a relationship, this is not the most important value that results from the interaction. The important thing, which often takes us by surprise, is that we find ourselves under these circumstances able more fully to experience the other's full value in an intense experience of quasi-aesthetic appreciation or awe. And the *physical symbolization* of this experience is actualized by concretely giving expression, not to our feelings so much as to the other's, with which we have identified in the space of empathy.

The notion that feelings and thoughts in spiritual partnership are symbolized by making oneself the vehicle for expression of the other's forms of consciousness allows this form of concrete symbolization to play a role analogous to a symbolic ritual that in turn symbolizes our admiration and compassion for the person's embattled authenticity, finitude, uniqueness, and irreplaceability. (It is presupposed here that this voicing of what the person feels does not merely project our own feelings onto her or manipulate her into feeling what we want her to feel—which would eclipse our view of her consciousness and destroy the space of empathy.)

The key to the concretion of quasi-aesthetic awe in this way is to make oneself into a mouthpiece for the other's patterns of consciousness; it thus allows our own being to flow in the pattern of the other. This remains true even if the other can fully enact his or her most authentic forms of consciousness only when with us in the space of empathy. By allowing ourselves to flow in the other's pattern of consciousness, to express this person's ideas and feelings as if they were our own, we in effect make our own physical system of language-body-behavior serve as a large part of the physical substratum of *the other's* consciousness, just as this same physical system would normally serve as substratum for our own consciousness. By having this alien system of language-body-behavior at its service, the other's consciousness is allowed to break the bonds of previous habit, so that things are perceived and felt with a new vividness, as if for the first time, or as an artist sees her subject. At the same time, the other's consciousness is now given voice by someone who regards this consciousness as very valuable and important, and therefore brings energy, intensity, and motivation to the task of explicating and expressing it.

In sum, each person's body becomes the instrument for the other's self-symbolization, and thus for the focusing, actualization, and intensification of the other's authentically directed pattern of unfolding consciousness. Since spiritual partnership must be mutual and reciprocal for the reasons discussed earlier, both simultaneously use their own language-body-behavior system as an instrument for the expression of the other's forms of consciousness. For example, each may give verbal expression to the other's feelings as enacted through empathy and, by expressing them, both intensify them and underscore their importance. As a result, both partners effectively use this process to symbolize their feelings of quasi-aesthetic awe toward each other's intrinsic value.

However, it seems obvious from empirical observation that there are serious difficulties regarding the ability to sustain this process indefinitely. Later we shall analyze these difficulties, and the ways in which primary spiritual partnership must lead to further developmental stages beyond itself if its effect on the ontological dilemma is to be sustainable. These further developments are the spreading effect and the abstraction of the value system motivated by and grounded in the transcendent value experience, which then creates a 'realm of the sublime' in the midst of daily life as guided by those values.

Spiritual partnership in the primary sense, then, is an intense mutual admiration-through-compassion, felt between spiritually complementary (and often oppositely polarized) subjects, within a completely nondirective and nonjudgmental space of empathy. It is concretely symbolized not by means of sexual feeling or behavior, but rather by means of using one's own body-language-behavior system to help the other person express her consciousness in the different and complementary (and often oppositely polarized) forms for which one feels intense admiration through compassion. The concretely symbolized, awe-stricken, and quasi-aesthetic feelings that result when we focus on the other's finitude provide such a powerful direct experience of positive value (in a non-egocentric sense to be further clarified as we proceed) that this positive experience more than compensates us for the harshness of the ontological dilemma, including our own inevitable finitude in the form of relative powerlessness, alienation from others, and impending death. It thus in principle can serve the same primary purpose that traditional religions were supposed to serve, without the need for self-deception or systematic denial and distortion of the facts of our ontological predicament. Later, we shall see that many other purposes that traditional religions once tried to serve are also facilitated by the experience of spiritual partnership.

The intuitive sense that spiritual partnership has the power to address such issues, combined with its tendency to present itself as a possibility between oppositely polarized individuals, is the essential reason for the increasing 'sexualization of religious experience'—that is, the use of romantic love as the central spiritual event that is expected to be so intensely positive as to override the negativity of the ontological dilemma. However, the use of overtly *sexual* behavior and feelings as symbolization for the love is an all-too-easy way of expressing it, so that the more sophisticated interrelation between people as spiritual partners per se, with its own appropriate form of symbolization as described above, is less likely to be developed far enough to accomplish its purpose. As far as spiritual partnership per se is concerned, it is not even necessary that the two people also engage in a romantic or erotic relationship; in some cases, it may be more likely to accomplish its purpose if they do not. This issue will be considered further in due course.

In order to quell certain preliminary reservations, perhaps I should say a word at this point about what happens when a spiritual partnership ends. Finite human beings, after all, are prone to die, move away, drift away from each other for extraneous social or economic reasons, or neglect existential needs by succumbing to the popular culture's demands for conformity or egocentricity. It will become clear, however, that the relationship of spiritual partnership is not a static situation that must persist unchanged, but a dynamic process that runs a certain course and accomplishes certain spiritual changes in both people. In essence, they learn how to love non-egocentrically in an intense enough way to provide a quasi-aesthetic, worshipful, and awe-stricken reverence for the positive value of conscious beings other than themselves—a tragic-yet-positive experiencing of value strong enough to fully compensate for the brutality of the ontological predicament. This admiration-through-compassion for conscious beings in general then forms the basis for a strongly motivating value system. And this effect remains even if the primary spiritual partnership itself should be lost.

3. The Sense in Which the Experience of Spiritual Partnership Is an 'Experience of Positive Value'

It is important to clarify what it means and what it does not mean to 'have an intensely positive value experience' in the context of spiritual partnership. Paradoxically, positive value experiences are not necessarily productive of one's own happiness, pleasure or enjoyment of life. Few people leave *Death of a Salesman* in a 'happy' mood in any ordinary sense of the word 'happy.' Yet we positively value the experience. If given the choice to be a happy dog or an unhappy human being, most of us on most of our more honest days would choose the unhappy human being. Obviously, there is something that we positively value about being a human being other than, or in addition to, the happiness, pleasure, or contentment we may or may not enjoy. Of course, we value happiness and pleasure, at least to a certain extent, but there seems to be something else that we value as well—something that human beings apparently have more of than dogs have.

I am not referring to the Cartesian argument (which philosophers now have resoundingly refuted) to the effect that man has a 'soul' whereas animals do not, or that humans have consciousness whereas animals do not. But it seems clear that humans have *more* consciousness than dogs, and dogs more than mosquitoes. This is why we feel somewhat guilty if we kill a dog, but more so if we kill a human being. We have destroyed something that has more value because it is more conscious. In the case of the mosquito, we feel little guilt at all.

Neither am I implying, however, that the 'intensely positive' value experience of quasi-aesthetic awe by means of admiration-through-compassion toward a spiritual partner derives its value from its power to make us more intensely conscious. It is true that it does have this effect, and often the allure of the opportunity for spiritual partnership is motivated by a feeling that we have been sleepwalking through life, that we have not been 'fully conscious' or 'fully alive.' But the positiveness of the experience goes far beyond this effect. Once we grant that no amount of enjoyment, pleasure, or contentment can adequately or enduringly console us for the brutality of the ontological predicament (powerlessness, alienation, death, etc.), then we must also admit that, even if intensity of conscious existence comes a little *closer* to accomplishing this objective, it still cannot fully achieve it (unless we are at least partially in a state of inauthentic *denial* of the reality of the predicament). Many people cannot appreciate this point until they reach a time in their lives when the hitherto easy conditions for the fulfillment of these existential needs finally become precarious. (And, in the case of death, those conditions become more and more precarious with each step that the Grim Reaper takes out of the shadows and into his inevitable place in any realistic phenomenal field.) At this point, we feel the need to go beyond even an existentially fulfilled existence, just as previously we felt the need to go beyond the placid and contented existence.

The important point here is that fulfillment of the need to be 'fully conscious' is not the primary reason for the positiveness of the experience of a spiritual partner. The intensity of the positive value feeling in a transcendent value experience does not correlate primarily with the extent to which either the fullness of self-actualization or the pleasantness of *our own* consciousness is enhanced; the intense positiveness of the experience correlates essentially with the extent to which the other is experienced as *having* intrinsic value. The intrinsic value of the other person is something that we appreciate not because our own experience of her has value, but because *she* has value. The reality of the other's value is not dependent on our subjectivity, but exists independently and then is perceived by us in the subjective act of focusing on the person's embattled finitude, thus her uniqueness, fleetingness, and irreplaceability, including the 'tragic' nature of this irreplaceability. Then, if only we can set aside egocentricity well enough to elevate this extreme positive value that we have experienced *above our own* (whose positive value we cannot appreciate to this extent, as explained earlier), we then fully appreciate this value and are moved by it in such a way that we feel that such extreme positive value is well worth the trouble and grief inflicted on us as we bear up under the adversity of the ontological dilemma.

In essence, the experience of the other in a transcendent value experience is a 'positive value experience' precisely when and to the extent that we enact the form of her consciousness in ourselves by means of empathizing with her. In this way, we experience the extreme positive value of her consciousness just as if it were our own. It follows that, to the extent that we are able to establish empathy with the spiritual partner, we also experience our own being (i.e., our own consciousness) in an intensely positive way. By feeling admiration through compassion toward the other more intensely than we could toward ourselves, we are impressed with the extreme value of being, and thus are inspired by it to the extent that our entire outlook is transformed to one in which the negativity of the ontological predicament is more than overshadowed by this positive appreciation of the worthwhileness of being as instantiated in that person.

Other than this non-egocentric awe in which a spiritual partner is considered more important than ourselves, the main other times most of us can usually experience our own consciousness in this positive a way and on a sustained basis are in the four instances cited earlier: romantic love; traditional religious ritual; appreciation of worthwhile artwork; and altruistic behavior toward ordinary friends, family members, or humanity generally in principled moral and political action. But these experiences all have inherent limitations with regard to the extent, permanence, authenticity, and/or concreteness of the ways they can sustain intense experiences of quasi-aesthetic awe and lead to a sustained spreading effect. Only a relationship of spiritual partnership in the primary sense can initially facilitate a concretely symbolized and mutual space of empathy that is not systematically subjected to the kinds of sociocultural, interpersonal, and moral conflicts that in other types of relationships would tend to either erode the space of empathy, remove the opportunity to symbolize empathic feelings, or (ending in these same outcomes) destroy authenticity.

At the point when we have learned to directly experience the other's value in this positive way, the important thing is not primarily to 'live for' the other in the sense of making her well-being into the most important concern in our own lives. It is not merely or even primarily her well-being that is experienced as so extremely valuable, but her very existence. In fact, to devote *too much* of our energy to the service of her well-being would be counterproductive to preserving the essential nature of the spiritual partnership relationship, which must be a relationship between equals who respect each other's autonomy and independence. To pressure the other person to become dependent on our benevolent actions (as many husbands do to their wives, for example) threatens to reduce both her autonomy and our own. More important still, we cannot allow *ourselves* to become dependent on the other in the sense that a cult follower is dependent on the cult hero, or that a masochist is dependent on a sadist, or that an overprotective parent is dependent on the child. In this case we would undermine our own autonomy, and thus render ourselves less able to maintain our own agency. Agency, in the sense of accepting responsibility for directing one's own stream of consciousness, is necessary for the skills needed to avoid self-deception, neurotic defenses, and an inauthentic shifting onto the other person the responsibility to live our own lives. This is not to say that a spiritual partner does not feel intense altruism and often act on it. The point is that we cannot allow the meaning of our own life to become defined completely in terms of these altruistic behaviors or dependent on them.

On the contrary, the way the experience of a primary spiritual partner enables us to live more meaningfully is not that it substitutes benefiting the partner in place of our other goals, but simply that it allows us to live with the attitude that the unavoidable tribulations of life are justified by the positive value that we have experienced in the spiritual partner's full value. To experience this positive value, it is necessary only to *contemplate* the other's positive value in a mindframe of quasi-aesthetic awe. This does require that we periodically symbolize our admiration and compassion through the vehicle of the space of empathy as practiced by spiritual partners. But it does not require that our whole life revolves around the spiritual partner, that we dependently 'cling' to her, that we follow her as a cult follower, possess her as a jealously guarded use-value, or define the structure of our goal-orientations primarily in terms of altruistically benefiting her.

In fact, the way we structure our goal-orientations may not be reasoned very differently from the way we did before entering into the spiritual partnership, except that the usual predominance of egocentric concerns that characterizes the 'normal' value system will no longer be so pronounced. The reason for this change is more negative than positive. We lose the obsession with acquiring ever more and more benefits (of whatever kind) for ourselves, because that obsession was caused by the fact that, in the absence of an adequate resolution of the ontological predicament, no amount of benefits we could ever acquire could possibly be enough to compensate us for such an abominable outrage. To try to come to terms with the finite dilemma of human beings by acquiring benefits is like trying to satisfy sexual need by eating, or to satisfy a need for romantic love through merely physical sexual pleasure. No amount will ever be enough, because we are trying to satisfy the wrong type of need with the wrong type of fulfillment.

Moreover, another, more subtle effect of spiritual partnership is that it leads to increasingly altruistic feelings toward humanity generally, because of the 'spreading effect.' Having witnessed the inspiring value of the spiritual partner by beholding her from the standpoint of embattled finitude, as 'too good for the world,' we then see the similarity of other conscious beings to her in the important existential dimensions (however different may be their individual natures), and thus are able to focus on their positive value more easily (although this may require ignoring their alienation, hostility, degradation, and sometimes obnoxiousness). One reason we are able to see people from this charitable perspective is that we ourselves are not as frustrated as before in the overall meaning of our own lives, and therefore can 'afford' to be benevolent. Also, once we have come to terms with the larger ontological issues that really determine the meaningfulness of life, the everyday problems that previously would have gotten our goat seem relatively trivial. And we are less inclined to pounce upon some trivial conflict as an opportunity to symbolize and act out deeper frustrations, because these deeper frustrations themselves are less pronounced now that we have faced up to the ontological dilemma and are no longer as frustrated by it. If spiritual partnership is fully realized by means of the symbolization process described above, then the spreading effect—that is, the spreading to other people of this intensely felt focus on their intrinsic value through compassion for their finitude—becomes more and more forced on us whether we like it or not, for reasons that will become clear in the following chapters.

4. The Roles of Sexual Attraction and Sexual Polarity in Experiences of the Value of Being

For reasons that will become increasingly obvious, the function of making possible the quasi-religious experience of intense positive value needed to override the negativity of the ontological predicament is often initially evoked in relation to a person toward whom sexual symbolization is possible, and/or whose 'sexual polarity' is opposite from one's own—especially in cultures which, like ours, particularly favor the kinds of interactions I shall describe in this context. If we are to understand the historical tendency toward the sexualization of this kind of positive value experience, it is necessary first of all to clarify in what sense the term 'sexual polarity' is relevant to the phenomenon of spiritual partnership and the way in which feelings of sexual attraction tend to help facilitate it.

It should be emphasized at the outset that there seems to be no reason to believe that spiritual partnership in the sense of a transcendent value experience must necessarily involve either opposite sexual polarity or sexual symbolization, but only that the possibility of spiritual partnership in the primary sense often tends to present itself in a stronger way, and more frequently, between oppositely polarized individuals and/or between those for whom sexual symbolization is possible. In some instances, polarization and sexual symbolization are *not* factors; for example, an older 'mentor' figure and a younger artist or scholar may strongly idealize each other, as in the case of Isaac Newton and the young mathematician Fatio. Although in our culture at this time such emotions do not as often tend to be as intense as in oppositely polarized relationships, they do sometimes appear to embody a good degree of spiritual partnership, because the mutually desirable differences in the two forms of consciousness motivate emotional intensity in the people's desire to vicariously experience each other's way of being. The younger scholar, for example, admires (and would like to replicate) the older one's wisdom, self-assurance, virtuosity, and so on, while the older one admires (and would like to replicate) the younger one's innocent enthusiasm, feeling of adventure, and open-ended potentiality (perhaps qualities the older person once had and feels a strong need to reactivate). Remember, however, that in the context of spiritual partnership this craving for a 'missing element' is only a seductive catalyst for the real effect—the realization that intrinsic value can be experienced more intensely in another than in oneself. Other kinds of relationships that embody spiritual partnership will also be discussed later. Most of these, however, typically lack the intensity to overpower the fundamentally egocentric perspective, as we shall see. (On Westfall's account, Newton certainly failed to allow his love for Fatio to generalize by means of a spreading effect, and became increasingly embittered when Fatio was no longer available to provide the needed transcendent value experience.) On the other hand, nonpolarized relationships may avoid the problems typical of romanticized relationships, as I have already mentioned. The remainder of this section will focus on the phenomena of sexual attraction and opposite sexual polarization.

It will be helpful throughout this discussion of sexuality to bear in mind that spiritual partnership in the primary sense requires such an intense direct experience of the other's positive value that this value is experienced *more intensely than one could experience one's own* value (for the reasons indicated earlier). This is a difficult inversion of the originally egocentric value system, in which one's own problems and concerns emotionally *feel* more important and central than those of others. Remember that being caught up in the circle of egocentricity does not require that we *intellectually believe* our own concerns to be more important, but only that we *feel* as if they were more important. It is this circle of egocentricity that must be overcome if the resulting value experience is to be intense enough to overpower the negativity of death, alienation, and the relative powerlessness and insignificance of the individual. Reflection on ordinary friendship, for example, suggests that these relationships do not initially 'pull us out of ourselves' relentlessly enough to overcome this egocentricity. Normally, a friend's value is experienced as *equal to* our own; we do not experience the friend's value in a way that seems infinitely more intense than the experience of our own value—as sometimes occurs, for example, in romantic or sexual relationships. Again, it is not that we intellectually believe that a lover's value is greater than our own, but simply that we directly experience this value much more strongly than we can our own.

The most obvious reason why opposite sexual polarization tends to correlate with a really intense pull toward the extreme positive value feelings of primary spiritual partnership is that males and females tend to be sexually attracted to each other. In the case of homosexuals, the sexual attraction to the *same* gender might enhance the possibility of spiritual partnership even where the sexual polarization of the two people is not different at all (whether it is physical or psychological polarization that is at issue). The reason sexual attraction tends to lead to a stronger likelihood that spiritual partnership will begin to develop is that the physical sensations involved in sexual love are available to be used as a concrete *symbolization vehicle* for the intensification of the feelings of admiration and compassion (which in and of themselves are not sexual feelings, but are felt toward the conscious being of the other). The physical sensations—butterflies in the stomach, flooding of hormones, continual yearning to touch, see, and be with the other, etc.—serve as a concrete, physical substratum for other originally nonsexual feelings whose object is the other's personality as a conscious being rather than merely the body as a sexual object (see my *Eros in a Narcissistic Culture*). This happens in the same way that the physical act of listening to Tchaikovsky's Sixth Symphony can symbolize feelings of despair (whose original object may have had nothing to do with the symphony), resulting in the intensification of the feelings. Sexual attraction, then, can symbolize and thus concretely intensify nonsexual feelings of admiration and compassion, and this obviously can increase the likelihood of spiritual partnership in the primary sense.

In the case of spiritual partnership pulled by and intensified by sexual attraction, however, there is also the danger that the sexual symbolization process may end up by *dampening* the very feelings that they originally intensified. We have already seen that spiritual partners need to interact in certain ways within an uncompromised space of empathy in order to feel what they feel. Sexual behavior does not necessarily require a space of empathy in the sense of a nonjudgmental and nondirective yet intensely interested pattern of interaction likely to enhance unobstructed mutual visibility, which then pulls an intensified empathy. For this reason and others which we shall explore later, there is the danger that sexual symbolization of feelings may be used merely as a *substitute* form of symbolization in place of the more subtle forms of interaction needed to maintain the possibility of continued spiritual partnership (as the next chapter will explore in more detail). The important point for now is simply that the pull of spiritual partnership is often likely to be felt more strongly in cases where the two people either have developed their personalities in 'oppositely polarized' ways, or have sexual orientations that enable them to become sexually attracted to each other. (The notion of 'opposite sexual polarization,' of course, requires that we define what we mean by 'masculine' and 'feminine'—a complex problem to which I shall return in a moment.)

The fact that sexual attraction is available to serve as a concrete symbolization for overwhelming feelings of appreciation for the seemingly infinite positive value of another conscious being seems to be true regardless of cultural or historical context. On the other hand, whether people are psychologically able to *use* this opportunity in this way is obviously subject to cultural obstruction, as any cursory glance at the history of sexual relationships will clearly show.

But there is still another reason why opposite sexual polarization tends to lend itself to the development of primary spiritual partnership, and this other reason could possibly be as much a product of culture as of biology. I am referring here to the fact that women often seem to men (and vice versa) to possess some mysterious *personality characteristic*, which each so urgently craves in the other that the two genders feel 'pulled out of themselves' toward an overwhelming appreciation for the extreme value of the oppositely polarized *form of consciousness*. This phenomenon is much more subtle and more difficult to understand than simple sexual attraction, but it seems to be an independent factor distinguishable from sexual attraction and worth acknowledging in its own right. Not only is this 'opposite polarization' in people's forms of consciousness a separable driving force toward the use of oppositely polarized relationships to serve the 'religious' need for spiritual partnership; it is also one for which most forms of culture set the stage by imposing conditions that confront each individual with the choice to emphasize one sexual polarity and to de-emphasize the other in his or her overall pattern of consciousness. In fact, all forms of culture I have yet studied set up this pattern of 'opposite polarization' in styles of consciousness, in one way or another. Yet this in itself does not prove that opposite polarization is not a product of culture to some greater or lesser extent. It may even be that one of the motives for a cultural pattern of opposite polarization is precisely to make experiences of spiritual partnership more likely to occur. At the same time, however, too extreme a polarization ends up defeating this purpose, by creating gender relations in which a very pronounced 'space of empathy' becomes virtually impossible to establish and/or to maintain for very long.

The relevance of this issue in this context does not require us to decide whether the sexual polarity in styles of consciousness is determined biologically, or culturally, or family-dynamically, or through a process of operant conditioning, or in some other way—or indeed whether it would be theoretically possible for there to be a culture in which sexual polarization in styles of consciousness does not even exist, as Chodorow suggests in *The Reproduction of Mothering*. Though such a scenario might be *logically possible* (just as a planet that supports only vegetable life is logically possible), there are strong tendencies that drive consciousness to develop in a polarized way. Also, however one might define 'masculine' and 'feminine' *forms of consciousness*, it is obvious that both styles will exist to a greater or lesser extent in all conscious beings, whether male or female. If there could be a culture in which styles of consciousness were no different for males and females, this might only mean that the 'masculine' and 'feminine' styles would be exactly evenly balanced in everyone; in that case, what we now think of as 'masculine' and 'feminine' *styles of consciousness* would still coexist in each individual. In any case, whether it is logically possible for consciousness not to be polarized is not our concern here. Our concern is to understand why it is the case, once polarization does exist in styles of consciousness, that the pull of spiritual partnership so often manifests itself so strongly between oppositely polarized personalities. And, of all the ways in which the concepts 'masculine' and 'feminine' might be defined, in what sense are these concepts to be employed if we want to understand the strength of the pull toward oppositely polarized spiritual partnership?

For this purpose and in this context, 'sexual polarity' seems to mean something broadly similar to but not exactly identical with Jung's *anima-animus* distinction. (Later I shall discuss some important differences between my usage of the concept of sexual polarity and the ways Jung and the Jungians have developed the *anima-animus* concept.) In every conscious and living being, there seems to be a tension between two styles of actualizing consciousness and maintaining its survival against the onslaught of the material world's necessary perils. Both styles appear to be present in everyone, but to the extent that we develop and use one style, the other has a tendency to be neglected because the two styles are difficult to enact simultaneously. Since the nature of sexual polarity is not the central focus of this book, yet is a difficult and complex problem in its own right, it is discussed in more detail in the appendix. The assumption here is that readers who are willing to grant the sketchy definitions of sexual polarity presented in this section might prefer to skip the more detailed treatment in the appendix.

Let me emphasize that it is equally possible for either *biological gender* to develop both 'masculine' and 'feminine' *forms of consciousness* in the sense I want to define; in fact, psychological functionality *requires* that we develop both. The difference is only that 'feminine' forms of consciousness are those which are developed *with less practice and effort* for the biological female, and vice versa. I say this because recent neurophysiology increasingly shows that there are different emotional tendencies in the male and female brains. The extreme examples are found in the predominance of oxytocin circuits in the female brain, especially during pregnancy and after sexual activity, which tends to subserve tenderness and empathy. To a lesser extent, oxytocin has the same effect in the male brain, but vasopressin plays a more prominent role subserving both permanent bonding with a sex object and aggression toward challenging males (for an excellent presentation of these findings, see Panksepp's *Affective Neuroscience*).

The 'feminine' style of sexual polarity in the sense I shall use, which attempts to encompass the particular differences within a unified phenomenological description (roughly corresponding to Jung's *anima*), is the style that refuses to forfeit the quality in oneself that Levinas designates as "foreign to the world too coarse and too offensive" (1969, 256). As I said at the outset, all of us are equally too good for the world in this sense. This is an ontological or metaphysical too-goodness that has nothing to do with sexual polarity; the physical realm of famine, pestilence, war, and death is a harsh and hostile environment for such an essentially sensitive and vulnerable form of being as consciousness, yet consciousness is inevitably condemned to struggle tenuously in this brutal climate on its own crass terms. But what is different about the two sexual polarities is that the 'feminine' style *deals with* this too-goodness differently, takes a different attitude toward it. There is a sense in which the feminine style *refuses to give up* its foreignness-to-the-world. By this I mean that it refuses to reduce itself to a calloused and insensitive brute as a way of doing battle in a realm of insensitive brutality. It accomplishes this feat by withdrawing from direct confrontation with the conflicts inherent in materiality, retreating often into ethereality and the realm of emotional interiority, defusing conflict wherever possible, and sometimes by regrouping in such a way as to assimilate or incorporate the aggressor, as the ancient Sumerians preserved their culture by assimilating wave after wave of invading peoples. All these features stem from an *a priori* insistence on maintaining a basic core of spirituality (or conscious intensity) that will not be sacrificed in order to do battle in the crass world of brutality, alienation, and hostility.

By the 'masculine' style, on the other hand, I mean just the reverse tendency: The masculine style deals with the adversity of the world by attacking it head-on. It strives to repel the attacker at all costs and will resist penetration by any means necessary, even if this entails stoic resolve almost to the point of turning oneself into a feelingless warrior, a machine, or an insensitive, calloused, and unprincipled brute. And, just as the feminine side often wins the war by forfeiting the battle through the assimilation of the foe, so the masculine style often loses the war by winning the battle. The purpose of the war to begin with was to preserve the soul (i.e., the intensity and authenticity of consciousness) against destruction by the harsh, practical world in which it must survive—the world 'too coarse and too offensive.' But by becoming *like* this 'coarse and offensive' foe in order to combat it, the masculinized subject risks losing its soul (i.e., the intensity and authenticity of its consciousness).

The reason there are just two and only two conscious styles in this regard is that, in the struggle for the survival of the soul, there are two elements in opposition: the soul itself (i.e., the interiority of consciousness), and the crass realm of material conflict on which consciousness inevitably must depend for its functioning. The masculine style's motto is 'Ensure physical subsistence first; then worry about spirituality.' The feminine style's motto is 'Subsistence without at least some degree of emotional interiority would not be worth the effort.' I use the terms 'masculine' and 'feminine' to designate these styles, even though both are present in everyone, because there is a tendency for the biological male to require less practice and effort in developing the 'masculine' style (and to be pressured by his society to do so), and for the female to do just the reverse. Jaak Panksepp, Lawrence Miller, and Simone de Beauvoir, among others, have provided good analyses of the extent to which biology may be involved in this kind of behavioral gender differentiation. In Beauvoir's analysis, no specialized knowledge of new or obscure empirical facts is needed, but only a logical and coherent interpretation of them.

It is true, of course, that in many cultures, especially many of the earlier ones in the written 'historical' period, it has often been predominantly the men who spent more of their time discussing and theorizing about 'spiritual' matters. But this is because the men in these cultures *have* 'ensured physical subsistence first'—largely by forcing women into subordinate roles in order to ensure subsistence, thus allowing men the leisure to pursue spiritual matters. But men have used both the 'masculine' and the 'feminine' sides of their consciousness to theorize about spirituality. The masculine style is useful for this purpose up to a certain point: The combative nature of philosophical discourse sets up a dialectic in which *certain kinds* of self-deception can be rooted out. But, without the 'feminine' side, such discourse would not know what it is talking about, since the interiority of feelings would be too steeled for combat.

It is also obvious that women have excelled as warriors and athletes. But the fact that these women have developed superior masculine virtues ('masculine,' since they must suppress sensitivity during the hardship of training) does not necessarily prevent their overall personality orientation from being predominantly feminine. It will become increasingly evident that a well-functioning person must develop both sexual polarities, somewhat as an instrument can play more than one melody, and that the two polarities function in coordination and interdependence with each other, although one or the other polarity tends to predominate (we shall see why shortly). By the definitions I am using, then, Artemis actualized more of her 'masculine' dimension than Aphrodite, and Tristan actualized more of his 'feminine' dimension than Achilles. But this does not mean that Artemis is not a predominantly feminine person, or that Tristan is not predominantly masculine

It is important to acknowledge that not all gender differences can be explained on the basis of the special senses of 'masculine' and 'feminine' styles of consciousness to which I am referring here. A variety of culture-specific, psychodynamic, and socioeconomic factors may either exaggerate or distort these basic gender differences or even create completely artificial and unrelated sex roles that also affect the forms of people's consciousness. A very logical accounting of many of these distortions has been presented by the psychoanalyst Jessica Benjamin in *The Bonds of Love*, where she suggests that the behavior of parents (which is culturally influenced) teaches children to associate assertiveness with self-centeredness and maleness, and to associate the desire for recognition with submissiveness, dependency, and femaleness (5–8). While I am sure that some such dynamic as this does tend to exaggerate and distort the gender differences in forms of consciousness, the differences that concern us here are the more definitive and therefore more authentic ones. (As Benjamin makes clear, the constricted opposition of assertiveness, self-centeredness, and maleness versus desire for recognition, submissiveness, dependency, and femaleness is quite artificial and distorted, yet largely permeates our culture and psychodynamics.) It will become increasingly obvious that the elements in the oppositely polarized person that tend most strongly to pull spiritual partnership are the authentic forms of consciousness in the other that are developed only with difficulty or strenuous practice in oneself, and therefore appear as desirable. Obviously, a disturbed personality may be attracted to the inauthentic features of someone else's consciousness (for example, a masochist to a sadist—in the psychological as opposed to merely sexual-game senses of these terms), but such attractions do not lead to the authentic interactions needed for spiritual partnership to develop. What we want to consider in this context are primarily the masculine and feminine forms of consciousness insofar as they arise as *authentic* potentialities in people, not superficial behavior patterns, culture-specific rules of conformity, or prevalent and typical forms of inauthenticity and neurosis. We are therefore primarily interested in the differences between the most 'definitive' forms of consciousness in the two styles, not in the accidental roles developed by specific cultures or family dynamic systems, whether the purpose of these latter is to facilitate survival or merely to reproduce neurotic defenses (as Chodorow suggests).

By the definitions we are using, then, every normal conscious being uses *both* the masculine and the feminine styles of consciousness (in these 'definitive' senses) at different times and in different ways, yet certain forms are mastered with greater or lesser practice and effort by one gender or the other. A totally 'masculinized' character, devoid of any 'feminine' consciousness in the sense we are using, would completely lose his soul and become a straightforward bully, with no feelings beyond the simple pleasures of a submammalian beast. On the other hand, a person with no 'masculinity' whatever would become so self-indulgent in always experiencing the conscious interiority of each moment, regardless of the demands of material and interpersonal survival, that the world would destroy her. Tennessee Williams shows two characters who approach these extremes in *A Streetcar Named Desire*. But even Stanley Kowalski at least is still not too much of a brute to allow himself to feel, and Blanche does at least try to repel the adversity of the world by means of her psychological defenses, and she also represses many of her feelings in this way. To a great extent, both characters' problems stem from their attempts to suppress or refuse to develop the opposite polarity in themselves. Both fail to see that further development of a well-functioning masculine style *requires* that the same person develop his feminine style further, and vice versa, because in order to accomplish their respective purposes adequately the two styles must function interdependently.

But it is still true that, in any individual, one style or the other almost inevitably ends up predominating in the overall personality structure. One might at first suspect that people would be as likely to develop 'androgynous' personality structures as to develop predominantly masculine or feminine ones. But to strike such a happy medium is in reality very difficult because of the importance of habit strength in the development of character. Although stoic self-discipline is important for both masculine and feminine styles of consciousness, in differing ways for each, the important point in the present context is that stoic virtue cannot be turned off and on as if it were an electric light. The more it is used in a certain context, the better one is at using it in that context; and one becomes better at using it precisely to the extent that it becomes a habit. The less habitual it has become to use the stoic response in a certain context, the more difficult it is; therefore, the more habitual it becomes, the more enjoyable it becomes as well—or at least the less painful. But the practice of stoic resolve requires that we always challenge ourselves to develop it further, since an easy-to-accomplish instance of stoic virtue is by definition not very stoic. The house painter who stands back to admire his work falls off the scaffold. Once we begin the process of developing stoic virtue in a certain context, there is an inner necessity in the dynamic of this development, which drives us to develop always more and more of it. The more we develop it, the more habitual the stoic response becomes, and vice versa. Stoicism becomes a self-maintaining *Gestalt*, like a row of arches that mutually support each other: It tends to exist either in the extreme or not at all. Thus, up to a certain limiting point, the more the stoic response is used in a masculine way (i.e., in the service of steeling ourselves for battle within the crass realm of adversity which threatens the soul's existence), the more we tend to neglect and underdevelop our feminine side.

    I say *up to a certain point*, and this is a very important qualification. We must remember that a person who goes too far in this direction loses the war by winning the battle; i.e., he loses his soul through the non-feeling of emotions and nonthinking of thoughts in order to steel himself for combat. But a person with no soul eventually loses his capacity to make a good stoic as well. Without self-understanding and self-knowledge, the skills necessary to achieve stoic virtue cannot be practiced effectively. Repressed consciousness works against us in this regard. Once we repress our consciousness to the point where self-deception and other neurotic psychological defenses become prominent, these defenses begin to erode self-discipline at the unconscious level. If my thinking and feeling are not mobilized and integrated toward self-awareness, then it is all too easy to deceive myself that I have absolute self-control by focusing only on, say, my athletic ability, while behaving in an undisciplined, infantile, and utterly nonstoic way off the field—for example, as a profligate philanderer or helplessly addicted drug abuser. In these respects, the 'return of the repressed' works to undermine stoic virtue if we try to push it too far by suppressing our feminine side. True stoic virtue cannot coexist with too extremely 'masculinized' a character structure.

Nor do I mean to imply (as some Jungians seem to believe) that feminine characters lack stoic virtue compared with masculine ones. The difference is only that the masculine style mobilizes stoic resolve in the service of repelling an adversary; we use it to steel ourselves for combat. The feminine style practices stoic virtue toward a different purpose: It stoically resolves not to sacrifice our 'foreignness to the world' in order to engage in combat with it. Rather than stoop to its level, our feminine side is willing to suffer excruciating emotional agony if necessary. Excruciating agony, after all, is at least a form of intense consciousness, so that in experiencing it we preserve the existence of the soul rather than becoming a nonconscious being in order to do battle with the nonconscious realm. So, while the masculine side develops stoic virtue in the thick of battle, where it works toward the suppressing of the feminine side, the feminine side develops the habit of stoic virtue in refusal to let inner sensitivity and emotionality be destroyed in order to do battle—which thus works toward suppressing the masculine side. In both cases, there is a tendency to become more and more masculine or more and more feminine until the limit is reached beyond which it would become self-defeating to go further, for the reasons just discussed.

It is very common then, especially for the normal, well-functioning person, to have developed one style or the other to a greater extent, but not exclusively. This seems to be as true for homosexuals as for heterosexuals; there is no reason to suppose that the conscious style of a homosexual male, for example, might not be predominantly masculine. Also, it may be true that biological males (whether homosexual or heterosexual) do sometimes develop a predominantly feminine style, in the sense we are using here. It is not uncommon that when a group of homophobes physically attack a pair of homosexuals, the homosexuals, trained in self defense, turn the tables and beat up the homophobes. This suggests that biology does not absolutely predispose a person to emphasize one style or the other, although most of us, whether homosexual or heterosexual, end up *learning* to habitualize one style as our overarching organizing principle. There also seem to be biological determinants for the choice of style—male genes and hormones tending toward the angular pattern and the frontal assault, the ungiving strength/brittleness of the oak tree, while female ones tend toward the supple give-but-don't-break style of the willow, as Panksepp and Wilson suggest. But there seem to be social determinants as well: If the organization of a society requires that women devote too much of their energy to 'feminine' pursuits (for example, nurturing the young, maintaining the extended family structure, etc.), then women might feel deprived of the amount of masculine expression they would really like. And men might be deprived of much of the opportunity to develop and express their 'feminine' side because of the same kinds of social demands on their time and energy (for example, repairing toilets is not a pursuit that strongly encourages the development of 'feminine' virtues). But, whether the choice of predominant style is socially or biologically determined, it seems almost inevitably to occur.

At the same time, the masculinized subject senses his loss and either consciously or unconsciously regrets it (just as does the feminized subject). In order to exist fully, to exist to a much greater extent *qua* conscious being than he can do in the predominantly masculinized style, this masculine subject feels the need to allow his consciousness also to flow in the pattern of the feminine style. But this is something he can do effectively only with the help of someone who has strongly developed that style and is free of the kinds of habits that would choke it off at every turn, while at the same time possessed of the habits necessary for the refusal to give up consciousness for the sake of practicality in combat with the world.

This, finally, brings us to the point about sexual polarity that is important for our purposes: When a predominantly masculine subject in need of experiencing the sensitive, vulnerable, and ethereal 'feminine' pattern of consciousness makes contact with a predominantly feminine subject who (assuming well-developed communicative and interpersonal skills on the part of both people) makes this dimension of being suddenly available to him, he is overwhelmed with a quite realistic, legitimate appreciation of the value of what has occurred and of the person whose character embodies this valuable phenomenon. Because she has dropped her defenses for the space of empathy, she allows herself to exist this authentic form of consciousness all the more completely, and allows it to be completely visible for the other's appreciation.

Moreover, her feminine sensitivity is enhanced all the more by the simultaneous enactment of her masculine potential through empathy with the masculine subject; the entire structure of her unfolding consciousness is more courageously authentic in the face of combat, and because of this increased authenticity in such contexts, more intense and more fully alive—while at the same time it can be seen more clearly within the space of empathy with a completely trusted and nonjudgmental partner than it would ordinarily be. In the same way, if we assume that each gender has developed much of what the other intensely admires and wishes to empathize with, an analogous process would occur from the reversed-gender perspective. Thus, women would experience a powerful pull toward the opposite gender as well.

As I have already granted, it is entirely possible that dramatic differences between masculine and feminine character might not exist in every conceivable form of culture. The availability of sexual attraction as a symbolization vehicle for spiritual partnership, on the other hand, does seem to be culture-independent.

If interactions between oppositely polarized and/or sexually attracted people unfold in a certain way, each person may find himself or herself not only in a state of admiration for the other's form of being, but in fact swept away in an intensely positive experience of quasi-aesthetic awe. This experience is no mere Jungian 'projection,' but rather a more or less accurate perception of the positive value that really exists in the other's form of consciousness. If this occurs reciprocally and completely, both people have then achieved in relation to a concretely existing being, at least temporarily, the same purpose that traditional religions once were able to achieve through the intense positive-value experience they made possible through awe-stricken admiration for a conscious being beyond oneself, be it a saint, martyr, ancestor, or deity.

Up to this point, what I have been describing may sound to many readers like merely a deification of a traditional 'romantic love' object, or perhaps the nonsexual yet romantic worship of a 'Platonic love' or 'courtly love' object in some such way as described in Plato's *Phaedrus* or Ibn Hazm's *The Ring of the Dove*. While it is true that, especially in modern times, romantic relationships tend to be used for the kinds of quasi-religious purposes I am describing, it is also true, as Denis de Rougemont, Robert

Johnson, and others have pointed out, that romance by itself more often than not falls short of serving this essentially spiritual purpose very adequately on a permanent basis. Later, I shall explore some of the reasons for this failure and suggest ways that romantic partners could perhaps relate to each other more fully as spiritual partners in the primary sense (as discussed more extensively in *Eros in a Narcissistic Culture*). But the essence of the kind of relationship I am describing here is really completely independent of whether or not it occurs in the context of a romantic relationship. In rare instances, a relationship may be based almost exclusively on the spiritual partnership dimension. But it is not necessary that a spiritual partnership be 'pure,' in this sense, to achieve its purpose. It is only necessary that this dimension be pronounced enough to ensure four conditions:

First, the other dimensions of the relationship must not *erode* the spiritual partnership dimension (which they all too often tend to do, especially in erotic relationships).

Secondly, the motivation to appreciate the value of the spiritual partner's form of being *for its own sake* must be strong *enough* to overcome the circle of egocentricity.

Third, some way must be found to concretely 'symbolize' the love for the spiritual partner, in the sense of 'symbolization' defined above, other than through sexual feelings and activities.

And, finally, each person must learn to allow the feelings of admiration and compassion for the other's consciousness to spread toward other conscious beings, so that a concretely felt love for conscious beings per se can form the basis for a strongly motivating value system that unifies the self by directing it toward the future. In this way, a stifling, symbiotic dependency relationship is avoided, yet the strong feeling of the positive value of conscious existence is not lost. In the case of Newton's relationship with Fatio, only the first three of these conditions were met, and even then only temporarily.

Clearly, there is no logical necessity that only people of opposite sexual polarity can inspire such intense feelings of self-transcending reverence. It is only that, especially in the modern era, oppositely polarized people are initially more *likely* to pull such feelings from each other, for the reasons discussed above, and these feelings are then likely to be thematized along romantic lines. But the ultimate and lasting spiritual effect of these feelings does not flow merely from the initial feeling toward the original spiritual partner; rather, the spiritual effect results from the series of psychological developments which, if handled in a certain way, may be produced *by* these feelings—including, as we shall soon see, a 'spreading' effect in which we eventually learn to intensely experience the value of all conscious beings in quasi-aesthetic awe.

So far, we have discussed only the most basic features of four essential aspects of spiritual partnership, which can be summarized as follows: Section 1 showed how spiritual partnership makes possible the direct appreciation for another conscious being, by focusing on the person's uniqueness and irreplaceability, which is more intensely positive than any direct experience we could have of our own value (since focusing on our own finitude is more negative than positive); spiritual partnership thus makes possible a religious experience of quasi-aesthetic awe powerful enough to counterbalance the negativity of the finite predicament. In this respect, it functions analogously to the way love for Christ is supposed to function in Christianity (but all too seldom does, as chapter 5 will discuss).

Section 2 addressed the extremely important dimension of symbolization in the spiritual partnership relationship. Any feelings must be concretely symbolized in order to be felt with intensity. This is why, in the past, religious ritual, sexual behavior, aesthetic experience, and altruistic behavior have been the most familiar ways to intensify positive feelings so powerfully that, while we were under the spell of these positive feelings, they seemed to compensate fully for the harshness of the ontological insult that is our inescapable finitude. All these activities lend themselves especially well to the concrete symbolization of the feelings and attitudes with which they are associated. But, for various reasons, the intensity of these 'spells' cannot be authentically maintained in the face of the struggle and strife of our perilous existence in such a way as to permanently come to terms with the existential anxiety resulting from the ontological dilemma, so that it again becomes necessary to erect self-deceptive doctrines whose purpose was to deny reality. It is therefore crucial to understand how feelings toward a spiritual partner can be symbolized in their own appropriate way, so that we do not make the mistake of identifying spiritual partnership with some other type of function or activity, and so that these feelings can maintain their unique character and identity. This need for symbolization is the main reason for the incarnation of Christ in Christianity—to enable the believer to love God in a concrete way. And our inability to symbolize feelings of *human* love in any way comparable in power to physical *sexualization* is what led to the increasing turn toward the 'modern myth of romance' for the ultimate source of spiritual solace, as de Rougemont, Jung, and others have hinted.

Section 3 tried to define in a preliminary way the sense in which spiritual partnership can compensate *us* for the ontological dilemma even though it subordinates our own egocentric motives. In effect, it allows intrinsic value to be experienced in another, and indeed more intensely than we can experience it in ourselves, so that the circle of egocentricity can be broken. This will be explored much more extensively in chapter 4.

Finally, section 4 then attempted to clarify the notion of sexual polarity in consciousness, in order to lay the groundwork for understanding the tendency for oppositely polarized people to feel the pull toward spiritual partnership especially strongly. In my view, this interaction between opposite sexual polarities accounts for the increasing use of romantic relationships to meet spiritual needs that previously were met by religion—that is, the 'sexualization of religious experience.' This issue is discussed much more extensively in the next two chapters, and in the appendix.

What needs to be done now is to spell out in more detail what the relationship of 'spiritual partnership' consists of, how it functions, and why it has historically expressed itself primarily as the 'sexualization of religious experience.' The next chapter will address these questions.

3

Essential Dynamics of the Primary Transcendent Value Experience

The increasing use of romantic or erotic relationships to serve spiritual needs that were once served by traditional religions has been noted by such diverse theorists as Carl Jung, Otto Rank, Virginia Satir, Rollo May, Ethel Person, Denis de Rougemont, Joseph Campbell, John Haule, and many others. Every one of the thinkers just mentioned has also emphasized that, although romantic relationships now come closer than religion does to meeting many people's essentially religious needs, romance in itself ultimately tends to fail to get the job done in a very adequate way. The modern individual looks to a romantic partner to quell existential anxieties about the problems of finitude and the ultimate meaning of life, and such relationships at first appear to resolve these problems. But sooner or later—and usually sooner, according to all the theorists just cited—the romantic relationship balks at this tremendous weight, essentially because it is too unrealistic and unfair a responsibility for one person to place on another: It is unrealistic (these theorists say), because it dampens romantic feeling to ask another person to neglect so many other needs in order to play the role of omniscient benefactor. And it is unfair, because it places this burden on someone who is also expected to meet all the other demands on romantic partners in our form of culture. Different theorists present different pictures of the dynamics through which eros meets what I have termed religious needs less and less adequately as a relationship unfolds; I have discussed many of them elsewhere. In the present context, what seems clear is that people increasingly try to use romantic relationships as spiritual partnerships, but for various reasons they are not succeeding very well in the endeavor.

The central question of this chapter is whether, by exploring the phenomenon of spiritual partnership per se, we can develop a better understanding of the use of human relationships to meet these religious needs. By religious needs, in this context, I mean the need to come to terms in one way or another with the fact of our own finitude. Traditional religions have all too often tended to reconcile us with this unfortunate fact primarily by self-deceptively denying its reality. To a certain extent, the same religions simultaneously have also addressed the same problem in a more healthy way, by creating a positive value experience strong enough to counterbalance the negativity of the apocalyptic predicament of finite beings. But they have had great difficulty in popularizing this experience without the help of self-deceptive myths that ultimately lead to a denial of the problem rather than its resolution. Spiritual partnership, on the other hand, may also be equipped to create just such a positive value experience *without* the use of denial or self-deception. But to make such an experience possible would require overcoming certain counterproductive trappings of the romanticization of such relationships, which present two main problems: First, they erect alternative forms of symbolization that deflect from the forms suited to spiritual partnership, as well as extraneous purposes associated with romantic relationships. And secondly, when romance is the primary or only means of meeting existential needs, it does not seem to encourage a spreading effect, but tends instead toward the substitution of one romantic obsession with another. The first problem (substitution of sexual for more subtle forms of symbolization) renders the transcendent value experience presented by the erotic relationship all too temporary; and the second problem (failure to spread intense enough admiration-through-compassion beyond one romantic partner) prevents the necessary spreading effect that could relieve the pressure for the obsession with one love object to bear an unfair brunt of the meaning of life. The first step toward avoiding either problem is to understand the essential nature of spiritual partnership in its integrity as a phenomenon, without confusing it with eros or any other emotion with which it might frequently be combined or associated in certain forms of culture.

1. The Sexualization of Religious Experience in Relation to Transcendent Interpersonal Value Experience

If we study the ways in which romantic partners in various cultures relate as conscious beings, it is difficult to find any culture in which romantic partners relate as spiritual partners continually and throughout the life cycle to enough of an extent to resolve the ontological dilemma as explained in the previous chapter. Hence the almost universal need for self-deceptive interpretations of religious dogma in all developed cultures, and the frequent unhappiness and anxiety of those who eschew the 'opium' of these essentially fundamentalist (i.e., literalistic) interpretations. Of course, this analysis is not as relevant to very early primitive cultures as to more recent and more advanced ones. Quaint stories about reincarnation and individual immortality in the afterlife do not involve much self-deception in a culture in which logical and empirical thinking are too little developed to count as evidence against such stories; but, to this extent, the ontological predicament of finite beings is not as problematic for extremely primitive peoples, because in the absence of much evidence to the contrary it would not seem completely unreasonable to hold out considerable hope for a personal afterlife and for one's own relative importance in the scheme of things. It is only when the ontological dilemma truly *becomes* a dilemma because of a reliable assessment of the reality of finitude that such religions become increasingly 'self-deceptive' in the important sense. It is only at this stage of development that we can speak of the near universality of 'self-deceptive' forms of religion.

The important point for our purposes is that human love seems to have remained almost universally incapable of replacing such religious mythologies as a way to come to terms with the finite condition, although people have attempted to use romantic love in particular for this purpose. If romance per se were really capable of replacing religion, one would expect that it would have done so long ago, at least in some cultures.

It is true that those who subscribed to the Catharist heresy in Medieval Europe did seem to free themselves of much of the existential anxiety concerning their own finitude by providing themselves with an experience of positive value (through courtly love) so intense that it outweighed the loss of any eternal life that doctrinal Christianity could have offered. (See de Rougemont, for example.) But, in the first place, this freedom from existential anxiety was bought usually at the expense of earthly happiness, since the typical courtly lover lived his life hopelessly pining away in sorrow and woe over the unavailability of the love object, given that the spiritual effect of courtly love apparently could work only if the love was not consummated. (Hence the name 'Tristan,' which means 'sadness,' for the archetypal courtly lover.) Secondly, the Catharist heresy involved its own dubious and largely self-deceptive metaphysical mythology that worked mostly to deny the reality of the ontological dilemma, replacing it with its own doctrine of spiritual immortality and narcissistic self-aggrandizement. The courtly lover fancied that, by working himself into a frenzy of unfulfilled erotic passion, he increased his spiritual (i.e., conscious) intensity to the point of eschewing the physical (dark) realm in favor of a timeless and eternal spirituality (light) unbounded by the temporal. This theory seemed to fit the experience of courtly lovers, who felt that the inspirational effects of their passion tended to wane if consummation were allowed to advance too far. Examples parallel to the European courtly love tradition can be found in other cultures, such as in the "History of Arabs Who Died of Love" discussed by Stendhal, and earlier in Ibn Hazm's *Ring of the Dove*.

Similar impediments seem to enter into attempts to use physical sexuality in the interest of spirituality, such as the Taoist sects dating from the fifth century who practiced public rituals of "heirogamy or successive [sexual] unions of the members of the assembly in the chambers along the sides of the temple courtyard" (Needham 1956, 150–51). One Taoist sect is described in the following way in an Imperial edict of 1839 reported by Von Gulik: "They gather in the night many people together in one room, and without the lamps burning. Then they have sexual intercourse in the dark" (1974, 8–90). In these instances, as in the Catharist heresy, it is not that the erotic experience provides a positive value experience intense enough to *replace* self-deceptive religious dogmas, but rather sexuality is being used as a symbolic or concretely symbolizing ritual in the service of a complex edifice of metaphysical dogma, including a doctrine of the immortality of the soul. The same can be said for the ancient Baal worshipers and other fertility religions in which sexual symbolizations were used as religious rituals—as discussed, for example, in Rank's *Psychology and the Soul*. Also, the orgiastic and purely physical nature of the use of sexuality in many of these instances would certainly seem to suggest that the sex is being used not only as religious ritual, but also as a pleasant albeit temporary escape from the ontological dilemma rather than as a satisfactory resolution of it—just as we in the West try to escape through drugs, promiscuous sex, and other temporary forms of hedonistic gratification. We therefore cannot consider such occasional interrelations between sex and religion as examples in which a romantic or erotic relationship per se was able to serve the purpose of spiritual partnership—that is, the purpose of resolving the finite dilemma of conscious beings by providing a strong enough positive value experience to counteract the harshness of the facts without resorting to self-deceptive denial of the facts.

What we do seem to find, however, is that in many cultures, including ours, romantic partners do relate somewhat as spiritual partners initially, but the space of empathy cannot be fully maintained for very long in the face of the egocentric defensiveness of the partners. They sooner or later erect communication barriers that block the ability to reveal their most intimate thoughts, feelings, and existential questionings about life, and eventually refuse to empathize with or even tolerate each other's potentially threatening, socially condemned, or even *pragmatically inconvenient* feelings and ideas. (See Satir 1967; Broderick 1979; Sheehy 1976/1989.)

The reasons *why* the space of empathy tends to become eventually eroded in erotic couplings are somewhat complex, and will become more clear in the next section, where I shall discuss the fact that the ends of eros do not completely overlap with the ends of spiritual partnership. To briefly anticipate, there are both accidental and essential reasons for this. The accidental reasons involve the need for romantic couples to play nonromantic roles in relation to each other that are not conducive to preserving the space of empathy, as required by their culture or by the needs of survival. As an extreme example, if the culture requires that a woman act groveling and servile toward her husband while continually waiting on him, and that the husband wave her away casually with no sign of gratitude, the space of empathy becomes impossible because the woman's well-being requires that she become mistrustful, guarded, and defensive. As a less extreme example, any discussion as to whose 'fault' it is when something goes wrong will tend to be blown out of proportion, since each person naturally resists admitting guilt in relation to the other precisely because guilt toward another person tends to cut off the empathy between oneself and that person; moreover, guilt is almost impossible to assign when two people's entire life cycle is inseparably interwoven—it becomes like trying to assign guilt to a corporation. Thus the most trivial question of 'who is to blame' tends to become a major conflagration, and each person then becomes guarded in order to avoid future such instances. Many other such examples of these 'accidental' and culturally relative problems are discussed much more extensively in my *Eros in a Narcissistic Culture*, and there is no need to be too detailed about them here.

As for the 'essential' conflicts between eros and spiritual partnership, these revolve around the fact that, in eros, we need for the other person to remain able to idealize us for erotic purposes, and this involves the way she perceives our concrete, bodily comportment; thus there is a tendency to be cautious in the image we project to the other person, and this narcissistic concern may detract from our willingness to show our vulnerability or to be completely open for a full space of empathy with the other person. Also, in a long-term romantic relationship, it is necessary that both people maintain their separate individuality so that, as Simone de Beauvoir points out in *The Second Sex*, they are continually able to bring something new and interesting to each other and prevent their interactions from becoming lifeless. A relationship can occur only between two people, and its vitality depends on what each individual can bring into it from his or her interesting and separate activities. But this demand for separateness also sometimes fits uneasily with the need for a space of empathy between spiritual partners. There is the danger that too continual a demand for empathic interaction may ultimately lead to a complacent and life-choking symbiosis.

In obviously observable terms, the tendency at least in our culture seems to be that the two people begin to talk less and less to each other about the things that really, ultimately matter in life, and begin to confine themselves to the routines of daily survival, perhaps mixed with some idle banter for entertainment purposes. To the extent that a romantic relationship evolves in this direction, it no longer can serve very well as a spiritual partnership, because the possibility of symbolizing the experience through empathic expression of the other's forms of consciousness, as discussed in the previous chapter, becomes closed off in this case. Both people then must deal with their own ontological dilemma either by trying to compensate themselves for it through alcohol and drugs, by losing themselves in work, through a self-deceptive and fundamentalist form of religion, or through such temporary diversions as philandering sexual affairs; or, if one is really to confront the ontological dilemma head-on, one does so either *unsuccessfully*, through anxiety and neurosis, or *temporarily*, by entering into a new romantic relationship that serves at first as a spiritual partnership, but only at first.

It also seems evident, however, from observation of particular cases in our culture as well as in some others (e.g., see Broderick 1979; Sheehy 1976/1989; Mayer 1978; Watts 1958; Colegrove 1979; Johnson 1987), that some romantic relationships eventually evolve beyond this point. They seem to do so only if both people have somehow managed to maintain a certain amount of authenticity in communicating what is going on in their consciousness in spite of the destructive effect of the erosion of the space of empathy—and, even then, the space of empathy seems to survive only if one or both people clearly understand the forces that in a romantic relationship tend to undermine the space of empathy, and realize that these forces if not unchecked would deprive each person of the previously privileged vantage point on the embattled innocence of the other's endangered authentic consciousness in the face of the alienating ontic onslaught—that is, the vision of the person's uniqueness, contingency, and irreplaceability in the inevitable fleetingness and finitude of all beings. At this point they may determine themselves to maintain or reestablish spiritual partnership in spite of the sacrifices that must be made.

It appears from the case histories of relationship counselors (e.g., Broderick, Mayer), that some couples can maintain or reestablish a space of empathy, at least to some extent. In successful cases, elements of a spiritual partnership long ago destroyed are now reintroduced into the relationship. Talk is again about meaningful and philosophically important issues rather than only the banal and practical trivia of survival and entertainment. Each person again both admires and takes compassion for the other's embattled finitude, and therefore intensifies feelings of admiration in spite of previous conflicts.

Apparently, some degree of spiritual partnership is regained in many such cases, but usually not enough to completely eliminate the need for literal belief in the immortality of the individual's soul, compensation in the afterlife for unjust treatment here below, and so on—all of which literalistic religious beliefs serve to dull if not repress the harshness of the apocalyptic dilemma of finite beings. But this repression seems less pronounced than in the lives of those who achieve no spiritual partnership whatever, and therefore must become increasingly dogmatic and irrational in their religious beliefs. So, even in those cases where some degree of spiritual partnership is attained in long-term romantic relationships, it usually falls somewhere short of what would be needed to solve the finite dilemma (including death, alienation, powerlessness, and relative insignificance) without the need still for some serious denial, self-deception, or destructive escape mechanisms of one kind or another.

Perhaps more important, we must remember that the feeling of admiration-through-compassion toward a specific spiritual partner in the primary sense is not sufficient by itself to resolve the ontological dilemma. It becomes sufficient only if it serves as the beginning point of the spreading effect, leading to still further changes in the basic constitution of the self and its value system. This process will be considered in detail in a later chapter.

Obviously, in our culture, even moderate success in achieving spiritual partnership by means of long-term romantic relationships is by far the exception rather than the rule. In the United States, 50 percent of marriages, by ending in divorce, openly admit their failure even to meet the elementary needs for an acceptable level of happiness and existential fulfillment, let alone spiritual partnership. Among the remaining 50 percent, many achieve at best a dull routine in which open communication is suppressed for fear that conflict will erupt. And many of these couples obviously address their ontological dilemma either through a self-deceptive form of religion, or through drugs, alcohol, obsession with work or extramarital affairs, neurosis or psychosis, or other such ultimately inadequate responses.

A few authors (for example, Johnson 1987, Haule 1992, Colegrove 1979) have wondered about the possibility of achieving a relationship of *nonromantic* spiritual partnership in an oppositely polarized relationship *outside* of any ongoing romantic relationship. In our culture—as in all others I have studied with the possible exception of the Oglala Sioux Indians (as reported by Neihardt 1932/1988, 3–4)—the option of developing a relationship involving a substantial amount of nonromantic yet oppositely polarized spiritual partnership (in a sense strong enough to pull us out of egocentricity) is even more rarely achieved than is the long-term maintenance or restoration of a good degree of spiritual partnership in a romantic relationship. (According to Neihardt's reports of the sayings of the Sioux medicine man Black Elk, the myth of the White Bison Spirit Woman among these people may have recommended some sort of purely spiritual and nonsexual relationship with a member of the opposite sex, which might have resembled what I am describing as the possibility of a pure, nonromantic spiritual partnership.) The option of developing a relationship along the lines of a *pure* spiritual partnership, divorced from any romantic symbolization or use of physical sexuality as concrete embodiment for the feelings involved, does obviously present itself to many people from time to time even in our culture, but the categories of our culture preclude the notion of spiritual partnership without romantic or sexual symbolization. Instead of seeing such interactions as desperate attempts to compensate for the fact that 'romantic' relationships in our culture all too often are unable to meet the needs of spiritual partnership, or that they cannot meet them by themselves in our imperfect social setting, we unthinkingly try to categorize these interactions in terms of familiar cultural formulas. We say that the person is having or is being tempted to have 'an affair'—as if the only options were either to destroy and replace an already existing romantic relationship with one that will probably be equally unable to meet the needs of spiritual partnership (and for the same reasons), or to give up altogether the prospect of experiencing the unequivocal positive value of being through the intense feeling of admiration-through-compassion, and instead to find some other spiritual solution such as a dogmatic, self-deceptive form of religion as an escape from despair.

Since the initial motivation for spiritual partnership usually involves the fact that the other person instantiates a form of consciousness that is largely suppressed in ourselves, yet which we feel the need to develop, there is a strong tendency in most cultures (where psychological development is considerably polarized) for a potential spiritual partner to be someone whose predominant sexual polarity is the opposite of our own. Not only does opposite polarization often open up the possibility for the use of sexual feelings to symbolize admiration-through-compassion in a more concrete and thus more intensely felt way; but the urgency of the need to enact a neglected aspect of ourselves at certain times also becomes strong enough to overpower our usual defensiveness and egocentricity. However, we are so conditioned to interpret any positive feelings toward a member of the opposite sex as constituting only a sexual or romantic attraction, that we feel compelled to interpret the human needs that are trying to express themselves simply under the traditional categories of erotic or romantic feelings. Thus, when we find ourselves strongly pulled by the phenomenon of spiritual partnership in any context, we either symbolize it through sexual and romantic behavior, or reject it altogether. For example, if a male police officer has worshipful, idealizing feelings toward his female partner, many people—perhaps including himself—may have trouble believing that what is going on is not essentially sexual.

What presents itself in the spiritual partnership effect, in essence, is the opportunity to empathically engage another conscious being who allows us to be pulled out of the circle of egocentricity and to intensely experience the intrinsic value of this person's being within an unguarded space of empathy (not merely her extrinsic value as facilitating a more successful circle of egocentricity). Paradoxically, this is one of the strongest motives we have (because it is needed to overcome the harshness of the various problems of finitude) although almost all cultures have attempted to deny it because an egocentric personality constitution is needed for survival. Yet we cannot effectively fulfill this purely altruistic impulse in relation to our friends, lovers, or family members until we have first undergone a process that tears down egocentricity in a way that these other relationships by themselves seem all too often unable to accomplish, because it is easy and natural to function within them *from* the egocentric perspective.

In our culture at the time of this writing, it seems clear that, for most people, the main arena for experiencing and extensively working through the primary spiritual partnership process occurs in the context of romantic relationships. Yet it is crucial to remember that spiritual partnership does not have any necessary connection with sexuality or romantic love. In fact, it is often easier to understand a phenomenon in its pure form, undiluted by other elements with which it often tends to be intermingled, and therefore confused. Also, since the amount of spiritual partnership that does seem to occur in most romantic relationships almost inevitably fails, at least by itself, to permanently resolve the ontological dilemma well enough to eliminate the need for escape from the anxiety through other means, we should really think of spiritual partnership as a different phenomenon from eros per se (in spite of their typical interrelations). This will make it easier to understand how the romantic trappings of a relationship can get in the way of the selfless and nongrasping appreciation of the intrinsic value of a spiritual partner which, combined with avoidance of a crutchlike symbiosis, can lead to a spreading effect in which other people and experiences also are experienced with a much fuller appreciation of their positive value, as will be elaborated in the next chapter.

From observation of contemporary urbanized cultures, it seems likely that people are relying less and less on the self-deceptive aspects of traditional religions to address spiritual needs arising from the finite ontological dilemma of human beings, and are turning more and more to various forms of spiritual partnership as the starting point for an egocentricity-eroding process that could address these spiritual needs. Such an eventuality would seem to represent, in at least one sense, an improvement over the self-deceptive forms of religion mentioned earlier. Those religions were based on the assumption that there were essentially two main alternatives with regard to the ontological dilemma: People could either address the dilemma through denial, by riddling the entire structure of consciousness with the self-deceptions required by the dogmatic content of a religious myth interpreted as a literal ontological truth; or they could refuse to deceive themselves, with the result that their lives were lived out in a predominant condition of existential anxiety in the face of an apocalyptic ontological scheme of things.

But it is important to recognize that there are additional alternatives beyond these two which can alleviate anxiety in the face of the cosmic dilemma—again, not by denying its existence, but by creating an experience of positive value intense enough to override the negativity of the dilemma and then free that experience from its initial dependence on obsession with a specific love object. If we begin by introducing a substantial portion of spiritual partnership into romantic relationships (although this course is fraught with serious difficulty), we eventually discover that it is possible to extend the selfless appreciation of intrinsic value by means of admiration through compassion toward other human beings generally. It may also be possible to develop a relationship of primary spiritual partnership in a completely nonsexual way, with a person who is not a romantic partner, as in the psychotherapeutic positive transference—which then could enable us, ironically, to relate also to romantic partners as spiritual partners, because the resulting spreading effect could then teach us to be thankful for any opportunity to value another conscious being more intensely than we can value ourselves, rather than resenting it as a threat to ego integrity. Once this transformation of the emotional structure has been achieved, all people with whom we interact could become spiritual partners in a secondary or derivative sense, to greater or lesser extents. But the crucial obstacle to the possibility of primary spiritual partnership is the need to find concrete enough ways to symbolize the reverence toward a spiritual partner other than through sexual feeling or behavior. This problem presents itself whether the spiritual partnership happens to occur in a romantic context or not. Ultimately, a primary spiritual partnership can work its effect of resolving the ontological dilemma in a sustained way only if it becomes a way of intensely appreciating the value, not merely of the one person who allows us this unique vantage point on the interiority of that person's consciousness, but of all other conscious beings with whom we come into direct contact.

Up to this point, we have operated from only the most abstract concept of what spiritual partnership consists of. It is now time to develop a fuller and more concrete picture of the experiential nature of the phenomenon as such, without being distracted by any of its possible romantic trappings. The next section will attempt to provide a comprehensive overview of the phenomenon, and the remainder of the book will explore its most important facets and consequences in more detail.

2. A More Detailed Characterization of the Spiritual Partnership Effect

At the end of the first chapter, we arrived at an abstract definition of spiritual partnership. But a more detailed account will be required to justify the claim that the spiritual partnership process is capable of dismantling the circle of egocentricity—which must occur initially against our will—and facilitating a transcendent value experience strong enough to resolve the ontological dilemma. The fact that such an experience must occur against our will in order to break down the circle of egocentricity provides a clue as to the kind of relationship dynamics required. The motivation to enter into the space of empathy must be different from the outcome that is finally produced by it. Before discussing these motives and results, it will help to explore the space of empathy itself in a little more detail.

We have defined the 'space of empathy' to include the idea that each person's stream of consciousness is allowed to unfold in authentically directed patterns, without having its direction deflected and blocked at every turn by the threat of directiveness or judgmentalism. This space of empathy also sometimes occurs to a certain extent in other relationships, including ordinary friendships and merely erotic relationships, although it all too often tends to be ephemeral; but, to the extent that people become spiritual partners, it must become permanently possible to establish a space of empathy at will, at any given time. This is because the full acceptance of the other's feelings, in relatively complete defenselessness and honesty—nonjudgmentally and nondirectively—does not conflict with other aspects of the relationship as it usually tends to do, for example, in many erotic relationships sooner or later. In the space of empathy, we can allow our own stream of consciousness to lead in the direction it is authentically motivated to pursue, without fear that the other will judge us as inadequate or unworthy because she does not agree with, approve of, or like the way we think or feel in a particular context. Moreover, she values our ideas and feelings, wants to know about them, and wants to vicariously experience them. In this section, we shall explore the reason why.

Because the expression of these ideas and feelings exposes our vulnerability, the other person is allowed an unusual insight into the endangeredness and embattledness of our consciousness, which wants to maintain both authenticity and intensity in the face of the crass world of brutal materiality and interpersonal alienation that threatens to choke off and thwart the genuinely motivated direction of consciousness, so that we would be tempted to self-deceptively suppress our true ideas and feelings in favor of the artificial roles and defensive postures we must assume. In the space of empathy, because the other person not only completely accepts but also values and encourages our ingenuousness, we find ourselves exposing this vulnerability to the person in ways that we would seldom expose it even to a close friend in the ordinary sense. This affords the other a rare vicarious experience of our embattled authenticity in the face of the ontological dilemma (exacerbated by the contingent brutality and/or artificiality of the culture) and a direct view of our finitude.

Finitude implies fleetingness, uniqueness, and irreplaceability. And anyone who has ever felt a strong love of any type knows that the times when this love is felt most intensely are when we focus on this fleetingness, uniqueness, and irreplaceability—the fact that the person's being is a finite event that occurs only once in the history of the universe, cannot be repeated, and cannot be duplicated. The same is true of aesthetic awe in the face of a great work of art, or the intense admiration we feel for an epic hero at the moment of his heroic death. The admiration is intensified because it is combined with the compassion we feel for the finitude and vulnerability of the hero. This feeling presents itself most vividly at the moment when we are vicariously identifying with this consciousness in its full expression, in the face of an *ontological* embattledness, and thus toward which we intensely and concretely feel both admiration and compassion, and in such a way that the admiration and the compassion feed each other.

Since the way in which our stream of consciousness unfolds—the pattern in which it chooses its direction in each context—is our identity as a person, and since in the space of empathy this pattern is able to flow relatively unobstructed, as it is authentically motivated to flow, it follows that in the space of empathy we have the opportunity not only to be completely who we really are in relation to another person, but also to express this being symbolically. This symbolic expression has the effect of intensifying, focusing, and clarifying the subjective side of our ideas, feelings, perceptions, interpretations, and any other states of consciousness that may be important to us at the time.

But even this much does not reveal the real power of the space of empathy. While it is true that we *are* the pattern in the unfolding of our motivated stream of consciousness, it is also true that this pattern exists as a pattern of *change*. Consciousness cannot remain the same if it is to remain conscious, because it *is* in its essence a pattern of change. To remain too much the same is to lapse into a semiconscious state, an existential somnambulism which at first numbs us to our own consciousness, but eventually evolves into a quietly repressed desperation for radical transformation of the structure of our being. If at this point we are offered the opportunity to participate in a completely different pattern of consciousness that we admire and want to vicariously experience through empathy, we then feel pulled out of ourselves into just the kind of radical transformation that our consciousness has been secretly craving in order to reawaken from existential lethargy and therefore continue being conscious at the needed level of intensity. Such a need is felt most acutely at a time of existential crisis, when we are ripe for a fundamental overhauling of the structure of our being. And such an opportunity tends to be presented by someone with whom we can engage in *personal* interactions that are not determined by our *social* interactions, so that ingenuousness can be encouraged rather than threatened and constricted.

So not only does the space of empathy allow us the rare opportunity to *be* who we authentically are, and to intensify and focus our consciousness by symbolizing it; it also offers the even more rare opportunity to *transform* ourselves into a completely different pattern of being, which is precisely what consciousness is motivated to do in its most basic ontological structure. We learn to enact the other person's form of being in ourselves, through the particular kind of empathy with it that only a complete space of empathy can make possible.

Spiritual partnership in the primary sense therefore does not occur between just any two people at any given time. In order to break down the circle of egocentricity, which normally defends against allowing another too much power over us, the pull of spiritual partnership must catch us off our guard, and at a time when we have an egoistic motive to transcend ourselves. There must be a peculiar condition of readiness for it—a point in life when the time has come for radical transformation, a time of crisis in the definition of the meaning of life, and thus also of the self and its value system. Only at such times are we willing to risk loosening the former structure of our ego defenses, which places us in a vulnerable position, threatens to cause emotional pain, and may in the end leave us hovering directionlessly in a valuationally disinterested vacuum. We are all the more vulnerable in such a case because not only our ego defenses, but the very structure of our being, our motivational direction toward the future, our value system, and therefore our personality itself, have been disconnected, thrown into radical question, and in a sense deconstructed or dismantled. Such fundamental regrouping causes chaos and disorientation. In this condition of weakness and vulnerability under threat of abandonment by our habitual instrumental values, and in the face of the seemingly insurmountable problems of finitude, we become willing to risk letting down our defenses with someone who seems trustworthy (i.e., someone else who we perceive is in the same condition). And the letting down of defenses is further facilitated by the above-mentioned readiness to abandon the former structure of our being, including the usual defenses that were habitual for us in that structure.

It is at this point that we are lured into the surprise of the spiritual partnership experience. Having questioned the structure of the stifling stagnance of the old pattern of being, we now are suddenly offered the liberating opportunity to participate, through the space of empathy, in an alternative form of being that seems uncannily admirable—because our compassion for the spiritual partner's ontological endangeredness has intensified the feeling of admiration itself.

It would therefore do no good to go looking for primary spiritual partnership. There must be a peculiar condition of readiness for it, and when the opportunity presents itself, we know it because we feel pulled involuntarily by a strange force that may be disturbing at first because we do not understand it, and because it seems to overpower the usual defenses with which our now-loosened ego structure is accustomed to protecting itself. Moreover, we feel a vague intuition that the phenomenon of spiritual partnership—once we have directly experienced what it is like within a space of empathy (or perhaps preliminarily calculated what it would be like to have a space of empathy with that person)—that this phenomenon is potentially a more powerful force than the ego of any individual; that if we submit to it we will have submitted to one of those frightening elemental forces that sometimes engulf people from without, like a tidal wave or a war. It is partly because of our lack of control over our own need for spiritual partnership that the other person may suddenly appear superhuman or larger than life, like some strange apparition from another world, possessed of mysterious, magical powers. Such feelings tell us that the person is associated with a force stronger than ourselves, which threatens to possess and occupy our being with an alien power that we can neither control nor escape.

The fact that we ultimately end up directly appreciating the other person's positive value in such an acute experience of quasi-aesthetic awe that this non-egocentric positive value experience fulfills the religious need to counterbalance the negativity of the ontological dilemma—this effect occurs almost as an unexpected afterthought or side effect. We are pulled into the experience, not by this religious need at all, but by a selfish desire to live off borrowed existential currency from the other person in order to pull ourselves out of existential lethargy. The end result is that any self-interest on our part is subordinated to our appreciation of the intrinsic value of the other person, and this direct experience of the other's value—which we can experience more intensely than we can our own—shatters our egocentricity, at first painfully and reluctantly (because egocentricity obviously dies hard), but eventually leading to a transvaluation of our entire value structure in which the locus of intrinsic value is willingly experienced as outside of ourselves. Finally, and paradoxically, if this process is allowed to reach completion, we find ourselves able to experience the world as intensely value-laden precisely because we have relegated our entire egocentric project, with its self-evaluating masks and roles, to a relatively minor place in our value system. This imbues each moment of experience with the intensity of Unamuno's 'tragic sense of life,' so that we ultimately can end up appreciating the uniqueness and irreplaceability of each experience and person in somewhat the same way that we originally could experience only the primary spiritual partner. Not to belabor the point of the previous section, this shattering of egocentricity does not occur in many instances of 'erotic love' that are not mixed with the spiritual partnership effect.

When the opportunity for spiritual partnership first presents itself, it may be experienced as frightening and threatening, especially when mixed with erotic or romantic symbolization, for the reasons explained above. And at this point it can still be rejected in a number of ways. None of these escapes really allows us to circumvent the force that pulls us; they only change the form that the force takes. One obvious form of escape is to interpret the experience as one of merely sexual attraction (in cases where the relationship involves sexual polarization or sexual attraction) and either pursue or reject the prospect of a romantic relationship in the traditional sense. But we have already seen that the defenseless interaction characteristic of spiritual partnership has no essential connection with sexual or romantic trappings. The reason we in the modern West tend to connect such ideas with romance is that the closest we have been able to come to enacting such feelings has been with our romantic partners. We have therefore developed a quasi-religion of sexuality whose mythology dominates our lives. But this mythology does more to obscure the real phenomenon of spiritual partnership than to facilitate it, because the myth of romance holds that romance will bring 'happiness' for oneself, and therefore restores egocentricity to our attitudes at the very point when we need to overcome it in order to experience the other's value more fully than we can our own. The modern religion of sexuality also strongly tends to divert spiritual partnership from its main meaning—which has to do with transcendent value experience—into a frivolous kind of enjoyment which then lends itself to reduction to physiological explanations in terms of 'drives' and the 'pleasure principle.'

At this point, many people no longer even understand the distinction between the need for spiritual partnership and the need for pleasure—when the reality is that these two needs are in conflict with each other: Pleasure is a *reduction* of consciousness to a state of contented complacence (i.e., 'drive-*reduction*'), and therefore to *stasis*; the existential needs that motivate spiritual partnership, by contrast, tend toward *transformation* of consciousness into a more *intense, dynamic, and active* process of continuing change (the exact opposite of *stasis*), because consciousness in its essence *is* a pattern of change and cannot continue to be conscious in a state of *stasis*.

The confusion between 'romance' and spiritual partnership is further complicated by the fact that, for most people at most times of their lives, the opposite sexual polarization of the other's consciousness offers an opportunity to be pulled out of ourselves into radical transformation, because by vicariously experiencing the other's consciousness through empathy we learn to enact a realm of spirituality that lies dormant in ourselves because it has been suppressed, and whose actualization we strongly desire. It was this confusion that gave rise to the modern sexualization of religious experience and mythologizing of romance to begin with.

In many instances, the spiritual partnership effect fails for extraneous reasons. For example, we may try to engage the person in spiritual partnership, but find that we can do so only in destructive ways—for instance, by using the other person's complementary form of consciousness (such as opposite sexual polarity) not to *learn* from her to cultivate a pattern of consciousness that is largely lacking or underdeveloped in ourselves, but rather as a crutch—to *substitute* for what is lacking in ourselves; the relationship then becomes an unhealthy symbiosis that fosters personal inadequacy and a mutual dependence whose result is decay rather than growth in the people's consciousness—at which point the spiritual partnership effect dies away. One reason for these outcomes, especially for young people, may be that the two people are too immature or psychologically undeveloped to know how to relate authentically, meaningfully, communicatively, and autonomously; or, even if psychologically mature, they still may suddenly sense the terrifying aspects mentioned earlier, become frightened, and retreat. Another reason might be that the people live in a form of culture in which most social relations are so alienated that it becomes impossible to extend the concrete feeling of intense appreciation of value to conscious beings other than the original primary spiritual partner. In this case, the spreading effect cannot occur, and thus it is likely that the relationship to the original spiritual partner will become a smothering symbiosis.

There are still other possible escapes from the threatening self-destabilization of spiritual partnership. One way to deflect the experience is to cultivate antipathy and hostility toward the person, using our natural envy of her admirable form of consciousness to fuel the resentment. Or alternatively, we may shut out the person—for example, by avoiding the person—in which case we either relapse into existential lethargy, or are confronted with the opportunity for still another spiritual partnership with someone else.

There is still another reason why spiritual partnership can occur only rarely, unexpectedly, and when there is a reciprocal need for it. Since the space of empathy must be mutual in order to occur at all, it is obvious that to suddenly begin baring one's soul to just anyone who is not also in a similar condition of readiness would be both ineffectual and grossly inappropriate. Superficially, the defenseless exposure of ontological vulnerability and readiness to deconstruct the former self system may appear symptomatic of weakness of character or psychological incompetence. To someone not also in need of radical self-transcendence, such an exposure of vulnerability will very likely be seen not with compassion, but with disdain toward a perceived emotional weakness and lack of stoic virtue, taking a weakened personality *state* as a permanently weak personality *trait*. Such a person may seem clinging, inadequate, infantile, and neurotic.

But when both people *are* in the condition of readiness described above, each sees that the other's vulnerability stems from an ontological dilemma rather than from pragmatic inadequacies; it thus pulls empathy rather than aversion. Each admires the other's honesty as a strength rather than abhorring it as a weakness or a need for dependence. Each actively invites and encourages further such honesty by being nonjudgmental and nondirective, because each sees the space of empathy as the key to personal transformation and revitalization. Both people sense that this space must be provided in order for them to be who they are and can be, and each feels both admiration and compassion for the other's courageous but embattled authenticity and emotionality.

I have alluded briefly to the idea that the spiritual partnership effect is not reducible merely to some combination of more commonly occurring relationships with which it has certain elements in common, such as sexual love, friendship, psychotherapeutic relationships, or love for family members. It will be helpful to focus on the ways in which spiritual partnership is different from these other kinds of relationships. A good way to be clear as to the essential meaning of a concept is to be sure we can distinguish it from other concepts that may be similar to it in certain respects. By exploring these distinctions, the next section will attempt to

Essential Dynamics of Primary Transcendent Value Experience 137

understand why these other kinds of relationships usually do not completely serve the existential purposes that can be served by the sustained process of spiritual partnership.

3. Distinguishing Primary Spiritual Partnership from Other Interpersonal Value Experiences

Transcendent value experience is apt to be mistakenly interpreted as falling into some other category of experiences to which it bears certain resemblances, but from which it is crucial to distinguish it. The symbolization process in transcendent value experience, its aims, and its essential nature become more clear when we consider the differences between it and these other kinds of experiences. Especially instructive are our culture's abortive attempts to meet religious needs by using types of relationships that are *not* transcendent value experiences—such as the increasing sexualization of religious experience within the modern Western 'myth of romance' in the sense defined above. The main reason people feel prone to try to use such relationships for religious purposes may well be that these relationships bear such striking resemblances to spiritual partnership in certain respects. Still more confusion arises from the fact that, in *some* instances, such relationships do succeed in *doubling* as spiritual partnerships, at least to a certain extent.

For example, we have seen why it is likely that emerging spiritual partnerships will often be experienced merely as instances of 'falling in love.' In this case, the potential for full spiritual partnership can easily be missed, for the reasons discussed earlier, and the relationship becomes transformed into a conventional 'romantic courtship,' which then plays itself out in one of the typical ways that such relationships do—with all their culturally sedimented meanings and customs. In this case the sociocultural institutionalization of the relationship, the dynamics of sexual interdependence, reproduction, family dynamics, narcissistic factors in sexual relationships, and various inevitable conflicts between the interests and moral rights of family members (or 'couple' members) tend to erode the space of empathy to a greater or lesser extent. At that point, romantic partners who originally were or could have been primary spiritual partners find themselves increasingly unable to relate as such. Moreover, if one or both people were already sexually attached to someone else at the point when the potentiality for spiritual partnership presented itself, then the construal of the feelings as 'romantic' leads not only to missing the opportunity for spiritual partnership, but also to the destruction of a previously existing romantic relationship, which one now merely duplicates by relating 'romantically' to the potential spiritual partner.

Explaining the differences between these kinds of relationships also serves to clarify the nature of the symbolization process involved, because each type of relationship dynamic lends itself to a clearly different kind of symbolization. In romantic love, we use the intensification and bodily globalization of sexual feeling to symbolize our own emotional and valuational feelings toward the other person. To express the way we feel toward a spiritual partner, by contrast, we use our own body primarily as a vehicle of verbal and other behavioral forms of expression so as to serve as a system for the symbolization, not primarily of our own feelings, but of the other's feelings with which we have now empathized; in this way we concretely symbolize our intense appreciation toward the person's positive value as if toward a quasi-religious object—not entirely unlike a saint or deity, except that we are able to relate to this conscious being in real, concrete ways.

As another example, consider the ways in which *psychotherapeutic* relationships resemble both romantic and spiritual partnerships. The therapist, it is true, does use her system of language-body-behavior to help symbolize the other's feelings, but not in the service of a feeling of quasi-aesthetic awe toward the consciousness of the patient. The psychotherapeutic relationship is essentially a one-way and temporary one in which the therapist must not become too 'involved,' must not foster too much dependency in the patient, must clearly define safe boundaries for the therapeutic setting itself—respecting the person's privacy beyond this setting—and should not allow the patient to continue idealizing the therapist too much once the patient's 'transference love' (or 'positive transference') has been worked through. In general, each type of relationship uses its own unique form of symbolization, which is especially suited to actualize the ideas and feelings that are essential to the purposes of that type of relationship.

It is therefore important to understand the differences between primary spiritual partnership and other kinds of relationship dynamics with which it might be confused—especially erotic or romantic love; psychotherapeutic relationships; friendship in the ordinary sense; hero worship or 'cults of personality' such as the quasi-worship of politicians, military leaders, or movie stars; and relationships with family members, such as adored little children.

(a) Spiritual partnership and eros. It will be helpful at this point to bring in a few of the remarks I made about the nature of eros in *Eros in a Narcissistic Culture*. It follows from the analysis presented there that romantic relationships embody to a great extent some of the main elements of spiritual partnership. Just as in spiritual partnership, eros begins with a space of empathy in which each person feels free to express ideas and feelings authentically without fear of judgmentalism or directiveness, while at the same time our communion with the other person's form of consciousness 'pulls us out of ourselves' so that we are able to vicariously experience a form of consciousness that enables us to transform ourselves. This transformation is one of the most basic existential needs of consciousness, because consciousness in its essence is a pattern of change. The space of empathy allows each stream of consciousness to flow and transform itself in ways that would not be possible except through this completely empathic acceptance and freedom in combination with the vicarious enactment of the other's consciousness within our own. Therefore, in the presence of the other person in the space of empathy, we can exist to a greater extent than we could otherwise exist *qua* conscious being. Since consciousness must transform itself in order to be, the transformation offered by communion with the other's form of consciousness allows us to be. Thus separation from a romantic love object threatens our very being and precipitates existential anxiety in its classic form. But, since this process depends on the feelings of admiration and compassion for the vulnerability of the embattled authenticity and sensitivity of the other person in the face of the negative facts of the ontological condition, it follows that eros occurs only because we are able to focus on the finitude of the other. Because we can appreciate finitude in another being in this positive way, in a way that evokes awe-stricken admiration for the other's being (whereas we experience our own finitude in a negative way), conscious beings that have attained the degree of existential intensity and sophistication characteristic of human beings *need* this kind of positive value

experience as an inspirational experience to compensate for the harshness of the ontological predicament. This is why most of us would have trouble living without some semblance of some type of love, or at least the hope of some future love, or the memory of some past love.

Only after this *spiritual* relationship develops between two conscious beings is romantic love rather than mere sexual desire felt. At that point, the appreciation of the other's form of being within a space of empathy becomes such an acute and such an urgently valued experience that we 'sentimentally and sexually fetishize' every aspect of the person's physical presence. If a woman is fair-skinned, the man suddenly is sexually attracted only to fair-skinned women; if she is thin, only to thin women. If she has a sun spot on her thigh, this sun spot is attractive. The reason is that her physical presence is associated with the consciousness that is expressed through it, and he is using his own sexual attraction to her body as a physical matrix for the symbolization of his appreciation of her as a conscious being—i.e., for his admiration and compassion for her embattled sensitivity and existential aliveness. Thus the intense physicality of sexual attraction to a particular romantic love object (by preference over other sexually attractive people) is mostly derivative from the spiritual relationship between the consciousnesses of the two people, or at least the hope or fantasy of such a relationship.

The similarity of this spiritual relationship to what I have described as spiritual partnership is unmistakable. To a certain extent, a romantic relationship of this sort is functioning as a spiritual partnership. In fact, the intensity of romantic love and the long-term success of the relationship depend largely on the extent to which the relationship is a spiritual partnership. The key requirement for spiritual partnership is appreciation of the other's positive value as facilitated by the space of empathy. And it is precisely to the extent that a space of empathy *continues* to maintain itself in a marriage or long-term erotic relationship that the two people are able to feel this love for each other in an intense way and maintain intensified and bodily globalized sexual attraction as a symbolization matrix for this spiritual process.

Nonetheless, this spiritual relationship between romantic partners is only one of many needs that a long-term romantic relationship is asked to fulfill. Romantic relationships serve many other important needs, and many of these needs conflict with the need for spiritual partnership. To say that a good romantic relationship includes a strong element of spiritual partnership is like saying that good politicians should understand moral philosophy. Indeed, they should, but this is only one of their many skills, and in some instances the compromises they must make in the real world of political wheeling and dealing will inevitably conflict with their moral principles. Moreover, if they devote too much effort to the study of moral philosophy, they neglect the other equally important activities of politicians. It would be counterproductive for them to become experts in philosophy in the way that a professional philosopher is, because then they would have to sacrifice all their other functions to this one.

Romantic partners are spiritual partners only to the extent that an athlete training for the decathlon must be a good long jumper. A decathlete is expected to be a jack-of-all-trades, not a specialist at one. Athletes who want to become excellent long jumpers must use a very different practice routine from someone who wants to perform adequately at all the events of the decathlon.

Romantic partners are not only expected to fulfill the need for spiritual partnership. They are also expected to be friends in the ordinary sense; they must fulfill sexual desires; they must get along as roommates, cooperate harmoniously in housework, combine efforts to make toilets work and keep bills paid. They often raise children together and help care for each other's aging parents. They invite friends and business relations into their home and delegate practical responsibilities to each other. When their interests conflict with each other (as when one person's career demands relocation to a different city, or when children are to be brought up in one or the other of their different religions), compromises and sacrifices must be made. And, not least important, they must continue throughout all this to appreciate each other's sexuality.

There are many opportunities for these diverse functions of romantic partnership to conflict with each other, and many of them conflict with the spiritual-partnership function. Each time these various role-relationships cause the moral rights of the romantic partners to come into conflict, each individual must protect his or her rights from being violated. For example, if all family members throw clothes on the floor in the expectation that a particular member will pick them up, they fail to respect that member as a person and therefore violate her rights. If one partner pressures the other to convert to a different religion so that children can be reared in that religion, the second partner must protect her right to autonomy. And many other value-priority decisions will present similar conflicts. There will naturally be differences of opinion as to how such issues are to be resolved, especially where social interrelations with third parties (including children) are concerned. The human weaknesses of each partner will further exacerbate such conflicts through no one's purposeful ill intention, and so will unavoidable misunderstandings resulting from missed communication.

To a greater or lesser extent, all these problems cause each person to become cautious and defensive in the exposure of vulnerabilities. Thus it is inevitable that the space of empathy will be eroded to a greater or lesser extent as each person begins to guard the vulnerabilities, and to just that extent spiritual partnership declines. The romantic partners hopefully can maintain a certain amount of spiritual partnership in their relationship, but to the extent that the space of empathy is eroded for these reasons, the concerns of spiritual partnership are sacrificed to accommodate the other roles that romantic partners must play in relation to each other and the other needs that they must help each other to meet.

A more essential factor that causes romantic partners to become guarded and defensive toward each other is that the romantic relationship itself would be threatened if either partner should be allowed to focus too much on the other's ontological vulnerabilities—a continual danger when people spend a great deal of time together. The threat is that the person would come to seem weak, dependent, and thus less sexually attractive. Thus each partner tries to protect these vulnerabilities from too much visibility, and as a result becomes defensive, holds back from ingenuous expression, and therefore reduces the openness required for a full space of empathy.

The central reason for this effect is that we need for a romantic partner to be sexually attracted to us to at least enough of an extent that this sexual attraction can be amplified into the bodily-globalized sexual feelings that she uses to symbolize her feelings toward our conscious being. For example, a spouse needs for the other spouse to see her as heroic and self-reliant, not as bumbling and pathetic, since these latter qualities are not viewed as very 'romantic' or 'sexy.' Thus, if she allows herself to appear too vulnerable in too many respects, there is the danger that his attraction to her may wane. Sexual attraction, unlike spiritual partnership per se, depends on our being able to present an image to the other person that is more attractive or admirable than it is ontologically vulnerable. This objectification need not be *extremely* attractive, but we must not allow it to be seen as so erotically disrespectable as to kill the possibility of the other's using it as raw material for amplified feelings of erotic attraction and admiration. The danger is that we therefore become all the more selective in disclosing to and hiding from a romantic partner, and this selectiveness inhibits the fully exposed authenticity of the space of empathy.

Someone may object that women have less of a need to avoid the appearance of weakness and dependency than do men. It is true that some cultures try to cultivate a weak or dependent image of women, or even to construe this image as sexually attractive. Our own culture tended in this direction up until less than a century ago. But we have already seen that such a lack of reciprocity itself inhibits the space of empathy, and a moment's reflection will reveal that, in any culture, a woman lacking in the strengths and competencies for at least the activities available to her gender loses rather than gains in admirability. At best, an incompetent being can be an object for physical sexual gratification, not for inspiring feelings of erotic love. This issue is discussed in more detail in the appendix, which deals with the thorny and difficult problem of sexual polarization.

In a sense, the need for a romantic relationship is more pressing than the need for spiritual partnership per se in that a romantic partner is a person on whom we depend to help us meet a vast array of different needs that may become important at different times, whereas spiritual partnership per se fulfills only one (though an extremely important one). So, while it is true that a romantic partner may play the role of a spiritual partner to a certain extent, and conversely we may sometimes symbolize love for a spiritual partner through romantic feelings, it also remains true that the more we relate to someone romantically, the more the demands of the romantic relationship will tend to threaten the conditions needed for a complete space of empathy, which is essential to the functioning of spiritual partnership.

Thus one of the most obvious differences between spiritual partnership and eros as such is that in eros we need for the other person to relate to our 'mask' in a different way. I do not mean 'mask' in a pejorative sense, as in pretending to be what one is not. By 'mask' in this context, I mean the objectively observable manifestations according to which the world *judges and evaluates* us. This includes our physical appearance, our speech mannerisms, the roles in terms of which people perceive us, the ways we comport ourselves, gesture and 'pose,' the entertainingness of our 'act,' our intelligence, strength, social prestige, and generally any behavior that may be evaluated as 'attractive' or 'repulsive,' 'friendly' or 'overbearing,' or any other *evaluative* term. By the concept of a 'mask,' I do not mean to include qualities that usually are not evaluated, such as hair color or a baseball player's habit of knocking mud out of his cleats before stepping into the batter's box. Instead, the mask includes evaluated features, such as an attractive or unattractive haircut, or the baseball player's tendency to look 'underconfident,' 'scared,' or 'full of false bluster' when he steps into the batter's box, or his ability to hit the ball. These are the kinds of physical manifestations by which people are judged. The mask, in this sense, consists of the perceptible aspects of ourselves that we are able to present to others, whether in an honest or a dishonest way. There is nothing inherently false or disingenuous about the mask; yet the other's perception of us through it can deviate to greater or lesser extents from who we are. The importance of the mask in eros is not so much its use to hide ourselves, but its use to show ourselves. Even an honest mask is the perceptible exterior of our being.

The reason masks become problematic in eros is not that they are more *present* in this context than in others, but because feelings are intensified through physical symbolization processes that take the loved one's total mask (i.e., the aspects of her that one can envision as the *object* for feelings of erotic admiration) as part of the physical symbolization process. For example, it makes sense to cite intelligence, strength, or physical beauty as things one loves about an object of eros, but not stupidity, weakness, or physical repulsiveness; the things we love in the *erotic* sense, and symbolize erotically, are distinguishable from the things that are loved in other senses of 'love,' many of which are also felt toward the same person, such as agape, friendship, or spiritual partnership.

The mask—that is, the manifestations that are judged—may or may not have anything to do with who the person is in his consciousness or personality. We may judge someone as attractive because he has wide-set eyes, or beautiful blond hair, even though these features are in no way within the person's control. Or we may respect a college professor more than a butcher even though the butcher would have been a college professor if he had not happened to get his Ph.D. at a time when the job market was especially tight, or had to drop out of school for financial reasons, or lacked the political connections to land a teaching job.

Obviously, we normally want to present the best possible 'mask' to a romantic partner, since it matters how positively or negatively the other judges our objective and bodily presence. A woman, for example, may be content that a man focuses on her good points while cognizant of the bad—that he sentimentally fetishizes her features, judging them as attractive even though she suspects that to the disinterested observer these same features may be indifferent or even ugly. And she may be content that he sees her as brilliant, heroic, and fascinating even though she may suspect that to the disinterested observer her interpersonal performance is pedestrian, ordinary, and uninteresting. But what she cannot tolerate is that a romantic partner should see her as completely ugly, drab, and out of control of her destiny—as manifesting an utterly unattractive and powerless ego-persona, yet 'love' her in spite of these acknowledged shortcomings. This would be the wrong kind of 'love'—not eros, but something like pity, ordinary friendship, or a 'mothering' attitude toward a weak and inadequate being. She may insist at some point on showing him some of her less-attractive features in order to assure herself that his love is dependable or that he does not love *only* her mask, but she is still generally concerned with his approval of the mask. The relationship between a person, the person's mask, and a romantic partner is therefore one in which the romantic partner evaluates the person partially according to the way her mask appears to him; he finds her 'attractive' or 'unattractive,' 'interesting' or 'dull,' although it is true (luckily) that his judgments of these things may be largely determined by the way he feels toward her in other respects.

The relation between this person, her mask, and a *spiritual* partner per se is completely different from this, and a substantial amount of conflict results when we try to combine spiritual and romantic partnership in the same relationship. A spiritual partner, as such, identifies with the subjectivity *behind* the mask rather than viewing the mask from the outside; he sees her mask from the inside, as something that must be presented to the world, very much in the same way that he relates to his own mask.

It might help our understanding of this difference between romantic and spiritual partnership to consider both types of situations in relation to a concrete example. Suppose a baseball player allows the winning run to score against his team by committing a humiliatingly stupid error: He may not then be consoled or enheartened to hear that his lover was in the stands to witness this humiliation. In fact, he may be much more humiliated by her seeing him in this way than by the many others who saw it. But if he learns that a spiritual partner was in the stands, he is not only consoled, but in fact compensated for the humiliation, because he knows that the spiritual partner cares only about the way *he* feels about the incident, and does not care in the least how the crowds of others feel about it. There is the danger that the romantic partner may think at this point, 'perhaps I was wrong after all to commit myself to this pathetic clod'; the spiritual partner only reconfirms her commitment all the more strongly, because she both admires and takes compassion on the subjective fortitude required to engage the existential dilemma in battle—win or lose.

The reason for this difference must certainly be that spiritual partnership is a relationship that bypasses masks, in a certain way that eros per se cannot. It is true that eros can allow the perception of the other's mask to become more positive than it would otherwise have been, because of the mask's association with the person's conscious personality, which is the primary object of the love—just as an otherwise indifferent piece of music might take on magical qualities just because it is associated with feelings toward a love object. For that matter, eros may even distort evidence in order to avoid perceiving the other as a pathetic clod. (The baseball error, for example, was not a stupid blunder, but an almost-successful attempt at a miraculous play.) But the positive feelings toward the mask in romantic love are nonetheless essential to feelings of eros; an erotic partner cannot be indifferent to the mask, because the realm of sexual attraction and excitement is the concrete matrix of physical symbolization that is used to intensify the experience of eros, and sexual feelings inevitably relate to the love object's physical presence and comportment.

In spiritual partnership, on the other hand, the method of symbolization is completely different. In this case, we symbolize and intensify the feeling, not by making the other's body serve as the physical symbolization for *our* feelings, but just the contrary: We convert our own body into a mouthpiece for the expression of the other's feelings and interpretations with which we have unqualifiedly empathized, in order to express the autonomy-enhancing altruism discussed earlier. The way that we symbolize the feelings of admiration and compassion is by becoming the concrete matrix for the expression of the other's feelings and interpretations, so that in helping to symbolize feelings and interpretations that the person could not express without a spiritual partner, we contribute to the intensification and actualization of these potential forms of consciousness in the other, and thus also in ourselves.

Although spiritual partners do of course perceive each other through physical manifestations (since that is the way people perceive each other), they focus on those physical manifestations that best reflect what really is going on in the consciousness and personality of the other person. Skin blemishes or unflattering clothes are of no interest; the focus is on facial expression or body language, not as attractive or unattractive, but as expressions of inner subjectivity to be interpreted.

By distinguishing between eros and spiritual partnership, I do not mean to imply that a romantic partner cannot be a spiritual partner, but only that eros is not the same thing as spiritual partnership. I remarked in the first chapter that in some historical contexts romantic relationships can work somewhat well as spiritual partnerships, and I mentioned earlier in this chapter that the intensity of romantic love is really a result of its serving or promising to serve the needs of spiritual partnership.

It is not that the tensions between spiritual partnership and the other aspects of erotic love must necessarily destroy spiritual partnership. But the tensions do exist. In some historical contexts, the cultural attitudes exacerbate these tensions so much that they do make permanent juxtapositions of eros with spiritual partnership the exception rather than the rule. In other historical contexts, the tensions are minimal and can be handled more easily, and those are the ones in which marriages based on eros *do* often work permanently as spiritual partnerships, at least to a great extent. But even in those periods, this is by no means universally the case. In many instances, a marriage may serve as a spiritual partnership to a great extent, but still may fail to pull each individual out of egocentricity to *enough* of an extent to completely overpower the negativity of the ontological predicament of finite beings throughout the life cycle, and in the absence of a sugar-coating form of religion.

It would thus seem that we can summarize the relationship between eros and spiritual partnership in the following way:

1. Not all romantic relationships, even intensely moving ones, can necessarily work well enough as spiritual partnerships to serve the spiritual purpose we are considering here.
2. Not all spiritual partnerships are romantic relationships.
3. When I speak of a 'merely' romantic relationship, I mean one that is *not both* eros and spiritual partnership (at least not to enough of an extent to resolve the ontological dilemma).
4. *Some* of the elements of eros and spiritual partnership that do *not* overlap with each other sooner or later will conflict *to a greater or lesser degree*. Ideally, of course, the degree will be lesser and can be resolved. But, increasingly in Western culture, the degree is greater than this, as evidenced by increasing divorce rates and extramarital affairs (though of course I am well aware that other social factors are also partly responsible for these trends; but the other social factors such as economic insecurity or increased access to extramarital sex without unwanted pregnancy also interrelate with the factors that erode spiritual partnership).

Some readers at this point may suspect that spiritual partnership differs and even conflicts with eros in these ways because such a completely nondirective and nonjudgmental empathy as it demands can exist only in psychotherapeutic relationships or close friendships. Still other readers may think that the selflessness of spiritual partnership exists only in relationships between family members. But it is important to see just how different spiritual partnership is from any of these other relationships in their essential features, even though the same person may accidentally happen to be both a friend and a spiritual partner (occasionally), or both a relative and a spiritual partner (even less frequently, in our culture). Let's focus first on the extreme difference between spiritual partnership and psychotherapeutic relationships.

(b) Spiritual partnership and psychotherapeutic relationships. In some respects, spiritual partnership in the primary sense may sometimes resemble a psychotherapeutic relationship. One person helps the other to 'get in touch with feelings' by reflecting them back empathically, by being nondirective and nonjudgmental, showing unconditional positive regard, and so on. The phenomenon of 'transference love' or 'positive transference' in psychotherapy is also very much like the idealization of a spiritual partner (for example, see Kohut 1985, Bollas 1989, Ornstein 1991). The therapist as object of transference love may become a magical, fascinating, larger-than-life, and almost deified being—at least temporarily. But in fact the therapeutic relationship also shares these features in common with healthy friendships, romantic relationships, and relationships with family members

These similarities notwithstanding, the aims of psychotherapy are fundamentally different from those of spiritual partnership. Psychotherapy makes no attempt to provide the patient with a positive value experience capable of overriding the acknowledged negativity of the ontological predicament, and thus of serving the function that traditional religions were meant to serve. Quite the contrary, transference love in psychotherapy must be 'worked through' so that the therapist is again seen as just another person, like any other. The usual goal of psychotherapy is precisely to end the psychotherapeutic relationship, but in doing so to enable the patient to engage in other kinds of fulfilling relationships. Although spiritual partnership does accomplish somewhat similar results, because it helps both people to become more self-aware, more able to own feelings, and so forth, this is not really its ultimate purpose.

In spiritual partnership, the ultimate purpose is to be found not in the results produced *by* the relationship, but in the relationship itself. Whereas psychotherapy tries to help us function more adequately to reduce alienation and powerlessness and to increase our courage in the face of death and other uncontrollable evils, spiritual partnership's main purpose is to *compensate* us for the tragic but inevitable facts of alienation, relative powerlessness, death, and other uncontrollable evils—to make us feel the extreme positive value of being.

In concrete terms, what keeps a psychotherapeutic relationship from becoming a spiritual partnership is that the therapeutic situation sets tacit boundaries or limits to the ways the two people are expected to interact. These tacit boundaries create a 'safety zone' that encourages the client to let down the usual defenses without fear that this vulnerability will be taken advantage of. Therapists and patients therefore play roles in relation to each other, and the therapeutic situation itself is both defined and delimited by these roles. There is a tacit understanding that both people will strive to be as honest, open, and authentic as possible with each other during the therapeutic session itself; but it is also understood that, beyond the boundaries that mark off the therapeutic situation from the rest of life, neither person has a right to press for much more intimacy or investment of time with the other than would normally be expected between two people working together on any other project.

This remains true even if the therapeutic situation is a reciprocal one, in which either person may play the role of the helper or the helpee—for example, as is the case with 'focusing partners' using Gendlin's 'focusing method,' where the partners take turns helping each other focus. (See Gendlin's *Focusing* [1980], part 3.) During the focusing session itself, complete intimacy is not only allowed, but also expected. The aim is to focus on innermost states of consciousness in order to discover more about what they mean. If one partner has concerns relating to her husband's impotence or her own sexual frigidity, for example, the other must encourage her to explore the entire emotional meaning of these issues as frankly and openly as possible, and will remain completely empathic, nonjudgmental and nondirective as she lowers her defenses to expose these sensitive issues. Thus, during a focusing session, each person has a very clear and unencumbered view of the other's soul—that is, her overall pattern of consciousness and way of relating as a conscious being to the ontological predicament. In this respect, a focusing partnership resembles a spiritual partnership.

But what makes focusing partners different from spiritual partners (whether the two people are of opposite sexual polarity or not) is that, when the two people meet beyond the tacitly delineated boundaries of the therapeutic situation—at the snack bar or at a bus stop—they are not expected to press for this degree of intimacy. They may be closer-than-usual friends as a result of the contact they have made, but neither person would therefore assume that this gave the other the right to entertain worshipful feelings, or to infringe too much on the other's personal time and space. To presume such a degree of intimacy outside the therapeutic situation would be as inappropriate as to assume the right to relate erotically to the other person.

In fact, the tacit guarantee that exposed vulnerability will not be taken advantage of outside of the professional context is one of the main things that helps the person feel safe in opening up *within* that context. This professional respect for the other's privacy is one of the main reasons it is considered unethical to pursue a sexual or romantic relationship with a psychotherapy client, a student, a parishioner, or any other kind of client in a professional setting that breaks down people's defenses and allows for the possibility of the helper's 'preying on the vulnerability' of the helpee. (For excellent discussion of this issue, see Edelwich and Brodsky 1991.)

Imagine the reaction of a psychotherapist when a client calls on a Saturday morning and says, 'Since we're such good friends now, let's play tennis today, so that we can enjoy each other's company more!' The therapist's reaction to this invitation clearly spells out the difference between a therapeutic relationship and a spiritual partnership.

But does the locution 'good friends' not capture just what is missing in psychotherapeutic relationships and present in spiritual partnership? I think not. The problem here is primarily that we cannot appreciate the value of a friend in the usual sense *so much more intensely than we do our own* that the experience tears down egocentricity and fills us with such gratitude as to override the negativity of the ontological predicament. It is important to consider this difference somewhat carefully.

(c) Friendship in the ordinary sense. Spiritual partnership in the primary sense can be clearly distinguished from friendship in the ordinary sense, although a friend (especially if oppositely

polarized) may occasionally double as a primary spiritual partner, and of course much more readily as a spiritual partner in the secondary or derivative sense (see chapter 4). The difference seems especially obvious in the case of same-sex friends, since this difference is tied in with the reason people of opposite sexual polarity are especially suited to spiritual partnership, at least initially. In essence, the difference between friendship and primary spiritual partnership hinges on the fact that the relationship to a friend is a relationship of *equals*, whereas we experience a primary spiritual partner as *more than equal* to ourselves, in an important sense. We see a friend's values as being equal in importance with our own, and we see the value of the friend herself as equal to our own. But we experience a primary spiritual partner as having much *more* importance and value than we can experience ourselves as having, because the structure of the symbolization process in spiritual partnership allows an intense direct experience of the person's finitude and 'tragic' irreplaceability in Unamuno's sense—not just an abstract intellectual acknowledgment of it, but a direct experience of it. Since we directly experience the spiritual partner's value so much more intensely than we could our own, there is a sense in which the person seems more important to us than ourselves.

Later we shall see that this empathic compassion for the other's existential endangerment, which facilitates the intense appreciation for the person's extreme positive value, tends eventually to spread to other people, including friends, family members, and even people we hardly know. But it is initially a spiritual partner in the primary sense who jolts us out of ourselves and therefore *teaches and enables* us to love in this way, because this relationship forces us almost against our will to grant the other's superior value in spite of the normal tendency to feel ourselves and our own interests as more important to us than anyone else's. For many, this experience may be a fleeting and ephemeral one that occurs several times during adolescence, and it seems to be common across cultures. For example, according to Neihardt's Black Elk, "Say I am a young man and I have seen a young girl who looks so beautiful to me that I feel all sick when I think about her. . . . I keep feeling worse and worse all the time. . . . I tell [her father] how many horses I can give him for his beautiful girl, and by now I am feeling so sick that maybe I would give him all the horses in the world if I had them" (1932/1988, 67). In case anyone thinks that Black Elk's young man is interested only in sex, we are told instead that he waits outside her tepee all night hoping simply to *talk* to her.

A spiritual partner in the primary sense can make possible a complete space of empathy in which the kind of communication that facilitates the concrete symbolization of the feeling could occur with no impediment if the relationship is pursued in that direction. It is true that a space of empathy may exist between friends in the ordinary sense, but it is not used to empathize with the friend's feelings as more important than our own, as clearly the young man in Black Elk's story experiences the girl as so important that he would sacrifice all the wealth he can imagine for her. Neither the space of empathy nor the need for it seems to be felt as urgently or symbolized as completely in a friendship in the ordinary sense.

It is also true that a friend may be highly *admired*, but not in the same sense in which spiritual partners are admired. We admire a friend's competence to deal with problems, whereas we admire a spiritual partner because of the tragic nature of the problematic universe for which the person is too good, and with which no one can deal. It is an admiration for the person in the turmoil of finitude; we admire the other precisely because the cosmic insult of finitude focuses the person's fleetingness and irreplaceability.

To some extent, these two kinds of admiration may even conflict with each other. To admire someone's finitude is to focus on the person's ultimate powerlessness and inability; admiration for a friend tends to focus on the person's competence, ability, and self-sufficiency. This is why, among friends in the ordinary sense, too much compassion is viewed as pity, and therefore as an insult.

By contrast, the compassion of a spiritual partner is more like the compassion of a lover, which is a form of admiration for embattled authenticity and finitude. We want a friend to respect our power to solve problems, our competence; the relationship with a spiritual partner hinges on the kinds of problems that cannot be solved. For primary spiritual partners as such, solving problems only enters the relationship to the extent that altruistic concern demands it, and because either partner welcomes the chance to use altruism as symbolization of worshipful feelings. Friends have little desire to be worshiped by each other.

The essence of the difference between friendship and spiritual partnership, then, is that a friend is experienced as having equal value with oneself, whereas a spiritual partner is experienced as more intensely valuable than one could ever experience one's own value as being. Thus love for a friend in the ordinary sense is much less likely to fulfill the religious need—the need for an overpowering enough positive value experience to override the negativity of the ontological dilemma.

If the same person functions as both friend and spiritual partner, there will thus be a certain tension between the two simultaneous relationships, as in the case of Isaac Newton and his friend Fatio. Although a friend is not in essence the same thing as a spiritual partner, of course this does not mean that the same person may not be both a friend and a spiritual partner, nor that a friend cannot function to a lesser degree as a spiritual partner or vice versa. In fact, it would be unusual for spiritual partnership to develop between two people who did not previously already enjoy some sort of intimacy. Many friendships involve some degree of spiritual partnership, especially in the derivative sense.

In many cases, a friend may be a spiritual partner in the derivative sense: it is possible that the love for an original primary spiritual partner may spread to many others to a lesser extent, and then the original spiritual partner dies or becomes unavailable; in this case, the need for spiritual partnership is then fulfilled by a number of diverse individuals, no one of whom may necessarily be prized as unreservedly as was the original spiritual partner, but all of whom together serve the need more or less adequately. In the case of each friend, colleague, relative, and so forth, we are in quasi-aesthetic awe of the finitude and thus the uniqueness and irreplaceability of the valuable but embattled being, although the space of empathy is not complete enough with any one of them to allow for the intensity of feeling that the original spiritual partner made possible by almost forcibly jolting us out of our egocentric perspective in the way that Black Elk describes. Thus it seems that a friend in the ordinary sense cannot jolt us out of egocentricity (at least not in the sense of undermining a basically egocentric overall perspective on life), although a friend may be appreciated with intense, quasi-aesthetic awe *after* we have been jolted out of egocentricity by some sort of primary spiritual partnership. We shall see later that this jolting out of egocentricity leads to a complex sequence of important personality and value system changes that no less-jolting relationship can bring about.

A same-sex friend is usually different from a spiritual partner in still another way. We initially identify with a spiritual partner's form of consciousness largely because it is one that we admire, but cannot enact in ourselves except by participation with her in the space of empathy. This is the main reason for the trend toward using *romantic* partners as spiritual partners when traditional religions lose their ability to meet spiritual needs. A further problem in the case of friends in the ordinary sense is that they normally cannot use the realm of sexual symbolization (and often cannot use differing sexual polarity) for the spiritual partnership effect, even if they happen to be of opposite sex.

Opposite sexual polarity often seems to intensify the aesthetic dimension of admiration in a way that a person of similar polarity does not. Of course, this effect is further increased if one is 'sexually attracted' to the person in the ordinary, physical sense. However, as I have already emphasized, spiritual partnership per se needs to bypass the mask, and thus cannot be based exclusively or primarily on sexual attraction in the physical sense. In spiritual partnership, we admire not the physical sexuality of the other person, but the oppositely polarized *patterns of consciousness* that we perceive. We find this form of consciousness 'beautiful' in a way that we cannot directly and intensely appreciate our own as 'beautiful.' Here again, the urgency to enact a form of consciousness that we intensely crave, yet cannot enact without the other's help, seems largely to determine the intensity with which we appreciate it when we do manage to experience it through empathy.

In contrasting friendship with spiritual partnership per se, the key again is the difference between the ways in which consciousness is symbolized. When talking to a friend, we use our own language-body-behavior system as the physical substratum for our own ideas and feelings. The friend may then reflect them back to us, but does not use this process to symbolize his or her own feelings of quasi-aesthetic awe toward us (in fact, such feelings hardly even exist between friends). Friends must remain more equal and in a sense more separate than that. They must remain comrades in arms in the struggle against the ontological predicament, not occasions for ceasing the struggle in order to be consoled. For a friend to become too compassionate toward a friend would violate this pact; it would be pity, which would seem like a form of disrespect. And for a friend to idealize a friend too much would be servile and groveling, which is a form of self-disrespect.

The reason we cannot as easily or as overpoweringly admire the quasi-aesthetic beauty of our own form of consciousness is actually very complex. In essence, the extreme intensity of feelings of admiration arise initially from the prior intensity of our desperation to enact in ourselves a fundamental dimension of consciousness that can be fully enacted only through empathic and intimate participation with the other's. This remains true even though this egocentric motivation eventually ends up tearing down the circle of egocentricity, so that we appreciate the positive value of the other in a way that we could never have appreciated it from the egocentric perspective. It seems that to love another person of similar sexual polarity in most instances involves too little urgency and neediness to allow this love to reach the intensity of quasi-aesthetic awe.

We can now see even more easily why, historically, there has been such an increasing tendency to play out the need to intensely appreciate another conscious being's extreme positive value in the context of relationships between lovers in the erotic or romantic sense. In the relationship between people of opposite polarity, the impediments just mentioned are much less likely to occur. The reason is that, even as the predominantly masculine person, for example, encourages the other to fully express her own sexual polarity, he simultaneously remains well-grounded in his own sexual polarity while empathizing with the other. Thus spiritual partners of opposite polarity allow each other not only to experience each other's opposite polarity—thus completing themselves—but, perhaps more important for our purposes here, each allows the other to exist in his or her *own* sexual polarity to a complete extent, in combination with the opposite one, and thus allows it to express itself fully and to fully be. The feminized subject is able to be fully 'foreign to the world' because the bringing out of her masculine dimension assures that this foreignness can be successfully protected with stoicism-in-the-thick-of-battle, while simultaneously the masculinized subject enjoys vicariously the fully feminized form of consciousness, and thus experiences his own 'foreignness to the world.' Similarly, the masculinized subject is able to drop his defenses to an extent not possible else-

Essential Dynamics of Primary Transcendent Value Experience 157

where, because his participation with her femininity prevents him from losing his soul in order to become a warrior to protect it. Thus the masculinized consciousness is able to appreciate the beauty of the feminized consciousness in an intense way because he is 'attracted' to it in this nonphysical sense. And it seems that the feminized consciousness admires the masculinized form because she is similarly 'attracted' to it, and thus finds it 'attractive,' that is, quasi-aesthetically beautiful. So, although I have said that spiritual partnership can and sometimes does occur between similarly polarized subjects—especially when each has something crucial to learn from the other's form of consciousness—the most frequent and most intense instances of it usually occur between oppositely polarized subjects, especially in our culture at this point in its history.

To conclude our distinction between friendship and spiritual partnership, then, too much compassion for a friend in the ordinary sense seems insulting because it encourages a kind of wallowing in self-pity and a giving up of the struggle, since in this case no one continues to 'stand guard' with stoic resolve as the two people both throw down their arms to indulge in an emotionally weak kind of oversensitivity. Such sensitivity without stoic virtue tends to seem not beautiful, but contemptible or pitiable. For the same reason, the admiration for a same-sex friend's form of consciousness is too similar to admiring *our own* form of consciousness. But we cannot admire ourselves this intensely—at least not for very long—because to do so would be to lapse into an inert complacence in which we cease to seek transformation And it requires that we ignore our own tragic finitude, whereas to intensely love a being requires that we not ignore but rather focus on its finitude, so as to appreciate its uniqueness and irreplaceability. Here again, in experiencing a being of opposite polarity, we are able to focus on this being's finitude in a positive way, whereas focusing on our own finitude (or that of a being of too-similar consciousness to ourselves) tends to be a negative experience because it implies giving up the struggle.

It also seems that, when we empathize with a being of opposite polarity, we are not so much *substituting* the other's consciousness in place of our own, but rather *adding* that form of consciousness *to* our own in the experience of quasi-aesthetic awe. Because the other is oppositely polarized, we are offered the possibility of adding to ourselves something radically different from what we already possess, yet which is a natural part of our wholeness as a conscious being.

What has been said so far about same-sex friends is also true of opposite-sexed friends who are friends only in the ordinary sense. In this case, we relate to the other just as if the person were of the same gender as ourselves. We do not predominantly allow our opposite polarities to interact in the ways spiritual partners do within a complete space of empathy, and with the quasi-aesthetic awe of spiritual partnership concretely symbolized by giving expression to each other's unformed ideas and feelings. Certain tacit limits are placed on the degree of intimacy to be achieved, and transgression of these limits is usually considered an invasion of appropriate privacy. We can by no means commit to the risk of spiritual partnership with just anyone, whatever the person's sexual polarity.

It is also true that the opposite sexual polarities of same-sex friends do interact in important ways. In fact, it is possible, especially at certain times of life, that same-sex friends can relate as spiritual partners. These cases occur when the other person, although similarly polarized, still manifests some very essential and pervasive realm of spirituality which we ourselves feel that we need in order to become fully actualized, yet cannot develop except through intimate and empathic participation with the other's pattern of consciousness. But even in these cases, because of the similar polarization and the complications just mentioned, we do not usually experience the all-consuming and overpowering emotions that opposite-sex relationships tend to facilitate. Even a spiritual partnership between same-sex friends therefore tends to lack the ability to undermine our fundamental egocentricity, which thus remains largely intact in such cases. This undermining of egocentricity is essential to the ultimate effect of the spiritual partnership process.

(d) Hero worship and cults of personality. Cults of personality—the quasi-worship of heroes, religious leaders, rock stars, and the like—are a common perversion of the need to value another being more enthusiastically than we can ourselves. They thus underline the pressingness of this need. What cults of personality have in common with spiritual partnership is that, by worshipping the hero of whatever kind, we experience him or her as having

more value or importance than ourselves. The problem is that we do this not by making the experience of the hero into an extremely positive value experience, but by reducing our own existence to a valueless status—in fact, by reducing our own existence per se. This is completely different from a real and reciprocal relationship of open communication in which the conscious beings of two personalities really interact with each other. The cult of personality involves only a fantasizing of interaction with the hero. No space of empathy exists, thus neither person's consciousness is really known by the other. We therefore project onto the hero whatever traits we would like to imagine ourselves as having, or would like to imagine a friend or lover as having. If we then fancy that the hero really meets our emotional needs, we do so only by means of self-deception, and therefore reduce the field of our conscious awareness by blocking out the truth and distorting experience. Systematic distortions of our entire worldview will then be necessary to prop up the illusion.

Cults of personality, as Eric Fromm and others have emphasized, are used to serve a variety of psychologically dysfunctional purposes that are obviously at odds with the positive value experience and intensified consciousness in spiritual partnership. We vicariously live through the hero in order to avoid the responsibility of living our own lives. We adopt the values of the hero unreflectively and uncritically as an excuse to remain thoughtless about them. We allow the hero to make our decisions for us so that we will not have to make decisions ourselves. The result is mindless authoritarianism or conformism—processes that reduce authenticity and reduce consciousness. Only because our consciousness is so thoroughly reduced by the herdlike mentality of the cult following are we able to delude ourselves that such an experience is a positive value experience at all. In reality, it is a confidence game in which we are manipulated or duped, and allow our entire pattern of consciousness to be governed by bad faith. This requires the same kinds of distortions of logic, denials of obvious realities, and self-deceptive defense mechanisms that fundamentalist religions at their worst have required.

With regard to social trends toward political cults of personality, such as the relationship between Hitler and the German people, Kohut describes the conditions leading to them as follows: "Creativity in all fields is choked off. There is no one in touch with the [narcissistically] diseased group self. This points toward the increasingly worsening condition of the group self (corresponding to the disintegration threat of incipient psychosis in individual psychology) and leads to pathological *ad hoc* solutions" (1985, 84). The failure of the intelligentsia and artists to help people solve narcissistic problems in a constructive way, by developing their self-image around morally constructive ideals, creates a vacuum in which any figure who provides a vicarious experience of grandiosity may step in.

In effect, cults of personality allow us to fulfill the need for religious experience—that is, the need to intensely experience the positive value of another conscious being so as to override the negativity of the finite predicament—by requiring us to forfeit our authentic consciousness and personality. The hero worshipper may well avoid existential anxiety, but at the sacrifice of the intensity and complexity of his or her conscious being itself.

For the reasons discussed earlier, spiritual partnership can be accomplished only in a two-way, reciprocal relationship between real human beings. One cannot arbitrarily select some public figure as the object of spiritual partnership feelings, any more than one can engage in a meaningful friendship with an imaginary friend.

For the same reasons, we cannot allow ourselves to unilaterally worship a dominatrix who would sadistically control and manipulate us. Such a relationship would destroy the space of empathy and occlude the reciprocal empathic perception of authentic consciousness. We have seen repeatedly the reasons why spiritual partnership can never accomplish its effect unless it is substantially mutual and symmetrical. This problem of symmetrical reciprocity also serves to distinguish primary spiritual partnership from still another kind of relationship with which it might otherwise be confused, because of the prominence of compassion and empathy: relationships toward children.

(e) Spiritual partnership and compassion toward children. In a sense, the normal love for children or other family members may serve as a learning experience in the kinds of attitudes that are present in spiritual partnership. These kinds of love show certain similarities to the admiration-through-compassion for a spiritual partner. Children are especially instructive in this regard. The 'cuteness' of children derives precisely from their uniqueness and

irreplaceability, on which we focus to the extent that we do not yet hold them responsible to become problem solvers. Their vulnerability evokes an intense altruism, which is a positive feeling, and this positive feeling attaches itself to the uniqueness of the features of the child, so that this uniqueness is experienced in a very positive way. As the child grows older and becomes more self-reliant, the vulnerability that originally sparked the altruism fades, but the altruism remains, along with a continued appreciation of the uniqueness which, once seen, is not forgotten.

Yet the difference between the love for children and the love for a spiritual partner is crucial in that spiritual partnership fulfills the quasi-religious need described earlier (i.e., fully compensates us for the non-self-deceptively acknowledged harshness of the ontological predicament), whereas the love for a child, despite the above similarities to spiritual partnership, normally does not by itself accomplish this result. The main reason for this difference seems to be that the relationship to a child is not a symmetrical one, and therefore the space of empathy works in only one direction and is thus limited. Even if a parent succeeds in allowing a child to express ideas and feelings in an open atmosphere of nondirectiveness and nonjudgmentalism, the child cannot allow the parent to express the parent's own ideas and feelings with this open attitude. The child, like a spouse or romantic partner, depends on the parent to play certain roles and serve certain instrumental functions for the child, and any thoughts or feelings that threaten the dependability of the parent for these purposes will fail to elicit the child's empathy. The child must demand that the parent change attitudes that are perceived as not in the child's interest. For the same reasons, just as in the relationship between husband and wife, conflicts arise between the *moral rights* of family members, and individuals often must protect their rights from being violated. Children and their parents are even more in conflict with each other than are spouses in this regard, because children are less able to understand the moral rights of others. Thus, if parents did not protect their rights against children, the children would gladly take the opportunity to effectually enslave the parents, and this enslavement of parents would inhibit the development of agency, self-responsibility and stoic virtue in the child.

As the child approaches maturity and autonomy, these empathy-destructive conflicts may diminish or (in rare cases) disappear, but even at this point a complete process of spiritual partnership usually still does not occur. Now the child must establish independence, and therefore cannot identify with the differently structured (and/or oppositely polarized) spirituality of a parent's consciousness. Also, in most cases, the parent is too concerned with maintaining the child's affection and respect (which now are in danger because of this thrust toward independence) to let down defenses for a completely uninhibited space of empathy. Overconcern with the child's perception and evaluation of them precludes complete honesty. This seems usually to remain true even in those rare instances where the parents are able to overcome their own habitual judgmentalism and directiveness toward the adult child.

In very rare cases—perhaps, for example, in the relationship between Thomas More and his daughter—it is conceivable that an exceptionally mature and emotionally well-balanced adult child might become the spiritual partner of a parent. But, if so, this occurs in spite of the normal relationship between parent and child, not because of it. As in the case of ordinary friends, here too, adult children and parents may intensely admire each other, but the admiration is usually different from the admiration of a spiritual partner. Spiritual partners concretely symbolize both their admiration and their compassion for each other by means of the ways they can interact verbally *within a complete space of empathy* (which includes full expression of ideas and feelings that could not be expressed except with the help of the spiritual partner). A space of empathy does often exist between friends, family members, or romantic lovers (in fact, it is indispensable to a genuinely felt romantic love in the sense of admiration combined with compassion), but in these relationships the space of empathy usually is not used in the same way that spiritual partners use it. Only if one person concentrates his or her concretely symbolizing resources in the service of expressing the other's consciousness, and at the same time symbolizes the love for the other in this way, does spiritual partnership occur. To the extent that this does occur, the friendship, romantic relationship or familial relationship is beginning to double as a spiritual partnership, or is beginning to be transformed into a relationship whose main character becomes one of spiritual partnership, and therefore is concretely felt in a different way from the way friendship, romantic love, and love for family members per se are usually felt.

We have as yet to discuss the most important reason for the claim that spiritual partnership, as it unfolds, is able to produce such a miraculous transformation in one's entire worldview that the brutality of the finite dilemma of death, alienation, powerlessness, and relative insignificance can be fully compensated for in a sustained way without being limited to a stifling symbiosis with a primary spiritual partner. What we have seen historically is mainly a 'sexualization of religious experience' that is not fully aware of what it is groping toward, and therefore does not achieve this effect very adequately. In order to consider the full effect that spiritual partnership is capable of bringing about, we must see how spiritual partnership unfolds *when allowed to run its full course*, not choked off by the conflicts and complications that are all too prominent in romantic relationships in our culture, and indeed in most cultures. And in this case, we shall see that the effect becomes much more pronounced because, when allowed to run its full course, the process leads to a spreading effect and to an emotional commitment to the set of ethical abstractions that then can flow from a transcendent value experience.

4

The Spreading-Out of Non-Egoistic and Nonhedonistic Valuation

It seems increasingly obvious that the relationship of spiritual partnership will tend to be a somewhat ephemeral one unless supplemented by what I have called the 'spreading effect.' Let's turn now to a discussion of how this spreading effect works. Although the transcendent value experience of spiritual partnership in the primary sense initially appeals to egocentricity by facilitating the growth and existential fulfillment of the self, it quickly becomes opposed to egocentric motives; at the same time, it continues to pull us out of ourselves, because it has in a sense tricked us into a non-egocentric attitude by making us experience the other's intrinsic value in a way that far surpasses the experience of our own.

There are two different phases in this erosion of egocentricity. In the first phase, on which we have already touched, we are confronted with an experience whose disconcerting or even disturbing aspect is that it causes us to elevate another person's positive value above our own. If egocentricity can be compromised to this extent, we then face the second phase, which we have not yet discussed, and which may well be still more challenging—the need to avoid a condition of symbiotic dependence on spaces of empathy with one particular person as the *only* quasi-religious experience of value in life—but to avoid this condition without thereby forfeiting the strength of the feeling that life's value is positive enough to override the negativity of the finite condition.

In our previous discussions of the first of these two phases, we focused primarily on its pleasant rather than its painful aspect. The pleasant aspect is that the intensity of this positive value experience, at least initially, is adequate to compensate us for the negativity of the ontological dilemma. But we must now consider the problematic aspects. Not only is there resistance against allowing another person so much power over us, but also, the attempt to go through life with the experience of a specific individual as the only motivating value is obviously and inevitably doomed to failure. We are thus compelled whether we like it or not to renounce this simplistic valuational and motivational system. Paradoxically, only by renouncing both egocentricity *and* this dependency relation are we forced to emotionally intensify our appreciation for the positive value not just of one chosen person, but of all conscious beings, of life per se, and of the moral direction of our own lives. Without such moral direction, primary spiritual partnership itself would eventually collapse under the weight of its own symbiotic inertness. In this chapter, we shall see that, at the end of this often painful double renunciation, the renunciation first of egocentricity and then of a clinging dependence on spiritual partnership as the only value in life, we finally find ourselves ironically able to fully appreciate the value of the present moment, not insofar as it serves egocentric motives, but for its own sake, in spite of and indeed because of its fleetingness and thus its irreplaceability and uniqueness. In Heidegger's terms, we then experience ourselves as one among many beings *within* the world, rather than privileged observers *of* it (as if from without).

The painful and disturbing side of the *initial* stage in the erosion of egocentricity is already fairly obvious: The appreciation of another's value more intensely than our own means that the other is more important to us than we are to ourselves. At this point, we find ourselves dependent on the opportunity to view the other's value, as if we were an electrical appliance dependent on a power source. Such an inversion of the normal priority system leads to contradictions within our value system and motivational structure that cannot be resolved except through a radical restructuring and deconstruction of the self, along with its normal motivational structure, value system, and defenses against possible external opposition. The self-system whose value experience was formerly centered within the self must now be replaced with one in which our own *experience* of value is less important than *that which* is valued. The safety of normal ego defenses is thus replaced with a sense of the unimportance of the self and the threat of a lack of control over what the self values. In that initial phase, we may perceive this lack of control as an assault on a now vulnerable and defenseless ego structure, by someone who at this point seems to dominate our destiny in an almost unfair way that insults our ego integrity and leaves us with a need that cannot be fulfilled unless an irreducibly *other* consciousness willingly chooses to indulge it.

What is more important for our purposes here is that no sooner is this first phase in the erosion of ego integrity worked through than we are assailed by a second one, which at first is even more problematic. After the relationship of spiritual partnership has been established, is somewhat stabilized, and is reciprocal, we are then confronted with an internal dilemma that inevitably is built into the nature of spiritual partnership in the primary sense per se: If the spiritual partnership is to retain its character as such, rather than becoming a symbiosis, then a complete space of empathy cannot be indulged in at all times, and must not be forced to bear the burden of supplying the entire meaning of life, for a number of reasons that will become clear in this chapter. First of all, a symbiosis cannot support the aims of spiritual partnership. One of the preconditions for primary spiritual partnership to function as such is that each member must maintain an interesting, meaningful, and value-expressive life *outside* of the dyadic relationship itself in order to continue injecting life *into* the relationship, so that it does not stagnate into an inert *stasis*. This requirement would not be met if both people were completely dependent on the relationship itself for the only meaning and motivational direction in life.

Moreover, in a symbiosis, each person uses the other's different form of being or opposite polarization as a crutch to *avoid* developing and fully experiencing his or her own corresponding conscious potential, rather than using it as a catapult *toward* such development. But that which is not experienced is also not consciously appreciated in the intensely value-laden ways we have been discussing here. Also, we must remember that (especially if the spiritual partnership is to double as an erotic relationship) full spaces of empathy will become less frequent as the quality of the space of empathy is permeated and contaminated by the various effects of the fabric of sociocultural and pragmatic interrelations. This last point is well dramatized in cultures where members of the community make noise and throw vegetables or other objects at the tent or house of the newly married couple throughout the wedding night. The couple must be reminded that their marriage is only a small part of their total life cycle, and that this life cycle must still be worked out in terms of the fabric of the couple's larger social context.

This chapter will thus attempt to describe this multistage assault on egocentricity, from the initial experiencing of the other's value more intensely than one's own, to the inescapable necessity to forfeit the addictive pleasure of focusing the quasi-religious experience almost exclusively on the person of the primary spiritual partner, so that the experience of that person is no longer the one and only definitive locus of value capable of eliciting awe and reverence. In chapter 2, we discussed the sense in which the feelings involved in spiritual partnership constitute an 'experience of positive value' in such a way as to compensate us for the negativity of the ontological dilemma, provided that egocentricity is abandoned in order to selflessly appreciate the other's value with a feeling of quasi-aesthetic awe in the face of the partner's uniqueness and irreplaceability (i.e., the person's finitude, for which we feel both admiration and compassion in such a way that they intensify each other). But the proviso that egocentricity be abandoned to this extent is a major one, and we did not explore at that point what it entails. This chapter will therefore trace this egocentricity-eroding process. If the process is allowed to run its complete course, it ends with the development of what I call the 'ultimate spreading effect,' which occurs through a process of relinquishment and leads to nongraspingness through humility, generalized agape, and finally a strongly emotional valuation of abstract ideals.

1. Resistance against the Threat to Egocentricity

When the need to establish a transcendent value experience through spiritual partnership is first felt, the meaning of the feeling may well be a disturbing sense of powerlessness or challenge to the normal state of being in control of ourselves. The idea of valuing someone to a considerably greater extent than it is possible to value oneself implies ultimately that in a sense we also emotionally feel the other's ontological predicament as more important than we do our own. This follows because the feeling of awe-stricken admiration, which we experience as such an acutely positive feeling, is inseparably dependent on our compassion for the other's embattled authenticity in the face of alienation, conflict, powerlessness, and death. The focus on this finitude is precisely what facilitates quasi-aesthetic awe because it allows us to directly experience the person's fleetingness, uniqueness, and irreplaceability in an intense way. We cannot intensely feel admiration of this kind without also feeling an urgent pull to such a powerful positive valuation of the embattled being that this value is felt as more important than any of our other values in life—even the self-serving ones. We may of course still cling to abstract moral principles because of intellectual commitment, or because life would be meaningless or absurd without the moral principles; but when it comes to the subjective values of our individual lives, which are motivated more by feeling than by abstract thought (the 'material' rather than the 'formal' values in Scheler's sense), the degree to which the value of a spiritual partner overpowers other motives correlates with the degree to which our experience of the other's positive value is more intense than our experience of any other positive value.

This is most certainly true when it comes to the most egocentric values, which depend for their priority on our being able to subjectively *feel* our own self-interest as more pressing than anyone else's. While a strict utilitarian may believe her own happiness to have the same value as that of others, she does not necessarily donate 95 percent of her income to the poor people of the world in order to increase the general happiness. Aside from intellectual justifications for this privileging of the self's position, there is also the sheer fact that we subjectively feel that which affects us personally. Thus it is disconcerting when we experience the prospect of spiritual partnership as a giving up of the power to define our own values and to control our own destiny and identity—that is, to control the direction of our future.

In valuational terms, the new value system that this experience demands is in virtually incommensurable conflict with the older, 'normal' value system, in which the interests of all ego-subjects are equally important, and the key question of morality concerns how much one ego-subject should be willing to sacrifice for the greater benefit of others. What I mean by 'normal' in this context is simply that we do not give all of our money to the poor, or treat our own family members as exactly equal in importance to everyone else, but rather skew our behavior somewhat toward centering ourselves in the moral universe, while expecting others to do the same. Indeed, this is part of holding people responsible for themselves. This normal value system is inseparable from the assumption that social relations are relations between ego-subjects, each having its own self-interest as the paramount motivating force, and interested in others only to the extent that this interest can somehow be motivated by the ego-subject's desire to embrace some abstract moral principle. The abstract principles, of course, may be supplemented by the fact that to benefit others may benefit the self by making it into a more fully functioning ego-subject in some sense. In this normal value system, one may intellectually recognize the value of justice and of others' well-being, and therefore promote these values, but not when they conflict too much with one's own 'self interest'—that is, when the motivation to be moral (though such a motivation does exist) is overpowered by other motivations that sometimes may happen to be stronger (see my *Coherence and Verification in Ethics*). By contrast, the relationship to a spiritual partner demands that we give up the centrality of the importance of the ego-subject itself. It demands that we experience the central place of value—the place in terms of which other values are derivative—as being intrinsically in the other, not primarily in ourselves.

This whole development is necessarily experienced as a challenge to ego integrity. It demands a radical overhauling of the motivational dimension of consciousness, which in turn largely determines the pattern of unfolding in consciousness through motivated selective attention, and therefore the very nature and identity of the self, since the self is distinguished by the peculiarities of the patterns in which its conscious experiences unfold. A transcendent value experience is thus felt as an upheaval. We experience the other as someone who has an unfair advantage over us, and it makes sense to try to resist the restructuring and decentering of the ego that the experience seems to demand.

We may of course be reassured by the fact that primary spiritual partnership presupposes a space of empathy, and therefore that the other cannot easily take unfair advantage of this vulnerability on our part, since to do so would directly violate and even destroy the space of empathy on which the feeling depends. Also, primary spiritual partnership can occur only if mutual and reciprocal, so there is the consolation that the other person sees us as a central locus of value that also overshadows *her* own ego-subject. Thus it is not as though we were to give ourselves up to a sadomasochistic dominatrix or a cult hero on whom we make ourselves dependent in an unhealthy way.

But in the beginning, there is still an uneasiness about giving up the centering of the self in the valuational universe, and there will be some difficulty in making this shift away from egocentricity, so that there will be many occasions at first for spiritual partnership to present itself as a painful and perhaps even unacceptable (to the egocentric subject) metamorphosis. In many instances, the initial appearance that the other regards us as a relatively ordinary figure in her own valuational universe, which we assume still centers herself in her own normal value system, at the very moment when we regard her as more important than ourselves, can engender a variety of negative feelings. One may feel so covetous of the reciprocation of the needed space of empathy as to spark jealousy. Ironically, this is one of the times mentioned earlier when one may reject the potential transcendent value experience as an insult to egocentric values and thus too high a price to pay. Furthermore, if our previous personality structure is too riddled with inauthentic defenses (such as exaggerated narcissism, or a tendency to project blame and guilt, or an exaggerated perception that the interdependence in love relationships is a power struggle, etc.), we may react with childish rage against the person who has dealt our ego-subject such an intolerable 'injustice.'

This is perhaps one of the main reasons why the most common misconstrual of the potential for such a transcendent value experience is that we interpret the meaning of the experience only as an instance of being 'sexually attracted' to the person (as if there were some mysterious, magical force that would lead people to be sexually attracted only to a specific individual). In this way we try to preserve the integrity of the ego-subject by construing the relationship as one between two egocentric individuals who stand to gain something for themselves—something construed as some sort of 'need' for love, as if love were a kind of service that we need done for us in order to increase our happiness or sense of fulfillment. As I mentioned earlier, it is somewhat natural to interpret such feelings as primarily erotic, since intensification of the body's sexuality serves as an effective concrete symbolization for the appreciation of the other's positive value, as well as of one's own radical transformation—at least at first.

But if bodily sexualization is the primary symbolization process used to concretize the feeling, then the interactions between the *persons* are not structured in the way needed to sustain a space of empathy and to symbolize the specific attitudes that are characteristic of spiritual partnership. Moreover, we have seen that thematizing the relationship primarily in erotic or romantic terms leads to the complication of social roles and to social and moral conflicts in which each ego must defend its own integrity, so that to a great extent the space of empathy becomes a guarded one in which each ego's defenses block the conditions for spiritual partnership. Also, in a romantic relationship, a sense of the separateness of the two individuals is essential to the continued success of the relationship; without it, neither individual has anything new or interesting to contribute to the other, and thus the relationship becomes mundane, trivial, predictable, and somnambulistic. Yet the sociocultural institutionalization of a romantic 'coupling' (whether in or out of wedlock) tends to tear down the separateness of the two people, so they must engage in an uphill struggle to avoid losing the ability to infuse life into the interactions between their consciousnesses. For all these reasons, the romanticizing of an opportunity for spiritual partnership may well send the relationship into an entirely different dimension, whose importance of course should not be belittled, but the outcome is usually somewhat divergent from the one to which spiritual partnership in a full sense would lead.

Romanticizing a spiritual partnership is also a typical response even if one or both people already have a romantic partner. I believe that, in our culture at the time of this writing, this need for transcendent value experience through spiritual partnership, which is then eroticized, is the main reason for the prevalence of rapidly alternating serial monogamies and the quickness to 'trade in' one romantic partner for another. The tendency is that one merely repeats the same pattern with the new romantic partner, thus largely eroding the conditions for spiritual partnership in that case too. Eventually, one then ends up in the exact same condition as before, with a romantic partner who fulfills spiritual needs only as well as one's own psyche and the pattern of social interactions for romantic partners in the given culture will allow. The main reason for the quickness to trade in one romantic partner for another is that the spreading effect, as discussed in the remainder of this book, is not understood as a natural complement to the spiritual partnership itself. As a result, the latter becomes a symbiotic dependency relationship, and the tendency is that we can imagine replacing it only with another symbiotic dependency relationship.

Conversely, unless the space of empathy in the original romantic relationship has already become hopelessly eroded, a complete working through of the spreading effect can sometimes ironically feed back into the romantic relationship itself; one can then relearn to appreciate a romantic partner's value by directly experiencing her uniqueness and irreplaceability. It may then become possible to reestablish even a seriously eroded space of empathy. A clear example of this principle occurs in Claude Lelouch's popular film *Vivre pour Vivre (Live for Life)*, in which the protagonist must learn to love in a non-egocentric way before he is able to love his wife fully enough to no longer need to engage in extramarital affairs—a lesson he learns by empathizing with the suffering of victims of the Vietnam war. Another reason for this effect is that, when the entire meaning of one's life is not invested in one relationship, pressure is taken off that one relationship, so that it can again function in a more healthy way. One no longer resents the romantic partner's failure to accomplish the impossible task of single-handedly meeting all interpersonal needs, 'making one happy,' and serving in effect as the entire interpersonal matrix in terms of which the 'being-toward' and 'being-with' dimensions of life are given their meaning.

But we have seen that to accept a spiritual partnership as such, whether in a 'romantic' context or not, requires a holistic revamping of personality structure, the ultimate outcome of which is a loss of the definition of the self as the center of value and as the most important person to oneself. The fear that may be felt in the face of such a prospect is not unrealistic.

Moreover, certain inevitable structures built into the nature of spiritual partnership make it still more punishing to the ego-subject than even what we have considered so far. The ego-subject senses the danger of this terrain in the same way that we may intuit the conclusion of a geometrical proof before logic is able to get us there. The next section will explore the most difficult part of the process of egocentricity erosion: the fact that, even after giving up the centrality of the self, we then learn that it is still impossible to define the meaning of life or overcome the negativity of the ontological predicament simply by means of complete dependency on a symbiotic obsession with one particular love object.

2. The Spreading Effect as the Intensifying Edge of the Generalized Experience of Value

We can now confront the most difficult, but also the most morally important and potentially the most valuable aspect of the spiritual partnership process: In the real world of material brutality, interpersonal alienation, and sociocultural practices and traditions, to define life in terms of a continuing and uncompromised relationship of spiritual partnership is for the most part pragmatically impossible—as Tristan learned in the archetypal myth of the courtly lover. This pragmatic impossibility delivers the ultimate death blow to the egocentric valuational perspective and leads to the ultimate spreading effect, in which we find ourselves finally able to revere the uniqueness and irreplaceability of all people and experiences with the same kind of quasi-aesthetic awe that initially characterized only the experience of a primary spiritual partner. Thus, I learn to experience the intrinsic value of my old high school classmate who grew up to be a serial murderer in a way that is very similar to the way I experience the intrinsic value of my wife and children. This section will attempt to explain why this transformation occurs.

From what has been said so far, it should be obvious that the phenomenon of primary spiritual partnership is a somewhat tenuous one in the real-life context of conformity to necessary cultural practices, interpersonal alienation, conflict, and the struggle for both physical and existential survival. There are two possible cases. Either the spiritual partnership is played out in the form of a romantic coupling—in which the space of empathy may indeed be impressive, but is then gradually and increasingly compromised not only to avoid symbiosis, but also to make room for the many other important roles that long-term romantic partners must assume in relation to each other. Or the spiritual partnership occurs outside the context of a romantic relationship, in which case the space of empathy may seem more pure, but then working the spiritual partnership into the overall texture of life becomes difficult, because it does not fit into the pragmatic system of social practices that largely dominate serious forms of relationships in any culture. These alternatives were symbolized in the myth of Tristan and Isolde by the dilemma as to whether courtly love could still continue its effect of transporting the lovers to the realm of sublime spirituality if the love had been sexually consummated. They were damned if they did, and damned if they did not. The impediment to their union, Isolde's marriage to King Mark, is merely a literary device to represent this dilemma, which courtly lovers who practiced the Catharaist heresy believed to be inevitable under any circumstances.

Spiritual partnership in the primary sense exists primarily between the cracks of life. We have seen why this is true in a romantic spiritual partnership. But it is also true of spiritual partnership aside from any romantic considerations. Spiritual partnership itself demands that clinging dependence and choking of autonomy be avoided, so that each person must let the other live her own life unencumbered by the continual pragmatic participation of the other. Such continual pragmatic participation would be directive and would place the relationship into an interpersonal matrix in which all the conflicts discussed above would inevitably impinge on the purity of the space of empathy. If spiritual partnership is to avoid the same interpersonal conflicts and complications that also typically lead to a guarded and/or less-than-frequent space of empathy in romantic relationships, it must do so by existing outside of the matrix of interpersonal role-playing, utilitarian functions, and social institutionalization that so obviously impinge on the privacy and mutual defenselessness of romantic relationships in the same way as for spiritual partnerships in general.

On the one hand, the more a relationship becomes incorporated into the normal, everyday course of social life, the more this incorporation leads to conflicts, social role-playing, and utilitarian requirements that tend to erode or compromise the space of empathy. On the other hand, the more the relationship is to be *protected* from incorporation into the general fabric of social life, the more it is inclined to become an inert symbiosis. Hence the lamentable antinomy that, as a spiritual partnership unfolds (especially a romantic one, which is intensified by sexual forms of symbolization), we want and need to be in a space of empathy with the spiritual partner more and more, yet we cannot indulge this tendency as much as we would like, or attribute exclusive value to it, without encouraging a symbiosis and isolation, and thus eroding the conditions for the possibility of spiritual partnership. We have touched on the reasons for this in earlier chapters, and they are discussed more extensively in my *Eros in a Narcissistic Culture*.

In essence, the space of empathy tends to shut out the world, and for this reason primary spiritual partners are tempted to define the entire meaning and value of their lives in terms of spiritual partnership. But ironically, this shrinking of the realm of value and meaning to the confines of the primary spiritual partnership serves ultimately to cut part of the necessary foundation from underneath the relationship, so that it becomes inert and clinging, and thus can no longer sustain itself, given that the people themselves, functioning as independent agents, must bring meaning to the relationship.

In spite of this fact, no matter how much time we are able to spend in an uncompromised space of empathy with a primary spiritual partner, there seems naturally to be a strong tendency to want more. This point is most clearly obvious in a spiritual partnership where the main impediment to the space of empathy is simply the *physical* separateness of the two people, but we have seen that it also applies in a more subtle way to the impediments to the space of empathy in other contexts as well (for example, in the way that the culturally imposed nonerotic social relations and pragmatic functions of married couples increasingly tend to block their establishing a complete space of empathy). No amount of time in the space of empathy can be enough, given these practical impediments, because no state of being could be more gratifying. To be in a space of empathy means that we can trust the other person not to judge or condemn any idea or feeling we may express, so that the stream of consciousness can unfold according to its natural flow as authentically motivated by previous states of consciousness in the stream, and is not blocked, deflected, and thwarted at every turn. At the same time, in admiring the other person's conscious intensity (as facilitated by our own respect for the space of empathy, which then allows the other's consciousness to unfold authentically and intensely), we vicariously participate in the pattern of that person's consciousness, and this participation in an alien pattern of consciousness causes us to transcend ourselves. We are pulled out of stasis into radical change. Since consciousness *is* a pattern of change, it follows that consciousness, in desiring to exist with a certain degree of intensity, desires to unfold and transcend itself. Therefore, it is gratified in its most basic existential need when it is pulled out of itself by a perfect empathy with someone else's consciousness within a space of empathy, which at the same time allows one's own consciousness to unfold authentically. It is a state of flowing intensity, in the fullest possible actualization of the most important existential need, the need for authentically motivated intensity of consciousness through fulfillment of the exact type and amount of self-transformation that is motivated at each moment in the stream of consciousness—an experience of full being. No phenomenological description of such an experience could ignore the feeling that we float euphorically in the space of empathy in a complete freedom protected from any alienation, hostility, manipulativeness, or moral judgment that might threaten to choke it off. It is a liberating, intoxicated feeling that easily becomes addictive.

All of this, however, is what spiritual partners must be willing to limit and place within a larger context, not only because of pragmatic impediments to the space of empathy, but also and more importantly because of the demand to avoid symbiosis and isolation. A form of being that can exist only within a space of empathy is a form that, like Tristan and Isolde, must attempt in vain to shut itself off from the real world. Thus both respect for the spiritual partner and practicality demand acknowledgment that she is a separate individual with her own separate agenda, and that both people must define for themselves forms of being that can establish their meaning *outside* of the space of empathy.

Yet at the point in the process when this dilemma arises, we are able to enact our whole conscious potential only *within* the space of empathy, for the reasons just discussed. So to insist on the independence of the two people's being (as we must) requires being content with much less enjoyment of the space of empathy than would really be desirable in terms of fully enacting our whole conscious potential, and also avoiding centering all value around the space of empathy. And this resignation is therefore resisted at every moment by the most fundamental ontological structure of our being.

The spreading effect of spiritual partnership can therefore occur in a relatively pleasant or a very painful way, depending partly on whether we continue to insist on shutting out the world and resting the experience of value completely on the direct experience of the primary spiritual partner, or whether we relinquish symbiosis willingly. Also, an unhappy spiritual partnership (due to separation, estrangement, or other impediments) will lead to the spreading effect in a painful way, because the push toward the space of empathy, which is still frustrated in such a case, can remain so intense that the experience of value by means of the spreading effect seems at first to be a paltry consolation prize, and cannot be willingly embraced.

And yet, when we do finally learn to genuinely relinquish dependence on an exclusive obsession with the conflict-free and completely uncompromised space of empathy in which consciousness flows uninhibitedly and unobstructedly, it is precisely at this point (and in proportion as the relinquishment is genuine) that the full and lasting value of spiritual partnership becomes apparent. In this resignation to 'letting go' of the other in her separateness, we experience with complete directness and immediacy the tragic fleetingness and irreplaceability of *all* things, people, and experiences. This experience is not embraced by choice, but forced on us. Any escape (e.g., by 'trading in' the partner for a new object of obsession and symbiosis) would be illusory. Thus we find that each experience is now intensified by this poignant edge; yet our appreciation of the *positive* value of being—as still impressed on us by our experience of quasi-aesthetic awe in the face of the spiritual partner herself—exactly counterbalances the poignant feeling, so that we simply value each experience with the intensity of a concretely felt tragic edge.

The reason this experience occurs is precisely *because* of having allowed ourselves inadvertently to become dependent on continuous, completely unconditional empathic contact with the spiritual

Spreading-Out of Non-Egoistic and Nonhedonistic Valuation 179

partner for the concrete enactment of our authentic conscious potential. Because the ontological structure of our consciousness depends on this contact, we reach the point where we can completely be who we really are only in relation to the spiritual partner. To relinquish the space of empathy with her is therefore to relinquish our very being—until we discover the surprise on the other side of this abyss. The surprise is that, when we are forced finally to admit defeat in the attempt to maintain this ephemeral being that is able to thrive only under such pragmatically tenuous circumstances, we give up the one thing that is most important to us, the thing compared to which all egocentric values have become trivial. We then find that the structuring of our time, our attention-direction, and our goal-orientations are no longer eaten up with striving toward the earlier pragmatic outcomes that had been defined first in terms of the egocentric project (which now seems trivial), and then in terms of the obsessive symbiosis (which we now see is impossible). Everything is then seen afresh, as if for the first time, with the naiveté of a child marveling at an adventure film on the wide screen, or an artist lost in the colors and details of her subject. The colors we then see are tragic in the inescapable finitude that we now are able to admit to ourselves; yet their value is also positive because we have now learned to awe-strickenly appreciate the positivity toward which the finitude of an experience or (still more) a person now pulls our focus. Thus the positive experience is intensified by its tragic quality; it is both intense and positive—intensely positive. The feeling is similar to the cathartic moment of a great piece of artwork—a 'being-in' our finite destiny.

Such an approach to experiencing is made possible partly by the fact that the relationship to a primary spiritual partner has undermined the fundamental egocentricity of our value system. Thus pragmatic goal orientations no longer make us feel too busy, for example, to pause for a moment to watch the beauty of sunlight reflecting off a natural scene, and to focus our attention on this beauty itself rather than on ourselves and our future-directed strivings. Instead of orienting the motivational structure toward thoughts of personal accomplishment and others' perceptions of us, we free ourselves from the egocentric mask, no longer compelled to rush ahead into an ever-receding future bounded only by death at the other end, so that the experience of the tragic uniqueness of the present moment floods in on us in sharply focused intensity. We see the uniqueness and irreplaceability of each moment in the existence of each person or experience with the same tragic sense that we had previously felt only when perceiving the spiritual partner. This is the ultimate spreading effect, in which the poignant experience of quasi-aesthetic awe initially precipitated by admiration-through-compassion now spills over into our experience not just of others who bear certain similarities to the spiritual partner, but also of other people generally, and even to all things and experiences that enter our phenomenal field. The phenomenal field is permeated with a tragic spirituality resulting from the finiteness of all things, combined with the relinquishment of symbiotic dependence on the intensely flowing pattern of being that was not only possible but easy within a completely uncompromised space of empathy. But, although this resignation is regretful, it is also permeated with the quasi-religious awe and appreciation of positive value with which everything associated with the transcendent value experience must inevitably be permeated.

The main reason we are able to accept the misfortune that we must relinquish dependence on the space of empathy is that the 'ultimate spreading effect'—in which all things are experienced in their tragic finitude, uniqueness, and irreplaceability—now imbues all life with an intensity and meaningfulness, so that we experience being as infinitely valuable in spite of this misfortune. We may still require the experience of a spiritual partner (of one sort or another), as a periodic renewal of our sense of the degree to which being has positive value, since we gaze *directly and immediately* on this value itself when we are in the space of empathy with a primary spiritual partner, and thus can directly *see* her being for what it is. (In this case, our admiration and compassion for her embattled authenticity and sensitivity force this value experience.) The appreciation of other people and things is to a great extent indirect and mediate—that is, it depends on being permeated with the tragic-yet-positively-valuing view of life that is *derivative* from the experience of the primary spiritual partner. In viewing other things and people, we may forget over time how to appreciate this value, but in viewing the conscious being of a primary spiritual partner, we are confronted with it through no effort of our own, almost involuntarily, provided that the space of empathy is even occasionally possible. We will therefore prefer if possible to continue periodically experiencing a primary spiritual partner to remind ourselves how to experience other people and things from this standpoint. But it is not necessary for this purpose to be in a completely uncompromised space of empathy as frequently as we would like. We are able to forfeit the *pleasure and happiness* of this impossible ideal because spiritual partnership itself has enabled us fully to appreciate the *nonhedonistic*, and in fact *tragic-yet-positive* value of the world per se.

Conversely, this spreading effect, because it extends the direct and intense experience of intrinsic value beyond the spiritual partnership, also creates a 'realm of the sublime,' a context for action in terms of value that allows each person to bring new meaning into the primary spiritual partnership itself, so that the stagnation of inert symbiosis is avoided. The realm of the sublime and the primary spiritual partnership now mutually support each other.

As I have mentioned throughout, these processes do not necessarily work themselves out in a happy way. If a primary spiritual partner is someone who is unavailable or inappropriate, or is lost for one reason or another before the spreading effect occurs, then this spreading effect will tend to be a painful and unwilling metamorphosis. Moreover, under such circumstances, the primary spiritual partnership itself may have been an unhappy one from the beginning. Spiritual partnership does not guarantee 'happiness,' nor does it ensure that we will always be fulfilled in the process of self-actualization or self-realization. These problems must be solved independently of the spiritual partnership, just as they had to be solved before we entered into the spiritual partnership. What spiritual partnership does do is to restore an extreme subjective appreciation of the value of being, and thus solve the ontological dilemma in providing an inspiring experience of positive value intense enough to compensate for the inescapability of finitude. If we insist on using a spiritual relationship too much to maximize our happiness and pleasure in life, we risk distorting its purity and diverting it from its main value, which is to allow us to experience life in a powerfully intrinsically valuing way despite the harshness of the ontological predicament. No amount of happiness or pleasure could ever be enough to accomplish this purpose.

3. Transferring Value Feelings to Derivative Objects and to Ideals that Organize the Self

We saw in the last section that, to a great extent, we must allow a primary spiritual partner to remain *other*, independent, a separate person with a separate life, career, family, and place within a social fabric from which we may extricate the person for spaces of empathy only occasionally. Yet this very relinquishment threatens our experience of the value of being (which at this point has become contingent on the spiritual partnership), and thus splits off the experience from many aspects of our goal-orientedness. At that point, the experience of Unamuno's 'tragic sense' of the value of being in general intensely floods in on us, and the experience of the value of many *other* people (and other values derivative from the value of conscious beings, such as works of art or political ideals) forces itself on us as a sort of substitute for the experience of the spiritual partner's positive value. We are forced to experience that which is valuable in the spiritual partner as it exists in others as well, so that our generalized agape for them (which now can be felt more concretely and immediately than before) serves as an indirect access to the sharply felt positive value of the primary spiritual partner, which thus continues to override the negativity of the ontological predicament. In the remainder of this chapter, we shall also find that, in order to have the strength to face life's turmoils on these terms, we ultimately must be able to generalize this value feeling to the abstractions of a system of motivating ideals, without losing their emotional intensity in the transfer.

Obviously, a happy outcome would result if the idealization of the *person* of a spiritual partner could be transferred to our own set of personal ideals in the form of abstract *moral or valuational commitments* which could be cherished so strongly as to provide motivated direction, and thus meaning to life. In fact, one reason for the difficulty in relinquishing dependence on empathic contact with a spiritual partner is that the idealization of the spiritual partner is forced to shoulder so much of the burden of the sense of meaning in life, precisely because the radical reconstruction of the self that makes us ripe for spiritual partnership in the first place also leaves us with a shortage of guiding goal-orientations based on strongly cherished values. It thus seems virtually inevitable that, if spiritual partnership is really to restore a sense of meaning to life without becoming a clinging symbiosis, then the powerful valuation of primary spiritual partnership must be spreadable to secondary spiritual partners, to guiding values within oneself, and in some cases to future primary spiritual partners. And there does seem to be a way to accomplish these objectives. To see how this can happen, we must first consider the psychodynamics of the need to value transcendent objects in order to appreciate the value of being strongly enough to provide motivational unity and structure to the self.

It is possible to distinguish (and most psychologists do distinguish) at least three aspects of the self that are oriented toward valuational feelings. These three aspects of the self generate a motivated directness toward values and feelings that provides much of the unity and continuity needed to structure the self. First, there is the 'ego ideal'—the aspect of the self that holds up esteemed images of what the self ideally should strive to be like. According to many theorists, notably Kohut (and this is also consistent with casual, everyday observations), people often are able to love their abstract ideals (moral values such as loyalty, integrity, magnanimity, etc.) with an emotion quite similar to the idealizing love one feels for a person.

Second, there is the 'narcissistic self.' This is the aspect of the self that craves the attention and admiration of others. Since we all must first attract the attention of others in order to make contact with them to meet the need for meaningful interaction, there will always be a narcissistic self in anyone's personality structure. It is only when this narcissistic self becomes 'disturbed'—when infantile traumata cause the person to react cataclysmically and compulsively to any threat to the narcissistic self's craving for attention, approval, and admiration—that it becomes a neurosis or even psychosis.

Third, there is the 'idealized object image'—i.e., the image of some specific person in whom one feels are embodied the cherished qualities of the ego ideal and/or of the narcissistic self. It is an obvious phenomenological observation that we sometimes relocate values from our ego ideal to another person (who serves as an idealized object image), and vice versa. In the same process, we also relocate the investment of emotional commitment and energy that accompanies these valuational feelings. It has also often been observed (for example, by Reik and by Kohut) that, at times when the ideals that unify a self are faltering or are being committed to radical questioning, the person is likely to find a person whose idealized image serves as a stand-in for the now missing or weakened ego ideal. In concrete terms, a person who finds herself no longer able to be enthusiastically enough motivated and inspired by the abstract value beliefs that used to define the meaning of her activity and organization will then desperately cling to the meaning and motivational direction provided by falling in love, or by becoming a follower of a charismatic personality or political demagogue, or by becoming devoted to a spiritual partner, whether the latter be a human being, a deity, or the representative of a deity such as a saint or martyr. In effect, the idealized person is made to serve the meaning-structuring and motivational directedness that organize the self, now that the ego ideal is no longer able to serve as much of this purpose as it did in other times. When this kind of dynamic is heavily involved in a love relationship, the threat of the loss of the beloved person's intimacy threatens to issue in an extreme disintegration and unraveling of the basic fabric of the self, leading to a more or less psychologically unstable condition. Even well-balanced personalities often experience a disintegration of the motivated directedness of the self to a greater or lesser extent when they lose an important love relationship. But the difficulty of working through the resulting anxieties seems to be proportional to the fragility or weakness of commitment to the valuational feelings toward cherished long-term goals that could pull the person into the future and thus provide a sense of direction and continuity that could overpower the fragmentation and meaninglessness that would otherwise intensify the anxiety.

How is it that most people usually do work through the loss of love without too much of this schizoid disintegration? On the basis of the above reasoning, it would seem that, when the person is in love, the beloved is serving as the primary locus of unifying values for the self. Why, then, does the self not lose its unity when love is lost?

In some cases, we simply allow the passage of time to heal the wound, and at some point recognize the need to assert ourselves against forces that would overrun us if we remained in such a condition of disarray. But the type of case that is of most interest to us here is the one where, after a sufficient period of grieving, love is reinvested into a new love object. What happens here seems to be that, when the original love object has become completely unavailable, we at first feel a push toward disintegration of the self. But what eventually saves us from the hell of this condition is that our experience with the original love object has taught us *how* to love; we have learned to focus on the person's vulnerability, innocence, and finitude in awe-stricken admiration for her struggle to maintain authenticity and intensity in the face of this finitude. We then realize that these same qualities also have intrinsic value when exemplified in *other* people, if only we could vicariously experience them within a space of empathy so as to fully appreciate them. Finally, we allow ourselves to be open to a space of empathy with some particular admired individual toward whom we can feel this reverence by appreciating in that person, in a particularly intense way, the qualities that are intrinsically valuable in conscious beings generally. In essence, we abstract from the lost love object the qualities that we experience as valuable in conscious beings so that we can later admire those qualities as exemplified elsewhere.

I should emphasize at this point that none of this contradicts the notion that it is precisely the *uniqueness* of an individual that is loved, and not some abstract set of qualities (such as 'temperance,' 'wisdom,' 'courage,' etc.). Also, specific admired qualities may play a role in tearing down our defenses against empathy and the decentering to which we know it can lead. But the *way in which* we appreciate the person's uniqueness—her irreplaceability and unrepeatability in the history of the universe—is by focusing on her potential embattledness and vulnerability in the project of trying to maintain authenticity and sensitivity in the face of the ontological conditions that *all* conscious beings face, simply by virtue of being conscious beings. This ontological endangeredness will manifest itself in the guise of very different kinds of threats for different individuals under specific different circumstances, but the essential effect that it has in allowing us to intensely focus on and appreciate the person's value *qua* unique individual always follows the same dynamic. Since this dynamic is the *way in which* we focus on an individual's uniqueness in order to feel reverent toward it, we can therefore say that we learn to love by learning to directly experience the value of a conscious being *qua* conscious being, and that we can then learn to focus on this same value (which can be abstracted) in other conscious beings as well—provided that we are able to enter into and maintain a space of empathy with them. The preconditions of the possibility of establishing a space of empathy in the first place, of course, are somewhat strenuous, as discussed earlier.

This same process also serves to restore the stability of the ego ideal. When we learn to focus on the fact that the same qualities that are intrinsically valuable in the original love object can also be found in all other conscious beings, we adopt an abstract system of values based on the premise that the existence of conscious beings has intrinsic value, and including all corollaries derivable from this premise. The ego ideal then includes this set of values, and we find that by loving the person in whom we worship this value, we also learn to love the entire value system based on affirming this value.

We can clearly see, then, that the value placed on an 'idealized object image' and the values that guide the ego ideal are *the same values*—the irreducible value of the existence of conscious beings per se. This value needs to be seen as embodied in an example, and intensely appreciated there, so that it *can* be felt strongly enough to *be* the guiding ultimate value of the ego ideal. In fact, what could the definition of a 'healthy' ego ideal be if not one whose ultimate guiding principles are derived from the intrinsic value of certain qualities inherent in conscious beings? And the person with the healthy ego ideal, as defined in this way, will also have a healthy narcissistic self. That is, one will enjoy the image of oneself, not as a ravishingly beautiful or handsome, omnipotent, irreproachable kind of persona, but as a person who embodies the same ideals that the healthy ego loves in a spiritual partner—sensitivity, courageous authenticity, uniqueness, finitude, and moral sincerity. These are the kinds of qualities one will then enjoy having people see in oneself, and will thus enjoy seeing oneself as exhibiting.

The ability to make a positive and reasonable *choice* as to whom one allows oneself to love—rather than remaining involuntarily unable to grieve and let go of a lost or harmful love object—therefore correlates with the health of the ego ideal, with causation working in both directions. Commitment to a set of moral values based on the intrinsic value of all conscious beings allows one to focus more easily on the valuable as it exists in a specific potential love object. At the same time, to transfer love from a lost love object to someone else involves abstracting that which is valuable in both, and this abstraction strengthens the abstract moral standards of the ego ideal.

Since the process of abstraction of the values manifested by one love object enables us eventually to transfer this love to someone else, it is therefore possible to transfer the locus of value appreciation from within a beloved spiritual partner to secondary spiritual partners, or to a subsequent romantic partner, or to human beings generally, merely by focusing intently enough on the appropriate qualities in these other objects. A romantic object, for example, in effect can become a spiritual partner in the full sense, while at the same time offering the opportunity to concretely symbolize this love (for example, through sexual feeling) on a continuing basis. Furthermore, each time other functions of the relationship again tend to eclipse the space of empathy, it is possible to renew the space of empathy by again focusing on the qualities that one learned to admire in a primary spiritual partner. At this point, one has learned to love a romantic partner or even a derivative transcendent object in such a 'reverent' way that this positive value experience is continually intense enough to compensate for the harshness of the ontological predicament. The spreading of primary spiritual partnership to derivative value objects is thus extremely important, even in the case where the primary spiritual partner is not lost, because this same process serves to spread the love for a primary spiritual partner to the love for one's own guiding ideals.

It is beyond our scope here to go into the details of the way such an abstract value system would be worked out. There can be arguments and disagreements among philosophers in this regard. But as soon as the intrinsic value of conscious entities and their well-being is assumed as the basic driving force of a value system, it then becomes possible to designate as a prima facie 'good' whatever serves to facilitate people's self-actualization and well-being. Acts that we 'ought' to perform can then be thought of as acts that would be expected to enhance those ends. There will be conflicts between different ends, since some will enhance the good of some, while others enhance the good of others; resolution of these conflicts are the job of a theory of justice, which I cannot go into at this point, although I have argued elsewhere (e.g., *Coherence and Verification in Ethics* and *Just Results*) that such a theory is possible, given the initial premise just mentioned. Essentially, we ought not to act in ways that would distribute values merely in terms of their exchange value, but also should consider that goods with similar exchange value can have very different amounts of use value depending on the degree of need of their users. A very needy person's life will be enhanced considerably by the acquisition of even small amounts of new goods, whereas a rich person's life will be enhanced only negligibly by acquisition of those same goods, since the rich person's most important needs and wants already have been met. Thus a value system derived simply from a commitment to the value of human beings will not automatically lead to a pure utilitarianism of the kind that counts justice only as an instrumental value. As the reader will easily realize, the working out of a theory of justice, not to mention a good social and political system, will be difficult and complex. My point here is simply that a person inspired by the spreading effect of the spiritual partnership process will be emotionally committed to the project of discovering what is good and right, and then acting to further the objectives that follow from such a value system.

4. Nongraspingness and Gratitude

Many people in our culture (as in most cultures, but especially in ours) obviously have trouble understanding how it is possible to have nonhedonistic experiences of the positive value of being in spite of serious personal misfortunes (both contingent and because of the essentially apocalyptic nature of things). The reason for this misunderstanding is the same as the reason that people have trouble understanding the phenomenon of spiritual partnership itself. Both understandings require taking seriously an aspect of human motivation that is at odds with the ideology of a culture intent on getting people to jump through hoops to attain rewards. Such an ideology requires that people see the main purpose of life as attainment of rewards, and thus interpret their emotions as desiring to see certain objective outcomes in the world, the occurrence of which is supposed to increase happiness, contentment, or a feeling of belonging. To a certain extent, any culture that wants to get the maximum amount of diligent performance out of its members will find it advantageous to teach them that this simplistic hedonism is the meaning of life, so that it can then get them to do the work in order to obtain the benefits. Our culture is more determined to maximize this performance of superior accomplishments than most are; it therefore teaches that obtaining the material and social benefits it can offer is the *only* thing that a normal human being is really motivated to do, and constructs an entire edifice of atomistic-individualist, egoistic-hedonist social scientific theory on this premise, promoting it through its media at every opportunity. People are then so intent on 'proving themselves' that they become all the more egocentric and narcissistic (i.e., image-conscious).

We have already seen why this view of emotions is misguided and ultimately destructive of the meaning of life. It is misguided because consciousness is motivated more strongly and basically by the desire to fully *exist* than by the desire for happiness or pleasure. Many of the feelings that we misconstrue as aiming to achieve happiness and pleasure really aim simply to fully experience themselves. The purpose of the behavior they motivate is neither to achieve any objective outcome in the world, nor to achieve an increase in happiness or contentment, but rather to provide an opportunity to symbolically enact the emotion so that we can feel it as intensely as it desires to be felt.

For example, consider a supervisor who shouts at her office assistant and begins throwing things because, let us say, the assistant forgot to type a document. Did the assistant's failure to type the document *cause* the supervisor's feelings of frustration and anger? Would she have *not* felt frustrated and angry if he had *not* failed to type the document? Ordinary life experience teaches us that, in many cases, the person would have found some other opportunity to express her frustration and anger. She might have been forced to wait for such an opportunity until later that afternoon, when a business client failed to provide some requested item of verification—at which point she would have shouted at the client rather than at the office assistant.

In neither case is her emotion 'about' what she interprets it as being about or 'caused by' what she assumes causes it. If the real object of the emotion were the client's or assistant's failure to do his duty, the appropriate response would be a rational rather than an emotional one; she would use the power available to her in these relationships to negotiate an amenable agreement. Nor would the emotion of anger have failed to occur if its supposed 'cause' had not occurred. Nor is it motivated to achieve what she thinks it is motivated to achieve—that is, getting the client or the assistant to take their responsibilities more seriously. The anger and frustration are about something else entirely, and the occasion of the client's or the assistant's lapse of duty is only an opportunity to symbolize a constellation of emotions that she already felt, or wanted or needed to feel, through the concretely embodied activity of shouting at someone and throwing things.

In this way, she does not *achieve* anything in the sense of increasing her level of happiness or pleasure or eliminating the negative feeling through expressing it. Quite the contrary, she intensifies it and makes it more painful, while in the process sacrificing other hedonistic values (i.e., the pleasurableness of her relationships with coworkers) in order to intensify her negative feeling. What the feeling essentially wants is to be experienced, because it is part of the person's conscious being, for better or worse, and the first motivation of any conscious being is *to be conscious*—to experience its own consciousness with a certain level of intensity. What appears to be a strategy to get what she 'wants' is in reality an attempt through symbolic behavior to *be* what she *is*, to fully experience her consciousness.

The same thing is true for the feeling of love. What love wants first of all is not to possess the beloved, or to benefit her, or even to confirm one's faith that the love is returned. What love first wants is simply to be felt with a certain degree of intensity. But for an emotion to be felt requires symbolization in order to give it a concrete substratum of which it can be predicated as a pattern of change, just as a piece of music needs a physical medium—a vibrating string, air through which the wave is transmitted, etc.—in order for the music to really exist. Further, the symbolization medium must be appropriate to the form of the emotion that is to be symbolized, just as a musical medium must be appropriate to the pattern of the music. A Chopin sonata cannot be embodied in the vibrating snare of a snare drum (although the snare may irritatingly voice one particular note of the sonata each time that note is played in the same room with the snare drum). Similarly, if love is to be symbolized in such a way that the love can be continually felt at the needed level of intensity, the lover must have the opportunity to behold or contemplate the being of the person he loves. And this involves more than beholding her physical body or appearance (since a person is her *pattern of consciousness*, not merely her physical body or appearance). The main purpose of the space of empathy for spiritual partners is that through it we are enabled to perceive the value of being as revealed in the other, provided that we ourselves are in the right frame of mind to do so. (The space of empathy also tends to help us achieve this frame of mind, as explained earlier.)

This is why we crave to be with a loved one often enough to renew our envisionment of the form of her being, so that we can contemplate and appreciate it. For essentially the same reason, when we are away from the person, we must be able to envision her as being *susceptible* to such perception, and thus as still enacting the pattern of consciousness that we observed in the space of empathy. A lover therefore needs to be able to feel faith that the loved one will continue to reciprocate the love in order to be able to feel love for her when she is not present. This desire for reciprocation is already entailed by the need for the feeling, not to attain some outcome or increase its level of pleasure, but rather to find ways to symbolize itself in a concrete context so that it can simply *be*.

The reason this last point becomes important in this context is that we have now seen that psychological dependence on a spiritual partnership must be relinquished, at least for the most part. But the less we are to have access to a space of empathy, the greater must be our faith in its continuing availability. Conversely, the less strong the faith, the more difficult it is to resign ourselves to the spiritual partner's separateness.

To insist on symbiosis in an attempt to always be in an uncompromised space of empathy with a primary spiritual partner would essentially either cause a destructive and clinging stagnation, or it would cause the spiritual partnership to run the typical course of romantic relationships in our culture, which is that the partners depend on each other to meet too great a variety of needs and play too great a variety of roles without specializing in any one of them. In either case, the space of empathy then becomes eroded to a greater or lesser extent.

But if we do allow ourselves to engage in spiritual partnership as such, and not convert it into some more egocentric kind of relationship, then the separateness of the spiritual partner and/or the relative unavailability of a complete space of empathy are things that we must come to terms with at a certain point in the unfolding of the relationship. To accept this separateness requires a good understanding of the nonpossessive nature of the kind of love involved, and the nongrasping nature of motivation generally. It requires that we understand the value of the experience of the spiritual partner as an appreciation of her value for its own sake rather than as a desire to attain some outcome. To maintain such positive regard while forfeiting an all-too-tempting dependence on frequent contact within a complete space of empathy requires an amount of unselfishness that people in an advanced culture would be largely lacking, if it were not for the feeling of gratitude for the good fortune that spiritual partnership has enhanced the meaning of life as a whole so much as to compensate for the misfortune. Nonetheless, the amount of faith needed to get us past this relinquishment can be achieved only after a long history of interaction has proven that, no matter how long the absence, a complete space of empathy will always be accessible.

Timing is therefore crucial in the development of a primary spiritual partnership. If a complete space of empathy is achieved too soon, there is the danger that this space will become symbiotic before the history of the relationship is long enough to warrant the kind of faith needed to relinquish dependent modes of relating. On the other hand, only a history of repeated experiences of renewal of the space of empathy can support the kind of faith needed. And a considerable amount of trust is necessary to motivate both people to drop their defenses for an increasingly full space of empathy in the first place. To relinquish complete engrossedness in empathic contact too soon would tend to erode the space of empathy, but to refuse too long to relinquish it would delay the ultimate spreading effect so that the partners would become clingingly dependent on each other and therefore convert the relationship into a symbiosis. Also, the feelings of upheaval which, as mentioned earlier, are likely to accompany the initial phases of spiritual partnership must be worked through before one can begin to accept the additional hardship of relinquishing complete dependence on a continuous space of empathy.

Spreading-Out of Non-Egoistic and Nonhedonistic Valuation 193

Generally speaking, it would seem that the development of a spiritual partnership must begin with admiration-through-compassion for the other's (admirable yet ontologically embattled, and usually oppositely polarized) form of consciousness. This requires development of mutual trust that neither person will judge, direct, or condemn any consciousness expressed by the other, and at the same time that each will intensely want to explore the other's consciousness with increasing empathy. This in turn leads to establishment of a full space of empathy, in which each person begins to experience a radical transformation of his or her form of being that is possible only through the space of empathy. Then there naturally occurs a transvaluation of one's value system to accord with the new fact that the other's value is now experienced more intensely than one's own, which demands that we overcome the egocentric perspective. This entails working through negative feelings— resentment of the unfair amount of power that the other now has over us, insultedness that we experience her as more important than ourselves, and an instinctive refusal to accept that we cannot obsessively cling to the space of empathy as completely as we would like. Finally, there must be a relinquishment of complete dependence on continuous and uncompromised empathic contact, through a 'letting go' process that leads to the ultimate spreading effect. Then, the tragic sense of life can also be a positive one, because overcoming egocentricity guarantees the continued availability of a direct experience of positive value intense enough to override the negativity of the ontological dilemma (although it is not available as frequently as we might like).

As a result of this entire process, we are then able to experience any given moment of the stream of consciousness in a nongrasping and nonhedonistic way. We thus make ourselves into a relatively pure subject of the experience of the finitude and thus of the uniqueness, fleetingness, and irreplaceability of each event—hence its intrinsic positive value—rather than using each experience as a means to advance the agenda of an egocentric and self-aggrandizing mask (or, alternatively, a mask intent on proving that it is not inferior). We therefore avoid approaching experience with an overall project of getting the *self* to be valued *as an object* (for actual or hypothetical adjudicators). Such a self-objectifying project would lock us into identification with the mask and a corresponding loss of subjectivity or subjective ability to experience things outside ourselves in view of their uniqueness, fleetingness, and irreplaceability. This is why we must overcome the preoccupation with proving our own extrinsic or instrumental value in order to experience life in a tragic but intensely positively valuing way.

All these developments presuppose that experiencing the positive value of the being of a spiritual partner is so meaningful that it counterbalances the sense of meaninglessness that would otherwise result from a tragic view of things. Without this tragic view of things, we could not experience their value fully; but without the experience of spiritual partnership, the tragic view itself, in full authenticity (and without any sugarcoating self-deceptions), would be depressingly negative.

It follows from what has been said so far that the 'ultimate spreading effect' in spiritual partnership cannot be sustained permanently if we continue to resent the necessity to relinquish dependence on completely uncompromised empathic contact, and if we therefore persist in feeling unacceptably deprived by virtue of this sacrifice. A resentful form of consciousness cannot cease 'grasping' always for something a little better than what it has, some more advantageous situation in which the cause for resentment would be lessened. This 'grasping' attitude prevents the grass in one's own pasture from ever appearing quite green enough to fully appreciate it. Instead, the hope for a way of life qualifying as 'good enough' in this sense must always be postponed to an ever-receding future. Thus the full appreciation of present experiencing cannot occur in an intensely positive enough way to counterbalance the ultimate cosmic insult of the ontological predicament. We must feel grateful for what we have if we are to appreciate it fully enough for this purpose. As Melanie Klein says, "One major derivative of the capacity for love is the feeling of gratitude. Gratitude is essential in building up the relation to the good object and underlies also the appreciation of goodness of others and in oneself" (1975, 187).

A feeling of gratitude is also necessary if we are to transcend the egocentric overconcern with our mask. The person who feels ungrateful for empathic contact with a primary spiritual partner is presupposing that he 'deserves' better treatment than he is receiving in life. To see that this is true, imagine the ecstasy in which the Phantom of the Opera would revel if, in spite of his depravity and deformity, he were able to have full sexual relations with his beloved even two or three times in a month. Then imagine the attitude with which a successful and handsome American business executive might justify his philandering on the basis that his wife 'only wants to have sex two or three times a month.' The same experience that is devalued by the arrogant and prideful self-made man of American industry, because he 'deserves' something better, is embraced with joyous euphoria by the humble man who considers himself lucky to have what he does have.

We see, then, that the ability to appreciate the ultimate spreading effect requires a feeling of gratitude, and gratitude in turn presupposes humility. Humility is an acceptance of one's own finitude, but without self-pity. It means accepting that one is only a small and fleeting part of creation, not the whole of creation, not the Creator himself, and not even the most *important* person in the history of the universe. It means accepting our 'lot,' that is, the particular combination of physical and psychological virtues and vices that have been 'allotted' to us and that we ultimately did not create. Although it may be true that we can make ourselves what we choose, within certain limits, it is also true that what we choose is affected in turn by shortcomings we already possessed at the point when we made this choice—shortcomings that we could have prevented only if we could alter still *earlier* choices in life; and these earlier choices were affected in turn by already existing shortcomings that could have been prevented only by still earlier choices. Once we trace the series of choices back to early childhood, or perhaps even to genetically inherited abilities and features, we see that every choice we make is attributable indirectly to an original physical and psychological makeup not of our choosing, in interaction with environmental factors for which we can claim no responsibility. (The effect of the environment may of course depend on how we are predisposed to perceive and respond to it, but these predispositions already result from still earlier interactions between environment and heredity.) It is therefore meaningless to think—and absurd to feel—that we 'deserve' any better lot in life than what we have been granted, regardless of how virtuous, accomplished, or attractive we may be. If this were not true, there would be no reasonable explanation as to why 80 percent of convicted murderers were victims of serious child abuse earlier in life; or why the correlation between poverty and crime in well-controlled studies is one of the strongest and most reliable correlations in all the social sciences, especially if we factor in the effectiveness or ineffectiveness of local welfare programs; or why crime rates in U.S. cities are many times as high as in most other countries where such statistics are kept. (And many other strong correlations could be cited between environmental antecedents and behavioral patterns, as for example I have done more extensively in *Theories of Criminal Justice: A Critical Reappraisal.*) Are these statistical facts merely coincidental, or do they indicate that the kinds of attitudes and personality characteristics people end up having are caused by certain factors in the etiology of character development, including aspects of the social environment with which one interacts during the formative years? Our 'lot' results ultimately from luck, not from some self-created virtuosity.

To have stumbled upon a transcendent value experience is not a reward for merit, but simply a stroke of luck to which no other good fortune can compare, since without it any and all other good fortune would be spoiled by our inability to resolve the ontological dilemma of finite conscious beings. It is therefore natural to feel grateful for such unearned good fortune, provided that we are free of the hubris of the 'self-made man' or the self-important self-aggrandizer who identifies himself with an accomplished or superior mask, foolishly believing that to prove superior and pleasing attributes should earn the right to enjoy extra benefits in the cosmic scheme of things.

In terms of concrete phenomenological experiencing, this feeling of gratitude is present whenever lovers think to themselves some such thought as 'What good luck that not only did this wonderful person enter my life, but, almost coincidentally, and in spite of all my shortcomings, it turned out that this relationship initiated a transcendent value experience and transvaluation of all values.' As Theodore Reik points out in the context of romantic love, a man who has just succeeded in winning the affection of his true love is the humblest of all men. Later in the course of the relationship, the return of his narcissistic pride may again threaten the intensity of his feeling of love. One reason this happens is because (in the terms we are using here) pride makes him defensive and thus destroys the space of empathy. But another reason is that humility is required for gratitude, which in turn is needed in order to appreciate what we have as fully as we need to in order to prevent our own existential anxiety (and defenses against it) from spoiling this feeling of appreciation.

Ultimately, the way to ensure that we do feel this necessary gratitude is to remind ourselves that spiritual partnership comes our way or does not, not through any desert on our part, but simply as a stroke of good luck. In fact, for those who are especially inclined to *hubris* (as most of us in the modern West are), gratitude may be felt more strongly if we can convince ourselves that there is even a sense in which we do *not* 'deserve' the good fortune—that, objectively speaking, our character does embody many defects and incompetencies that would tend to conflict with anyone's feeling of admiration for us. For this purpose, it may be helpful to mentally rehearse the most foolish and embarrassing things we have done in our lives, and then reflect that a spiritual partner can still admire us in spite of these shortcomings (since love includes both admiration and compassion). Nor would she admire us more if we had fewer shortcomings, or if we were to write the Great American Novel or the greatest symphony in history. We know this because we know that, from our own perspective, any failings of the spiritual partner's mask or any worldly accomplishments on her part would neither add to nor subtract from our own feeling of admiration for her, since this admiration is not based on such considerations, but rather on her courage in trying to maintain the authenticity and intensity of her consciousness in spite of the onslaught of life's travails, both contingent and ontological. Her failures in life elicit compassion without diminishing admiration. To the extent that spiritual partnership must be a reciprocal relationship, we can therefore have faith in the forgiving nature of the spiritual partner's admiration-through-compassion. In this sense, the non-egocentric and non-narcissistic experience of spiritual partnership absolves us of all shortcomings in the same way that the forgiveness of a priest would do.

5. From Spiritual Partnership to Generalized Agape

Once we have appreciated the direct view of the extreme positive value of a spiritual partner's form of consciousness by means of the space of empathy, in which our compassion and admiration aim at the person's irreplaceability and uniqueness, that is, her finitude, this appreciation then spreads to other people and things. The intensity of our appreciation for other beings may initially appear, misleadingly, to correspond to certain similarities to a primary spiritual partner. In these early stages, before we have fully understood the phenomenon of spiritual partnership, we may find ourselves feeling more empathic than usual toward individuals who happen to share superficial similarities to the partner, such as forms of body movement, facial characteristics, vocal inflections, or peripheral personality characteristics such as leftist political views or an incisive logical ability.

But the more fully we have understood and experienced the phenomenon in all its facets, the more we understand that these peripheral characteristics are not the essential things we admire in a spiritual partner, but are only associated stimuli that please us because they remind us of the particular form of the conscious being of the spiritual partner—her courageously embattled refusal to give up the authenticity and intensity of her consciousness in the face of alienation, powerlessness, and death. The feeling of love, as Levinas says, aims at her finitude in this respect. Once we understand this, and yet have forced ourselves to relinquish frequent empathic contact (or, in the case of romantic spiritual partnership, to compromise the spiritual partnership aspect of the relationship to make room for other aspects), we are then in need of less direct ways to appreciate her value than by actually being with her in the space of empathy. At this point, we are motivated to turn our attention to the fact that the *essential* thing we most value in a spiritual partner (not her peripheral appearances)—namely, her embattled authenticity in the context of finitude—is present to a greater or lesser extent in all other people. The main reason we chose the particular person we did as a spiritual partner was not merely that she embodied this ideal so much more than others, or that she shared certain personal affinities with us that allowed the space of empathy to develop. As important as these factors may be, the crucial factor was that, for these reasons or others, she was willing to drop her defenses at least enough to make the beauty of her form of being *completely visible* to us. To a greater or lesser extent, a similar kind of beauty is also present in other conscious beings, but is not as visible to us because their defenses (both normal and neurotic) wall us out, so that we cannot get a clear view of their authenticity-in-the-face-of-finitude. Since love aims at the person in this finitude, in the form of admiration and compassion for embattled authenticity, we are initially unable to love most people fully because this view is hidden from us. But we know intellectually that they do embody this valuable phenomenon, and we have also had a chance to view the phenomenon in the person of the spiritual partner. We are now therefore more likely to focus on this phenomenon in others.

It is much easier to see something when (1) we have had a chance to view it before; (2) we know what we are looking for; (3) we know that it is there; and (4) we are motivated to look for it. With regard to the embattled finitude of people other than a primary spiritual partner, our repeated experiences with the spiritual partner in the space of empathy have led us to meet the first three of these conditions, and the ultimate spreading effect causes us to meet the fourth one.

The way we feel toward people when we view them from this perspective is similar to what Christians call agape, but with a slight difference of emphasis. In Christian agape, the emphasis is more on behaving morally toward people than on emotionally intensifying the experience of love for them. Judging from their behavior, the vast majority of Christians do not seem to feel agape with the emotional strength that a spiritual partner does once the ultimate spreading effect has occurred. Perhaps saints or holy men have felt it this strongly. This is not an indictment of the central insight of Christianity, as the next chapter will discuss. As Gandhi remarked, Christianity must be a great religion in order to have survived the behavior of its adherents.

When we do empathize with people generally to the extent that the spreading effect facilitates, we are then able to partially gratify the need for spiritual partnership in our concrete relations with them. We find ourselves lowering defenses in the attempt to establish at least a partial space of empathy with many of the people with whom we interact. Since we have also abandoned much of our commitment to the egocentric mask in learning humility and gratitude, we are able to lower defenses more easily because we feel less competitive and care less about the pragmatic consequences to our egocentric project if lowering defenses should make us vulnerable to hostile and self-serving attacks on the part of others. On the other hand, we still must preserve defenses to a certain extent, because if we invite hostility and self-serving attacks, the other's attacking posture erodes the space of empathy—which would be counterproductive—and the hostility and self-servingness eclipse our view of the positively valuable aspect of the other's conscious being in terms of which the person is similar to a primary spiritual partner. Granted this qualification, we are still able and willing to appreciate the positive value of others to a much greater extent than we could if the experience of a spiritual partner, combined with the relinquishment of symbiosis, had not led to this spreading effect.

This agapistic effect also leads to concrete action in the service of an abstract value system built up from the initial premise that the conscious existence of human beings has intrinsic value and thus ought to be enhanced and facilitated rather than thwarted, perverted, or destroyed. The reason we are emotionally committed to useful action in this concrete moral arena is that we now emotionally affirm moral ideals rather than merely intellectually cognizing them. A good part of the emotional investment in the primary transcendent object now has been transferred to these abstract values because they are based on the concrete feeling of love toward an intrinsically valued conscious being other than ourselves, and this love has now spread to all other conscious beings. Moreover, we are driven with an emotional intensity that is derivative from the intensity of our love for the primary spiritual partner, or transcendent value object, because this love has discovered its need to find other avenues through which to manifest itself than through a smothering symbiosis with the primary transcendent object. The abstract value system is now emotionally charged because in it we love the values that have been abstracted from that which we love in a primary transcendent object, and useful action in the service of this value system is a concrete way to symbolize this feeling of love through embodied action.

5

The Interdependence of Courage and Compassion

We began with the observation that it is contrary to the nature of conscious beings, once they become intelligent enough to understand the implications of their own impending death and relative powerlessness, to accept these facts or reconcile themselves to them. It is obvious throughout history that intelligent beings will resort routinely to prodigious feats of irrationality, neurosis, erosion of consciousness, repression of important feelings, violence, or denial of obvious facts if such maneuvers are necessary to maintain unconsciousness of the fact of one's own finitude. The entire history of human thought processes, cultures, and emotional orientations is largely a history of the various convolutions and permutations of attitudes and beliefs needed to maintain the illusion of immortality and to deny the reality of personal powerlessness and insignificance in the ultimate scheme of things.

But when the intense appreciation of positive value is made possible by the phenomenon of transcendent value experience through the spiritual partnership process, the illusion can be abandoned with cheerful equanimity. If life offers an intensely positive enough experience—not in the sense of happiness and pleasure, but in the sense of quasi-aesthetic and inspirational awe—then it is possible to face the outrageously tragic facts of life without denial, self-deception, or complicated metaphysical fantasies. Life becomes more than worthy enough to compensate for the misfortune of death, powerlessness, and alienation.

Consider, for example, our modern Western ideology, which is necessitated by belief in a radically free will—that is, a will whose nature presumably neither directly nor indirectly results from the causal influence of environmental or hereditary factors that were originally beyond the person's control. This belief in free will, necessitated by a religious system intent on denying the ultimate reality of evil, leads to a morality and sociopolitical philosophy based on the priority of guilt, blame, and retribution, rather than simply doing what is beneficial and distributively fair; it thus leads to a *laissez faire*, 'let them pull themselves up by their bootstraps' attitude that justifies blaming the victim on the basis that life histories result from the exercise of free will rather than from victimization by unlucky circumstances that cause people to develop inadequate skills or undesirable personality characteristics.

This retributive, victim-blaming outlook results from the belief in an extreme degree of free will in human character development, and the belief in free will in turn is required to make possible a dogmatic, self-deceptive form of religion. The reason is that, in order to believe that an all-good and all-powerful deity could create a universe as permeated with evil, pain, and suffering as this one is, we must reconcile these ills with the deity's power and goodness. Ultimately, such a reconciliation must posit that the existence of such ills is needed in order that humans have the opportunity to exercise free will by choosing how to respond to evil—by allowing our nature to be corrupted by it, or by learning from it to strengthen and ennoble our character (or so the conventional argument goes).

This chapter will discuss just a few of the convolutions of logic needed to deny the reality of genuine, irreducible evil in the ultimate scheme of things—more specifically, the reality of our own death, powerlessness, and alienation. For those who have not substantially undergone the inspirational positive-value experience resulting from the extended spiritual partnership process, including the spreading effect, the realization that the problem of evil cannot be logically reconciled with literalistic or dogmatic approaches to religion is likely to seem depressing, anxiety-provoking, or even unacceptable. But once we have been completely compensated for the misfortune of finitude—as an acute and direct experience of the extreme positive value of a being other than ourselves together with the results of the spreading effect can ultimately allow us to be compensated—then it is no longer necessary to deny the reality of this misfortune. Even if a primary spiritual partner has been lost, the transcendent value experience resulting from the entire spreading effect allows us to face these misfortunes cheerfully and with calm resolution. It no longer need pressure us either to distort our entire rational and emotional make-up, or on the other hand to suffer from permanent, inconsolate existential anxiety. The way will then be cleared for a new kind of value system, a new morality, and a new sociopolitical outlook—an outlook based on compassion rather than blame, collective opportunity enhancing rather than rugged individualism, genuine humility rather than the false modesty of the egocentric and prideful self-made man or woman, forgiveness rather than hatred, gratitude rather than envy, distributive fairness rather than a theory of justice based on a doctrine of 'desert' or retribution for its own sake, and love for others rather than ego gratification through materialistic achievement and narcissistic flamboyance.

Ironically, and by no means coincidentally, this is the very change in moral outlook that Christianity tried but failed to achieve in Western culture. It is no coincidence, because Christianity is the example *par excellence* of a religion that tried to create an extreme experience of positive value through a concrete feeling of love for a specific being other than oneself. It facilitated both admiration for the courageous authenticity of Christ and compassion for his embattledness and suffering. It promoted humility and gratitude for an *unearned* and thus purely fortuitous absolution, rather than smug complacence and self-congratulation for having achieved one's own salvation. It emphasized above all forgiveness of the ignorant and wicked through an empathic understanding that (in modern terms) we would have been exactly like them if we had had the exact same environment and heredity as they (if we had 'walked in their shoes'). It emphasized that no amount of happiness and pleasure (i.e., material benefits) could ever be enough to compensate us for the tragedy of finitude, and that these benefits therefore could not constitute the meaning of life. It taught that no one *merits* salvation any more than anyone else, and that it is thus better to believe in a merciful than a just deity. And all these attitude changes were to be effected by means of an emotional experience of love for a being other than oneself that would be so intense as to inspire an awe-stricken appreciation, a spontaneous gratitude, and a tearing down of egocentricity, so that the anxiety, frustration, aggression, and neurosis stemming from the dread of death and from the insignificance of powerlessness and alienation would naturally drop away.

The problem, however, was the same as with all popularized religions. In order to get people to engage in such an intense love for a being other than themselves, it had to get them to believe in a grand metaphysical system, so that they could gratify their egocentricity (for example, the desire for personal immortality) rather than abandoning it. The being whom they were supposed to love was too remote and ethereal. In order to love him, they had to believe, not that he had once existed, but that he literally still existed; that he would not only console them for their problems, but that he would actually solve the problems; that he would not just make life valuable enough to be worth dying for, but that he would eliminate death itself. In short, he became inseparably connected to the age-old omnipotent benefactor of all self-deceptive myths that invite the believer to believe that whatever we wish were true, literally is true. The believer then distorts thinking and feeling in general with all the convoluted defenses discussed in our first chapter, loses the sense of self-honesty, and therefore becomes incapable of the authentic and intense love needed for transformation and consolation. At this point, doctrinal Christianity thus becomes just another self-deceptive system of metaphysics that both erodes Christianity as a religion based on the concrete experience of love and compassion, and at the same time allows people to feel that these direct and intense value experiences are not *necessary* in order to compensate for the brutality of the ontological predicament—a predicament which at that point has been systematically denied by the self-deceptive metaphysics. This is why, as Randall Auxier (1990) explains, Dewey thought that the experiential component of religion should be separated from its doctrinal or dogmatic component, and that 'Religion' is the worst obstacle in the way of 'religious experience.'

The metaphysics and morality of self-deceptive, fundamentalist religions thus fit together into a coherent scheme, whose ultimate purpose is to deny one's own finitude and relative powerlessness in the ultimate scheme of things. From the metaphysical perspective, the belief in free will is needed to explain why an all-good and all-powerful deity would allow so much evil to exist in the world. And from the ethical perspective, this same belief in free will buttresses a retributive, victim-blaming moral outlook in which we condemn the wicked rather than feeling compassion for them in their psychic dysfunction. At the same time, practitioners of this form of religion do not *need* to feel compassion as a way to provide an intense experience of positive value (through direct appreciation of the finitude, vulnerability, and irreplaceability of other conscious beings) in order to override the negativity of the ontological predicament; they feel no such need because the self-deceptive form of religion simply denies the reality of the predicament by insuring immortality and the restoration of justice at the end of time. The belief that people with psychological or social problems deserve to be blamed and condemned helps to explain why there is evil in the universe, and also excuses us for not feeling compassion for such people, while nothing is lost by *not* feeling compassion, since no intense value experience is needed to overcome the harshness of finitude (which has been neatly denied). Thus a viciously competitive and cutthroat socioeconomic system is justified, as a system of rewards and punishments, and the self-deceptive belief that things will be better in the afterlife enables us to numb ourselves to the bleakness of the all-pervasive interpersonal alienation this system causes. No one piece of this ethical-metaphysical mosaic can be abandoned without causing its entire fabric to disintegrate.

The spiritual outcomes resulting from the experience of transcendent value through spiritual partnership, by contrast, render *all* the pieces of this age-old mosaic simply *unnecessary*. From the ethical perspective, retribution need not interfere with a constructive attitude of compassion, and the limitations of what can be accomplished in our short life here below need not erase the value of acting beneficially. Thus also the recognition that human psychology is essentially deterministic not only need not render life meaningless, but on the contrary facilitates the feeling of compassion—hence the intense appreciation of the value of conscious beings. The direct experience of this value both establishes the meaning and value of human existence, and at the same time completely compensates us for the negativity of our dilemma, since through empathy with valued beings we are able to subjectively experience this value with full intensity, as discussed at the end of chapter 2 above.

The present chapter will examine the logic of these two contrasting outlooks: on the one hand, forms of religion that operate by *denying* the harshness of the ontological dilemma, regardless of how many distortions of logic are needed to do so; and on the other hand, those that operate by creating an intense experience of positive value through compassion for conscious beings other than ourselves. We shall then see how easily the second of these two options, once it is realized, completely removes the need for the first.

1. The Problem of Evil and the Morality of Blame

In contrasting self-deceptive and non-self-deceptive forms of religion, it is useful to consider in a little more detail than we did at the outset the vast matrix of philosophical theories and assumptions needed to justify the self-deceptive worldview—that is, the kind of worldview that operates essentially by denying the ultimate reality of finitude. Such denial systems inevitably lead sooner or later to the 'problem of evil,' whose solution in turn requires an even more elaborate system of distorted reasoning and a rejection of even more obvious everyday realities. The essence of this problem is usually framed in terms of the following formula:

> God is all-good.
> God is all-powerful.
> There is evil.

The problem of evil as usually discussed in the philosophy of religion can be summarized with this apparent contradiction, but it is really much simpler than the volumes of logical intricacies on the subject would lead us to believe. The problem of evil, in essence, inevitably results from the fact that the original purpose of the self-deceptive kind of religion—dating virtually to the apes—*was precisely to deny the existence* of those evils which are so unpalatable that we cannot reconcile ourselves to them. Yet at the same time it is empirically obvious that such evils still do exist. Thus it becomes 'paradoxical' that what we have convinced ourselves *cannot* exist, *does* exist after all. On the level of reality, we must deal with evil every day in order to survive, while at the same time the meaning and purpose of survival are defined at a level of fantasy in which these everyday realities can have no relevance, and therefore no purpose.

For example, at the level of everyday reality, we believe that the preservation of human life is the most important of all intrinsic values. Yet our value system itself is supposedly based on a religious doctrine that denies the ultimate reality of death, maintaining, for example, that soldiers who die in war do not really die, but merely migrate to a metaphysical realm in which they live on eternally. How, then, can the death of a soldier—which is not even a real death at all—be considered *intrinsically* undesirable, rather than a mere pragmatic inconvenience to his family, his friends, and the economic system? After all, that which is intrinsically valuable—the soldier's life—presumably has not been destroyed. In short, how can that which has no reality, death, be considered an evil? But if not an evil, why try to prevent it? The suicide terrorists of al Qaeda are merely the reductio ad absurdum of this denial of the reality of death, which is correlative with the failure to value life.

The same question arises with regard to all other intrinsic values. We observe that, in the empirical realm of everyday reality, the wicked often flourish while the good suffer. But we know that an all-good deity would not *wish* such injustice to exist, and an all-powerful deity would *know how* to prevent it. We must therefore believe that any injustice that we humans are unable to prevent, through sincere effort and hard work, will be exactly compensated for in the afterlife. But if all injustice is to be eradicated in the hereafter, then there is not much point in our efforts to eradicate it here and now. Here again, that which in the ultimate scheme of things has no reality—in this case, injustice—also cannot really be an evil. In every case, it turns out that the meaning of life is *erased* precisely by the same metaphysical system that was supposed to give life meaning. If death is not really death, then what point is there in saving a life? If injustice is to be cancelled, why work so hard to fight it?

The classic Judeo-Christian solution to the problem of evil (and one also finds parallels to it in the Muslim, Hindu, ancient African, and most other theistic religions) is that God, in order to create the greatest possible amount of good, needed also to create the greatest possible *variety* of goods. It would not have been so good simply to create one very good entity—say, an angel—and then proceed to exactly duplicate this one being millions of times, thus bringing forth a universe that would consist of a vast array of precise duplications of this one being. Much better to create a variety of good things, even though this entailed creating both greater goods (for example, angels) and lesser goods (for example, the tsetse fly). This balancing act became precarious when the well-being of some of the lesser goods conflicted with each other; yet God calculated that more good would result from the existence of these conflicting goods than if he were to deny one or the other of them the opportunity to exist. And it is clearly better to have the opportunity to exist, despite whatever pain and suffering might arise from this unavoidable balancing act, than never to exist at all—especially if we assume that God rectifies the resulting injustices in the hereafter.

But this solution, posed in such a simple form, cannot easily withstand the numerous counterexamples to which it is subject, and therefore it must be dressed up a little. The tsetse fly is such a lowly, insignificant being that no humane and rational God—not to mention an all-good, all-powerful one—could possibly think that the existence of this nearly worthless insect (whose only biological purpose seems to be to cause sleeping sickness in humans) could ever outweigh in value the life of even one conscious human being, let alone thousands. Similarly, it is beyond credibility that an omniscient deity could not have calculated a way to avoid a tidal wave that destroys an entire city—especially if He has the power to create and destroy things at will. Why not destroy the tidal wave in the nick of time, or create some impediment to its striking—or at least warn the people that it is on its way?

To see clearly why free will becomes so indispensable to the solution to this problem, consider what is needed to explain the most troubling of all types of evil—the suffering and death of innocent children. Here we must grapple not only with a death that surely could have been prevented by an omnipotent deity, but indeed with the snuffing out of a just-emerging potential before it even reaches the fruition of its essential nature. It is for this very reason—because the child has not yet attained the age of reason and cannot be held responsible as a moral agent—that St. Augustine, in the official solution to the problem of evil accepted by the Catholic and most other Christian churches (*On Free Choice of the Will*), maintains that the innocent's death is not really an evil. Since the child has not attained the age of reason, it is not an actually existing, rational being, and therefore is not really a moral agent. According to Augustine, the purpose of such apparent evils as pain and suffering is to allow man to exercise his free will by choosing to either morally improve himself or become worse as a result of it. With regard to the suffering of innocents, the improvement of the parents is the important outcome to be accomplished. Augustine bears quoting in detail on this point:

> But the objection that ignorant men usually raise against this argument concerns the death of little children, and the bodily sufferings with which we have often seen children afflicted. They say, 'Why need the child have been born, since he died before he did anything of merit in life? How will he be judged in the judgment to come, since, having neither acted rightly nor sinned, he has no place, either among the just or among the sinners?'
>
> My answer to these men is as follows: In view of the encompassing network of the universe and the whole creation—a network that is perfectly ordered in time and place, where not even one leaf of a tree is superfluous—it is not possible to create a superfluous man. What is clearly superfluous, however, is any inquiry into the reward of someone who has merited nothing. There is no need to fear that there could be a neutral condition between right action and sin without there being a neutral sentence by the Judge between reward and punishment. . . .
>
> Because of their age, they say, children have committed no sins (assuming that their souls have not committed sin before animating their bodies). Hence they ask: 'What evil have they done that they should suffer so?' But what reason is there to believe that anyone should be rewarded for innocence before he could do harm? Since God works some good by correcting adults tortured by the sickness and death of children who are dear to them, why should this suffering not occur? When the sufferings of children are over, it will be as if they had never occurred for those who suffered. (1964, 139–40)

Note that the correction of the parents is the purpose of the suffering of the child. Augustine continues,

> Either the adults on whose account the sufferings occurred will become better, if they are reformed by temporal troubles and choose to live rightly, or else, if because of the hardships of this life they are unwilling to turn their desire toward eternal life, they will have no excuse when they are punished in the judgment to come. Moreover, who knows what faith is practiced or what pity is tested when these children's sufferings break down the hardness of parents? (140)

Augustine then compares this problem with the problem of the suffering of lower animals:

> These superficial questioners and careless students of such issues, these loquacious sophists, are also in the habit of harassing the faith of the less learned even over the sufferings of dumb beasts by saying, 'What evil have beasts done that they should suffer such great hardships? . . .' They say and think this because they think wickedly about these problems. . . . The pain that beasts feel shows the strength of their souls, a strength admirable and praiseworthy in their own class. . . . What else is this pain except a sense of resistance to division or corruption? . . . We would not see how strong was the desire for unity in lower animate creatures were it not for the pain suffered by beasts. (141)

In essence, Augustine's position is that the punishment of a child is inflicted in order to offer the parents an opportunity to change their moral and religious attitudes. The question naturally arises as to whether an omnipotent and omniscient god is not capable of calculating some more humane method of producing the desired effect in the attitudes of the parents, without resorting to the infliction of torture and death on an innocent child. Clearly, it is possible for people to develop the right attitudes without undergoing this particular kind of suffering, because we see that there are many people on whom God chooses *not* to inflict the suffering and death of a child. Why does God not cause the attitudes of the parents of the child in question to change in some way similar to the way He causes the attitudes of those other people to become correct, rather than causing it by means of the suffering and death of the child? Clearly, this would be possible for an omnipotent god.

But the answer, of course, is that it cannot suffice for God simply to *cause* people to develop the right attitudes. They must develop them for themselves through the exercise of their free will. The reason is that one of the intermediate types of goods that God decided to create, when He was in the process of creating as great as possible a variety of good things, was precisely the existence of beings with free will. This means that their personality makeup must not completely result either directly or indirectly from the causal influence of any environmental or hereditary factors over which they had no control. Their personality makeup must be free from causation by any combination of factors that are ultimately beyond their control, so that they can freely will themselves to be whatever kind of people they end up being. Only in this way does it become possible for God to justly pass moral judgment on them, rewarding the good and punishing the wicked. Without free will, morality itself (i.e., Augustine's completely retributive notion of morality, whose ultimate purpose is that everyone get what they deserve) would be impossible. Without the suffering of innocents, then, free will would not be possible in the moral correction of the parents involved, and without free will there could be no good or evil as far as human actions are concerned—again, defining 'good' and 'evil' in terms of a completely retributive system of ethics, in which "the ugliness of sin is never without the beauty of punishment" (123).

Notice that this notion of free will would *not* be necessary to make morality possible if we were talking about a nonretributive system of morality. And there are many such systems. For example, John Rawls's theory of *distributive* justice (as opposed to retributive justice) would prescribe that we distribute opportunities and benefits in a fair way, without attributing any *intrinsic* value to what anyone 'deserves' in the sense of a proportion between the goodness of their personality or actions and the rewards or punishments they receive (although such a proportion may *sometimes* have *instrumental* value in a Rawlsian-type justice system—for example, for purposes of deterrence or rehabilitation). A purely distributive rather than retributive concept of fairness would refer only to the value of allowing everyone to have a relatively equal chance to actualize potential and obtain benefits, without reference to any moral judgment of the people themselves (for further elaboration, see my *Just Results*). Another quite different nonretributive moral system is utilitarianism, which simply prescribes that we should do whatever is necessary to maximize human well-being, and minimize the suffering of humans and other conscious beings, again without regard to what anyone 'deserves.' Still another nonretributive system is the communitarianism of Muslim thinkers like Ibn Khaldoun, who advocated very strict punishments for criminals even though he believed in complete determinism—not because he thought the criminals 'deserved' harsh punishments (since their characters were predetermined by environment and heredity), but rather because the criminal justice system would be doing them a favor by making it easier for them to make the right choices; it is easier to make the right choice when we know that the wrong choice might lead to decapitation or loss of a hand. Most communitarians do not believe in the Draconian measures advocated by Ibn Khaldoun, but they do emphasize that the community produces its individuals and causes them to have the personalities they have, thus the community should take responsibility to provide the opportunities and resources needed for people to develop into good, well-functioning and morally positive individuals—which of course is very different from indoctrinating and brainwashing people. For example, since the U.S. society currently produces so many more people who are prone to commit crimes than other societies do, we should take the responsibility to find out why we are failing to produce more harmonious personality structures in our citizens and to make the necessary social and economic changes, such as making educational resources more equitably available, rather than merely blaming those who (much more frequently than in other cultures) turn out to be criminals.

The moral systems just mentioned are just a few of the many nonretributive moral systems that are theoretically possible. Such systems do not refrain from punishing criminals when necessary and demanding that people accept the consequences of their actions when this demand serves a purpose, but they have no need to blame and punish merely for the sake of giving people what they 'deserve.' My point in bringing up these possibilities at this point is to show that Augustine's reasoning holds up only if we assume (1) that God believes in a purely retributive system of morality, as opposed to the many other moral systems available; and (2) that such a thing as 'free will' is both logically possible and morally valuable. Only on these assumptions can any moral good depend on the existence of free will in humans.

The existence of pain, suffering, and death in cases where they could have been avoided by an omniscient, omnipotent deity would be completely nonsensical without the postulation of human free will. But if free will has any value—even as an intermediate good—then the being who possesses this free will must have opportunities to exercise it. The playing out of situations involving pain and tragedy constitute these opportunities. Hence the existence of evil—at least so goes the traditional solution.

The empirical claim that many instances of pain and tragedy seem to play no role in anyone's choice between good and evil will simply be denied out of hand by the dogmatic believer. And all of this could perhaps be maintained without self-contradiction, if the will really were as free as Augustine wants to maintain. Unfortunately, however, such a notion of free will not only conflicts with readily observable facts in the social sciences (as I have discussed more fully in the works cited earlier); worse still, the notion of contra-causally free will itself is a logical impossibility, as can easily be shown by means of a simple logical analysis. The next section will discuss this issue.

2. Fallacies in the Morality of Blame

The doctrine of a contra-causally free will is the fortress and the citadel of self-deceptive and fundamentalist forms of religion. In one stroke it makes possible not only a belief in personal immortality, but also a sense of self-importance and a virtually unlimited power to create ourselves as whatever we please, without any interference from the bothersome principles of psychology or physics. Free will is, as we have seen, the logical foundation for a religion in which the personal ego is invulnerable to death, master of its fate, and the absolute center of all moral value. It solves the problem of evil, explains the suffering of innocents, eliminates all injustice from the ultimate scheme of things, insures an afterlife that is not only a continuation but a vast improvement on the present one, and legitimates the condemnation, ostracization, and destruction of the wicked enemies of all the foregoing beliefs. No wonder that Western civilization has employed armies of philosophers sizable enough to rival the Crusades to argue and defend such a gratifying doctrine! There seem to be no comparable armies of philosophers to argue for the doctrine of psychological determinism. Perhaps determinism's threat to their own belief in personal immortality works to undermine their morale.

If there were such an army, they would join Ibn Sina, Ibn Khaldun, J. J. C. Smart, and a few other overwhelmingly outnumbered individuals who have defended arguments like the following one: In order to be attributed to me, a choice must result from my character—from the kind of person I am. But this raises the further question as to whether the kind of person I am at the point when I make this choice is itself brought about by previous causal influences (including the influence of previous choices I may have made), or whether on the contrary it results merely from nowhere, from mere chance or luck. If my character results from mere luck, then it does not result from any choice or action on my part, and therefore I cannot be blamed for it any more than if it were caused by the laws of physics. The only way that my character can be the result of my free will is if it results from previous choices I have made. But, in the case of each of these previous choices, the question arises as to whether the choice results from *previous causal factors beyond my control*, or from the *previous structure of my character*, or merely from *previous luck*. Of course, it is obvious that the only way the choice in question can result from my free will is if it results from *the previous structure of my character*, and the only way this previous character structure could avoid being predetermined by factors beyond my control would be if it had resulted from *previous choices* I had made at some still earlier time in my life. But, in the case of each of these previous choices, the question still arises as to whether the choice resulted from previous causal factors beyond my control, or from the previous structure of my character, or merely from luck or chance. Again, the only way the choice in question can result from my free will is if it results from the previous structure of my character, and the only way this previous character structure could avoid already having been predetermined by factors beyond my control would be if it had resulted from still earlier choices on my part. But, here again, whether these previous choices were free or not depends on whether they resulted from the structure of my character at the time when I made them, and whether my character at that time in turn resulted from still earlier choices I had made rather than resulting only from previous causal factors beyond my control, or perhaps merely from luck (perhaps an electron accidentally strayed from its statistically determined orbit). But, here again, whether each of these still-earlier choices is attributable to a character structure that is free of determination by factors beyond my control (including random chance or luck of the kind just mentioned) depends in turn on whether my character structure at the point when I made the choice in question was attributable to still earlier choices on my part rather than resulting only from previous causal factors or merely from random-chance occurrences, since in these cases it would still result from factors beyond my control.

Ultimately, the only way any of these choices can be free is if they can be traced sooner or later to some earlier choice which itself was free from determination by factors beyond my control. And the only way *that* choice could be free is if it could be traced to some still earlier choice that was free from determination by factors which at *that* point were beyond my control. But if we continue tracing backward through my personal history the sequence in which each choice results from the structure of my character at that time, which results in turn from still earlier choices on my part, and so forth, we can ultimately trace this whole series back to the first moment at which I existed as a decision-making entity. At that point in time, whatever choice I made may possibly have resulted from the character that I possessed at that time, but this character in turn could have resulted only from factors *beyond my control*. It could not have resulted from any previous choices on my part, because I did not yet exist as a decision-making entity prior to the time in question. But if my character at the first moment of my existence resulted from the influence of factors beyond my control, then any choice I made at that time results from the influence of these same factors. And any subsequent character development that results from any such choice therefore also indirectly results from the influence of these same factors beyond my control, in combination with whatever new factors beyond my control may subsequently present themselves throughout the course of my life and development.

For example, if I am an evil person because I chose not to go to church as a young man, then this choice must have resulted from the fact that I was already somewhat evil at that point. But why was I evil at that point? Perhaps because I maliciously and willfully chose not to have respect for my parents and therefore did not listen to them when they told me to go to church. But why did I not respect my parents? Perhaps because I had previously chosen to court the favor of an antisocial peer group who did not care for boys who respected their parents. But why did I choose to court such a peer group? Because I lacked self-esteem, social grace, or intelligence, and so forth. Ultimately, every choice I made resulted from some earlier choice, tracing all the way back to the time I made the first choice in the series. So if that first choice was not free, then neither were any of the others that ultimately resulted from it, in interaction with environmental influences to which I either did or did not choose to be subjected. (Either way, the subsequent choices can be no more free than the prior ones from which they result.) But if the first choice in the series resulted only from factors beyond my control (because there were no previous choices on my part from which they could have resulted), then *it* was not free. Thus, neither are any of the subsequent ones. So every choice I have ever made is indirectly but completely determined by factors beyond my control. (This point is discussed with more detail and technical precision in my *Coherence and Verification in Ethics*.)

If spiritual partnership leads to a sustainable transcendent value experience capable of meeting religious needs, so that none of the self-deceptions of the elaborate metaphysics developed by dogmatic belief systems were needed, then it should also become easy to cast a cold and logical eye on the notion of free will that props them up. For example, no one can raise to someone who has experienced spiritual partnership the emotionally charged objection that 'without free will life would have no meaning.' Once having directly experienced the extreme positive value of being as instanced in a spiritual partner, we know that to be an intensely conscious being has irreducible intrinsic value, and that this value remains regardless of whether she is what she is because the laws of physics and of psychology have caused her to be that way, or whether she created herself without help from the laws of physics and psychology. It is true that part of her beauty consists in the ability to train and condition herself through stoic virtue to become whatever she initially chooses to become. But this does not entail that the initial choice was not conditioned by some still earlier causal and/or random chance factors, such as genetic influences on the chemical structure of her brain or environmental influences that may have caused her to choose to become an athlete, a clown, or a ballerina. Nor does it necessarily preclude that the physical and psychological traits needed to carry through with a ballerina's training might have been predetermined by social, economic, genetic, and family-dynamic factors that influenced certain details of her personality development. Englishmen are Protestants and Arabs are Muslims, not because of free will, but because their environments caused them to become the kinds of persons who would choose in those particular ways. Imagine what an unlikely coincidence it would be if almost all Arabs were Muslims and almost all Englishmen were Protestants, not because of environmental influences but because they chose it purely out of 'free will!' But wouldn't it also be just as unlikely a coincidence if ten times as many Americans were to commit violent crimes as in most other countries, not because of systematic social problems in America, but because ten times as many people as elsewhere just happened to freely choose to do so?

But the fact that a spiritual partner may ultimately have been psychologically predetermined to become the kind of person she is, through a continual process of interaction with and learning from her environment in accordance with hereditary talents and predispositions, does not detract in the least from her intrinsic value as a conscious and sensitive being. Indeed, her inability to escape the limitations imposed by her heredity and earlier environment (if indeed personality is predetermined by such factors) would only increase our compassion for her in this added finitude and vulnerability, and thus also our admiration for her courageous authenticity in the face of this additional limitation of her power and even more insulting brutality of the apocalyptic scheme of things that confronts us all in the form of the ontological dilemma of our own finitude.

The objection that life would lack meaning without free will makes sense, if at all, only from the egocentric perspective of someone who has not yet fully faced up to the ontological dilemma in a way free of sugarcoated metaphysical doctrines. From the egocentric perspective, we cannot accept the limitation on our own power constituted by a psychological determinism, any more than we can accept the limitation that we must die. Death, power limitation, and the notion that we as individuals are relatively inconsequential in the ultimate scheme of things tend to erode our sense of the value of life because they spoil our frame of mind so sourly that we become unable to appreciate the value of being a conscious being. But, from the standpoint of the experience of the *other's* intrinsic value—that is, a spiritual partner's intrinsic value—the recognition of all these aspects of her finitude only intensifies our experience of her value, because we focus on her fleetingness and uniqueness, therefore her irreplaceability.

And the fact that we experience her as having this much value despite all limitations on her power confirms that conscious beings per se have value irrespective of limitations on their power. It is thus absurd to raise as an objection against psychological determinism that conscious beings would have no value if their nature is ultimately predetermined by luck (for example, the luck of the hereditary draw) and/or by causal factors beyond their control. What makes the notion that life would lack value without free will seem more compelling than it really is? The reason is that, if the doctrine of free will is needed to buttress a belief in personal immortality, then any objection against determinism becomes attractive even though it really consists only of little more than an irrational appeal to emotion.

As another example of the irrational lengths to which otherwise intelligent people will go when their personal immortality is at stake, consider the objection that a learned and usually astute philosopher once raised against me on this point. He said that, if I asserted that there is no free will, then I must believe that my denial of free will is a true statement. But if determinism were true, he said, then my belief in determinism would be caused, not by the truth of my belief, but rather by the random movement of electrons and protons in the physicochemical reactions in my brain. Therefore, if my belief in determinism is caused by such factors, then this belief itself cannot be true.

Of course, the same reasoning could be used to prove that no conclusion reached in a logical analysis carried out by a computer could possibly be true, since it is well known that the action of computers is determined by the causal processes of physics, and that no computer has free will. It is incomprehensible that such a simple objection to this argument could be missed by a distinguished professor of philosophy who has spent his life publishing important books and articles, unless his personal immortality were at stake in the outcome of the discussion. (Nor do I endorse the 'computational' approach to the philosophy of mind by using this example, as might be charged by someone emotionally motivated to turn my argument into a straw man. The point is simply that, if the deterministic causation of a system were to imply the invalidity of the conclusions it reaches, then the conclusions reached by a computer would always be invalid—which, obviously, they are not.)

Many philosophers have posed the following argument for free will: If determinism were true, then it should be possible in principle to predict in advance what someone is going to do, given enough knowledge of the person's heredity, previous environmental influences, and the laws of physics and psychology. But if we had complete knowledge of all such information, and on this basis predicted that the person would, say, rob a bank, then the person could simply refrain from robbing the bank in order to prove our prediction wrong. This assumes, of course, that the person knows what our prediction is and acts accordingly. This argument was used by Dostoievsky in *Notes from Underground*, and even the sophisticated cognitive theorist John Searle, in his *Minds, Brains, and Science*, has lent credibility to it.

Similarly, of course, it is possible to build a simple machine that would have 'free will' by this criterion. We simply program the machine in such a way that, if someone predicts what the machine is going to do, and this information is punched into the machine, then the machine automatically does something different instead. If the ability of this machine to falsify predictions about its behavior does not prove that the machine has free will, then neither does the argument in the previous paragraph imply that human beings have free will. (Here again, it would be a straw man argument to accuse me of asserting that the mind is like a machine. The point is that, if ability to consistently falsify predictions were to imply free will, then a machine could have free will.)

Augustine's argument for free will is more direct than these. He asserts that "nothing can make the mind a companion of [sin] except its own will and free choice" (1964, 22). The reason is that "[Nothing] lies more truly in the power of the will than the will itself" (24). Or again, "No one wills a thing unwillingly" (69).

Yet it is well known that 80 percent of murderers were victims of violent and serious child abuse earlier in life. Unless we wish to believe that this statistic is merely an amazing coincidence, then it seems clear that there must be some cause and effect relationship between the child's being brutally abused, and his growing up later to become a drooling bathtub killer. But murder is presumably a sin. Thus we have an instance where something causes the will to sin. Of course, even in this case, the drooling bathtub killer still 'chooses' to strangle women in their bathtubs. This is because certain environmental factors that acted on his development during childhood (the fact that his father threw him down stairs, tied him to a chair for days at a time, and smashed his face with a baseball bat) caused him to become the kind of person who would *choose* to strangle women in their bathtubs. Any one of us, if we had had the *exact* same heredity *and* the *exact* same environment as this person, would have turned out exactly like him, and would probably be salivating at the thought of our next bathtub murder even now. Augustine is therefore right to say that nothing can cause the mind to be a companion to sin unless the mind itself chooses. The catch is that something can cause the mind itself to be the kind of mind that will choose to be a companion to sin (for example, strangle women in their bathtubs).

But the belief in personal immortality (entailing the assumption of a contra-causally free will needed to make it credible) dies hard. People commonly raise two objections against this reasoning. The first is that, even if a person is victimized by child abuse, he can still choose not to be a bathtub killer, as evidenced by the numerous abused children who do not grow up to be murderers. The reason for this, of course, is all too obvious. Although their environment was similar to the bathtub killer's in this one respect, both their environment and their heredity were different in other respects. If their environment and heredity had both been *exactly* identical with the bathtub killer's in absolutely *all* respects, then they too would be bathtub killers. The fact that victimization by serious child abuse is *one* of the factors that in many instances cause people to become murderers is evidenced by the following reasoning: If there were *no* causal connection at all between child abuse victimization and later criminal behavior, then there would be no significant statistical correlation (in well-controlled studies) between child abuse victimization and later criminal activity on the part of the abused child. But there *is* a significant statistical correlation between child-abuse victimization and later criminal behavior. Therefore, there must be some causal connection between the child abuse victimization and the subsequent criminal activity. Thus serious physical child abuse must be *one* of the factors (among others) that combine to cause the extremely complex developmental history that leads someone ultimately to end up as the kind of person who would choose to strangle people in their bathtubs.

The second objection is that, even if this reasoning proves that there is a certain amount of causal *influence* on the development of personality, it does not prove that a person's personality is *completely* caused or predetermined. And if the will even has any tiny bit of freedom to choose to do anything other than what it has been causally determined to do, then this amount of freedom is enough to justify the inclusion by an omnipotent and benevolent creator of a certain amount of evil in His creation, in order to make possible the exercise of this freedom. Furthermore, there does seem to be reason to believe that some events in nature (for example, changes in the states of subatomic particles) are somewhat random, and thus are not completely caused or predetermined. Therefore it is plausible to suppose that human beings also have a certain amount of free will.

But this brings us to the crux of the whole issue. If there are choices on my part that are not caused by *anything*, then those choices are not caused by *me*. Any choice that resulted merely from some uncaused, random firing of a neuron in my brain would not be an instance of free will, because I still would have no control over it. In order to be a true instance of free will, it is not enough that a choice merely be uncaused; it must on the contrary be caused *by me*, but in such a way that factors beyond my control did not cause *me* to be the kind of person who would make that kind of choice.

It is currently fashionable for philosophers to base their arguments for free will on a Whiteheadian or Bergsonian notion that there is somehow a randomness or noncausality in the operation of physical events as understood in terms of some current physical theory such as quantum theory. But, even if there are uncaused events in nature, this would not affect in the least the central argument against the kind of free will at issue here. Suppose my choice to climb up on a tower and begin shooting people at random resulted, not from an orderly sequence of cause and effect events in my diseased brain, but rather from a series of random misfiring of neurons that in turn was not caused by anything. This would merely be another way in which my decision to climb the tower could fail to be caused by *me*, since in this case it would be caused by these random, uncaused neural events over which, again, *I* had no control. So whether physical events are strictly caused, or whether they occur in a random, uncaused fashion, really has nothing to do with whether human decisions and personality characteristics are free or on the contrary result from causal and/or chance factors beyond my control. It is easy enough to understand the logic of this situation, but it becomes more difficult if we are strongly motivated to end up buttressing a doctrine that would allow us to fancy ourselves personally immortal, more powerful than we actually are, and possessed of more moral centrality than is really the case. In short, the logic is easy unless we are still ill-prepared to accept the fact of our own finitude.

But if we have already addressed our finite ontological predicament, in all its facets and all its harshness, by means of a very intense positive value experience felt in the form of an intense direct appreciation of the value of a conscious being other than ourselves, and if we have undergone the often difficult process through which this feeling of reverent compassion is transferred to conscious beings generally—so that our entire value system and outlook are permeated with a strong feeling of the positive value of conscious beings despite their misfortunes—then we no longer need such self-deceptions. We can simply face the truth, and get on with our lives here below, defining their meaning in terms of the fleetingness and hence irreplaceability and uniqueness that are appreciated all the more sharply because of the inevitable vulnerability of all things here below. Life itself, in all its finitude, becomes well worth suffering and dying for.

3. Toward a Constructive and Nonretributive Sense of Compassion

The experience of transcendent intrinsic value and the courage to face with equanimity the complete truth and full brutality of the ontological predicament of our own finitude would seem to be virtually inseparable from each other, in the sense that it would be almost impossible for the one experience to occur without the help of the other. When the transcendent value experience occurs through spiritual partnership, the space of empathy creates a sort of protective cocoon in which our own being flows together with that of someone whose unique positive value seems undisturbed by that person's finitude. Moreover, the fact that the other's conscious style is utterly different from our own makes it as refreshing as a breath of fresh air, unpredictable in its future, and not rigidly ossified and entrapped by the same troubles and limitations that detract from our experience of the value of our own existence. That she is constrained by her own troubles and limitations does not subtract from this effect. Since we observe her in the space of empathy—and thus in a condition that allows her stream of consciousness to unfold undeflected by any directiveness, manipulativeness, or judgmentalism—we see her in the process of the very metamorphosis that we ourselves crave, and which we can accomplish by participating in the space of empathy with her style of unfolding. She thus seems dynamic rather than static, and by flowing together with this unencumbered being, we vicariously experience the value of such a being in a magnified way.

This finite value experience in turn gives us the courage to fully accept the brutal facts of finitude. The idealization of the spiritual partner's being pulls us out of ourselves and enables us to see our previous defense structure as unworthy compared with the awe-inspiring form of consciousness we now have discovered in the other. It makes little difference that to abandon these defenses is to indict ourselves as much more limited, powerless, ordinary, and in short more *finite* than we wanted to think of ourselves as being. We have now directly experienced a far more rewarding pattern of being that does not depend for its value on any such defense structure as those on which we previously depended. Quite the contrary, we appreciate the value of the spiritual partner by focusing on her finitude, that is, her uniqueness, fleetingness, and irreplaceability, and we understand that the space of empathy is facilitated precisely by *not* evaluating each other in terms of any such demands as those that the previous defense structure had placed on us—namely, that we be powerful, invulnerable, self-sufficient, and competent to the point of godlikeness. By basking in the beauty of the other's form of being in spite of and because of its very finitude, we cease demanding infinitude of ourselves.

When we have such a pronounced positive value experience as this, whatever its meaning and outcome, we feel that if only it could be sustained indefinitely we would be much more than compensated for even the worst of metaphysical scenarios—for example, the scenario in which our brief and humble existence on this inconsequential ball of dust is all there is. We find that our appreciation of the spiritual partner's quasi-aesthetic beauty and value is in no way spoiled by the unfortunate fact of finitude. Indeed, since we have given up our own sense of self-importance in favor of reveling awe-strickenly in the other's form of being, it now makes much less difference to us whether the ego-subject with which we previously identified ourselves will survive forever or not. Our own being with its silly demands for self-importance and self-aggrandizement is precisely what we have escaped in favor of living in the appreciation of the other's uniqueness and vulnerability in the face of finitude; we empathize with this uniqueness and vulnerability in the form of compassion mixed with admiration. In concrete terms, we esteem the other all the more strongly because she is finite. And if the spreading effect is successful, the intensity of this inspirational feeling is spread to the most abstract valuational commitments, which are grounded in the strength of our appreciation for the value of conscious beings generally.

In short, once we have experienced such extreme positive value as spiritual partnership makes accessible, we are *compensated* for the ontological predicament rather than needing to deceive ourselves that the predicament *does not exist*. Correlatively, the experience of spiritual partnership itself depends on our ability to face the truth. If we did not at some point bring ourselves to acknowledge that the ontological dilemma is a dilemma, then our compassion for the finitude of the spiritual partner *in the face* of this dilemma would not be intense enough to make possible a powerful enough value experience to motivate dropping our self-deceptions with regard to death, powerlessness, and alienation. This is why the experience in a sense can occur only by 'tricking' us into abandoning egocentricity. The primary spiritual partner initially pulls us out of ourselves by appealing to an egocentric motive—the need for self-transformation. This need for self-transformation is built into the structure of consciousness per se, because consciousness is in its essence a pattern of change and cannot exist as stasis. The egocentric subject must allow its being to be taken over and overpowered by the other's pattern of unfolding in order to pull itself out of existential lethargy and somnambulism. Even if submission to this transformation is threatening or painful, the ontological structure of consciousness in its motivational dimension impels us to do it. To be conscious is a more fundamental need than to be happy or complacent. Of course, one must already have attained a certain amount of self-honesty in order to be open to such self-transformation, or else one would merely trade one's being in exchange for dull comfort and inauthentic self-assurances.

A condition for the possibility of spiritual partnership is that conscious beings have intrinsic and absolute value. We do not need to experience spiritual partnership, or undergo any transcendent value experience, in order to know intellectually that this is true. The value of conscious beings is presupposed by all other valuational or ethical propositions for which any evidence or argument can be given. Without conscious beings, there would be no such thing as happiness (the utilitarian ideal), justice (the deontic ideal), or self-actualization (the personalist ideal). Moreover, if there is any such thing as value in any nonsubjective sense, any such value presupposes and depends on the value of the existence of conscious beings; but if there is not any nonsubjective value, then the only value there is must be subjective, and in this case too conscious beings would have value. So the fact that conscious beings have value is demonstrable in a purely abstract and logical way, and does not depend on any special phenomenological experience for its verification.

But to know intellectually *that* something has value is different from actually directly *experiencing* its value, just as the knowledge that Tchaikovsky wrote a Seventh Symphony, and that it was as great as his Sixth, is no substitute for directly experiencing the beauty of the Seventh Symphony by actually listening to a performance of it. Or again, to know that a city is beautiful is different from the concrete experiencing of its beauty.

The fact that we can experience the value of conscious beings accounts for the extreme moral importance of events here on earth despite the infinitesimal smallness of the earth in the cosmic scheme of things. As Trotsky eloquently put it,

> If I were one of the celestial bodies, I would look with complete detachment upon this miserable ball of dust and dirt. . . . I would shine upon the good and the evil alike. . . . But I am a *man*. 'World history which to you, dispassionate gobbler of science, to you, bookkeeper of eternity, seems only a negligible moment in the balance of time, is to me everything!' (1964, 40)

Once we have abandoned the sugarcoated metaphysical doctrines of the self-deceptive type of religion, we also no longer need the metaphysical dogmas that were necessary as *ad hoc* hypotheses to prop them up. The most important one of these *ad hoc* hypotheses was the doctrine of free will, which was needed to solve the problem of evil in the self-deceptive scheme of things, and therefore led to a predominantly retributive, guilt- and blame-oriented morality. This retributivism, as we saw above, kills compassion. One can easily see how damaging this retributivism is to the possibility of compassion by observing the dynamics of any long-term romantic relationship or marriage. One of the main problems that undermines the space of empathy between the two people is their insistence on shifting guilt and blame for all problems away from themselves and onto each other. Their need to avoid the other's blame then forces them to become so rigidified in their defensiveness that they cannot openly express feelings and ideas to each other without fear of condemnation and rejection.

The same problem can be seen in people's political behavior. For example, in most states in the United States, 99 percent of welfare recipients are children and single or divorced mothers who need to care for their children when not in school (and who also are required to seek and accept employment by all possible means on pain of losing their welfare benefits). Yet, year after year, politicians win elections by running ads that promise somehow to eliminate welfare or force welfare recipients to work—as if it were not a matter of public record that those who receive welfare are precisely those who, given present social conditions, *cannot* work, and in most cases should not be expected to do so because they must care for young children. Are these facts about welfare and poverty in our society so complicated that people who are sophisticated enough to manufacture rockets and make a complex economy function cannot understand them? That would be beyond credibility. The truth is that people in our culture are so obsessed with projecting guilt and blame onto someone, and insisting that people's problems are the result of their own free will, that we prefer to use our vote to express hostility toward the victims of social problems than to use them to elect someone who would try to develop solutions to the problems. We are more interested in finding scapegoats for our problems than in making the problems go away.

As another example, consider the problem of drug abuse. At the time of this writing, our culture shows virtually no interest in offering resources to help people overcome drug addiction, or to eliminate the social problems that cause people to become so hopeless that they would sacrifice their lives to an addiction, or even to find out what the causes of the psychological problems that lead to addiction might *be*; we instead spend billions of dollars to send armies and police to drug-producing areas to destroy crops or engage in shootouts with gangsters. Our culture manifests a need to engage in some sort of expressive action, no matter how counterproductive, to symbolize our hostile and condemnatory feelings toward people who deal in or use illegal drugs. But few are interested in expressing compassion or humanitarian concern for those who are addicted to drugs, let alone those who were unlucky enough to have their character determined by such negative environmental and/or hereditary factors that they would end up with immoral and criminal personality structures. The retributive, guilt- and blame-oriented morality with its emphasis on free will demands that we hate and inflict still further harm on such people—even if this means harming ourselves and other innocent people in the process—rather than pitying them and trying to calculate the most beneficial way to deal with them by taking into account all available facts of the case.

I do not mean to imply that an ethic of compassion would refrain from punishing or doing battle whenever such actions are necessary to produce socially beneficial outcomes. Sometimes compassion requires precisely that we *not* placate people's neuroses or make it convenient for them to dodge responsibility for the predictable consequences of their actions, so that they can learn the important virtue of agency. But the point is that an ethic of compassion would not rejoice in the infliction of suffering on the 'evil' and 'wicked' for its own sake, or for the sake of 'just retribution.' It would see the victims of unfortunate psychogenesis first of all as *people*, and secondly as people with psychological problems. As mentioned earlier, this is the kind of ethic that Christianity was originally supposed to create, but the Christian culture's emphasis on compassion had to be largely sacrificed to make room for an even greater emphasis on free will, retribution, and hostility toward the 'wicked' in order to prop up its self-deceptive metaphysical mythology. People were not yet ready to accept a religion that worked by creating a feeling of compassion at the expense of their own egocentricity and consequent narcissism.

What is needed, then, is a way to intensely and directly appreciate the value of real conscious beings other than ourselves, rather than projecting consciousness onto a metaphysical principle or force. We are presently drawing to the close of a historical period when the need to feel this love was enacted by projecting it onto a merely 'romantic' partner (as defined by a certain cultural tradition) in the form of sexual feeling. This was all too limited an attempt because the sexual symbolization served as an all-too-easy substitute for the more complex forms of symbolization that would make accessible the more sophisticated feelings toward the consciousness of the other person that primary spiritual partnership and its spreading effect both entail.

If, however, we understand why we felt so compelled to project such an awesome spiritual experience onto a sexual love object, we should then be ready to take the next step, which is to use the experience of spiritual partnership per se (whether in a romantic context or not) to pull us out of egocentricity, so that we experience the value of conscious beings other than ourselves intensely enough to compensate for the harshness of the ontological predicament. We can then abandon the metaphysical dogmas needed to support a self-deceptive denial of the predicament, along with the distortion of ethics that blocked us from fully feeling compassion toward others.

In sum, spiritual partnership enables us, not merely to know intellectually that conscious beings have value, but to immediately and movingly experience this value. We experience this value by allowing ourselves to feel both compassion and admiration for the person in her finitude. This in turn is possible only within a space of empathy, as we have seen. As the spiritual partnership experience unfolds, its dynamics lead us to experience directly the intrinsic value of all conscious beings with whom we interact. We feel compassion and admiration for their attempts to maintain an authentic consciousness as they battle the hostile conditions of existence that all conscious beings face. All conscious beings become 'spiritual partners' in a secondary or derivative sense, and through them we are able to commune indirectly with that element in all conscious beings that we originally learned to value so intensely in the primary spiritual partner. All experience becomes permeated with the reverence and awe that the spiritual partner taught us to appreciate in a much more intensely positive way than we could ever experience anything from the egocentric perspective.

Appendix
The Sexuality of Consciousness

One of the thornier issues in understanding transcendent value experience through spiritual partnership is posed by the tendency for the experience in its primary form to occur between people of opposite sexual polarity. I have argued, contrary to the belief of Jung and most of his followers, that opposite sexual polarization is not an essential element in bringing about the overwhelming feelings of admiration and compassion that I have been discussing. Rather, sexual polarization is only a helpful catalyst because, like sexual attraction, it is a handy way to symbolize the feelings involved in spiritual partnership, and thus one that is likely to be used toward this end, especially in certain forms of culture. To understand why this is so frequently the case—not only in our culture, but in many others as well—it is important to avoid unclarity as to what is meant by 'masculine' and 'feminine' forms of being. Toward this end, it is helpful to consider the essential reasons why the development of opposite polarization is a natural tendency favored by (but not necessarily required by) the survival needs and physiological patterns of conscious beings.

If the terms 'masculine' and 'feminine' are to have any consistent and coherent meaning with regard to styles of consciousness, then the terms must be defined in a way that bears some relation to maleness and femaleness in their biological senses. But a problem immediately arises for any such attempted definition: If we define the concepts *empirically*, that is, by observing the differences between male and female styles of consciousness at a particular time and place (or even at a number of particular times and places), then we have no guarantee that the patterns we are observing bear any necessary or essential relation to maleness and femaleness per se. On the contrary, these patterns may only accidentally correlate with gender differences, and reflect only the way a particular culture has taught its males and females to think, feel, and behave.

Moreover, the empirical fact that many males seem to exhibit effeminate personal styles, and even have brain circuitries and neurotransmitter systems similar to females (for example, oxytocin, vasopressin, and prolactin distribution) substantially muddles the attempted empirical definition (for example, see Panksepp 1998). Given this fact, it remains possible that what is considered 'masculine' in one culture might be considered 'feminine' in some other imaginable culture. In that case, what we would then be calling the 'masculine' form of consciousness would not be *conceptually* related to maleness in the biological sense any more than to femaleness, as Benjamin and Chodorow have suggested in the works discussed earlier. It would merely be a coincidental empirical fact that males in such-and-such a culture happen to behave in such-and-such a way; there might not be anything essentially 'masculine' about such behavior at all.

If we observe the diversity of personalities available to us in everyday life, as well as in psychological studies and in literature, we find that, given any personality characteristic or form of consciousness that we might want to designate as 'feminine,' we can find men who have developed that particular attribute very highly, whereas any form that we might want to call 'masculine' will also have been highly developed by certain women. Few women are more sensitive and emotionally delicate than Frederic Chopin, and few men are as aggressive as Queen Elizabeth I, or as forceful in military leadership as Margaret Thatcher, or as precise in their logical reasoning as Patricia Churchland.

Jung tries to solve this problem by positing that all people embody both 'maleness' and 'femaleness'; on this basis, it is supposed to be explainable why many men markedly exhibit features that Jung designates as 'feminine,' and vice versa. But does this move really lay the problem to rest? If Chopin (a heterosexual male with a preponderance of male hormones) is more 'feminine' than Thatcher (a heterosexual female with a preponderance of female hormones), then the term 'feminine' loses its connection to biological femaleness in any tangible sense—a connection which we said at the outset is needed in order for the term to be a meaningful one.

What bothers skeptics about Jung's solution is that Jung wants to say that there are certain forms of consciousness and behavior that are 'masculine' or 'feminine' by their very nature, whereas the empirical fact is that both men and women can and do embody all these forms of consciousness and behavior. Furthermore, even if men embody certain forms more frequently than women, we still would not know how much of this difference is attributable to biological maleness, and how much of it results from cultural traditions that bear no necessary connection to any biological gender differentiation. It seems highly questionable to designate some characteristic as feminine, but then to allow that the 'feminine' in this sense can be in principle just as much present in men as in women.

When we consider these reasons for people's reluctance to accept Jung's solution to this problem, we can also see what must be done in order to formulate the definitions in a workable and convincing way. We must begin with the fact that female *bodies* are different from male ones in certain respects, and that forms of consciousness require physical embodiment in order to occur. As Merleau-Ponty suggests in *The Structure of Behavior*, the relationship between the body and conscious processes is analogous to the relationship between an instrument and the melodies that are played by using this instrument. The structure of an instrument does not determine which melodies will be played on the instrument, and the same melody can be played on a variety of different instruments. But this same melody will sound a little different on a trumpet as compared with a violin. Also, certain patterns that can be executed with great practice and effort on the trumpet can be executed with less practice and less effort on the violin, and vice versa. It is possible to execute a forceful *marcato* on the violin, but to do so requires more practice and effort than on the trumpet—and also a different *kind* of practice. If one were to apply the same degree of disjointed, clipped movement in executing the same passage on the trumpet that a violinist must use, it would come off sounding *too* marcato—it would sound like a cartoonish stereotype of itself. In general, the type of instrument on which a melody is played does have an effect on the way the melody ends up sounding, and on the amount and kind of effort that must be marshaled to play the melody on that instrument.

We must define 'feminine' forms of consciousness, not as forms that cannot be executed with a masculine body, or cannot be executed as well with a masculine body, but rather as forms that would require *greater practice and effort* to execute with a masculine body. Given the similarities between the male and female brains (notwithstanding a slight difference in the development of the *corpus callosum*), there are many forms of consciousness that are executed with equal ease by both masculine and feminine brains and bodies. But differences in glandular function and neurotransmitter levels can lead to habitually different patterns of action, which in the long run can result in different patterns of personality. Again, this does not mean that the masculine person cannot execute all the same patterns of consciousness as a feminine one, but some of these patterns are executed with more effort and practice than his feminine counterpart would require, and others with less, and still others simply with a different *kind* of practice and effort. Also, in interpersonal contexts, the use of the masculine body to project, say, empathic feeling requires a more concerted effort because the masculine body is perceived as less empathic than the female one, unless the person inhabiting the body purposely compensates. For example, women normally make more direct eye contact with the person with whom they are speaking, whereas men more often tend to cast sidelong glances. Newborn infants show preferences for a female face. And a woman's personality develops from early childhood with the possibility in mind that she *might* someday wish to bear children, at which point hormonal changes (especially oxytocin increases) might be likely to make her wish to nurture this offspring. While she may of course choose not to develop in this direction, she also knows that there is a possibility for being motivated toward nurturing behavior here which would be, not impossible, but more difficult (all things considered) for a person with a male body; it would be less likely to be as strongly motivated or as easily perfected given his physiological constitution, which uses oxytocin more sparsely and in combination with different chemicals such as prolactin and vasopressin. Chodorow, in reviewing the evidence for the physiological basis of infant-nurturing behavior, shows that such nurturing is equally *logically possible* for both genders; what she does not show is that development of such nurturing ability is equally likely to be *motivated* and equally easy to *perfect* given their differing hormonal balances and neurotransmitter levels.

Not only the body's role as physiological substratum differs with gender, but also the way one must behave in order to communicate certain emotions to others through this body, and this difference will also be influenced by the way differently structured bodies are *perceived*. For example, a friend of mine, as a high school teacher just out of college, *looked* too young, wide-eyed, naïve, and tentative to command the students' obedience and cooperation, simply because of his slight build and lack of forceful-looking features (facial hair, body weight, etc.). He thus had to overcompensate for this disadvantage by behaving more forcefully, which he did successfully. But, after twenty years had passed, he saw a videotape of himself in the classroom: His demeanor now seemed much too hostile and threatening, because he no longer *needed* to behave as he had at the age of twenty-one in order to avoid seeming weak. The same effort with a different body produces a different interpersonal effect. And to produce the same effect with a different body requires a different kind of effort. This modification of the kind of effort required leads to a modification of the form of consciousness of the person who must exert the different effort. My friend in his older body had to begin feeling more relaxed and empathic than before in order not to seem hostile and threatening. Similarly, the kind of effort needed to produce an interpersonal effect through a female body may be different from what would be required to produce a similar effect through a male one.

What, specifically, are the differences between male and female bodies that make important differences in the ease with which these bodies can execute certain forms of consciousness? Are the differences in these forms of consciousness really important ones, or are they only peripheral?

The most consistent differences between male and female bodies, of course, are the differences in the balance of certain hormones (which in turn influence neurotransmitter balances). And it is possible that to produce certain forms of consciousness through a body with a predominance of male hormones requires greater effort and practice than would be required to produce those same forms of consciousness through a body with a predominance of female hormones, and vice versa. In spelling out the differences between 'masculine' and 'feminine' forms of consciousness, we are not necessarily referring to forms of consciousness that are exclusively or even primarily the province of one gender or the other; instead, what these terms refer to are forms that require less (or different) *practice and effort* for one gender or the other, given the effects of male and female hormone balances on long term habit formation.

Of all the differences that this difference in bodily substratum can make, the one that is crucially important for our purposes hinges on the ontological threat to any conscious being arising from the conditions of finitude, to which there are two possible responses: One of these responses will tend to be favored by the 'masculine' style, the other by the 'feminine' style: Suppose we assume that consciousness is motivated to exist—that is, to be conscious. This means that it must maintain a certain level of intensity and authenticity. This motivation to exist brings consciousness into conflict with the world, as does any being's need for survival. An array of difficult practical problems must be solved in order for consciousness to continue to exist (i.e., to maintain its intensity and authenticity). Many of these practical tasks demand that a conscious being stoically suppress any state of consciousness or range of states of consciousness that might interfere with the effective performance of these tasks—especially states of emotional consciousness; to be stoic is almost synonymous with being in control of one's emotions. And to suppress consciousness or a whole range of states of consciousness tends to lead to a reduction in the intensity and authenticity of consciousness.

The more the task in question requires that we suppress incompatible forms of consciousness in order to perform the task, the more conflict it creates, both internally and externally. This is especially true when the consciousness that must be suppressed is emotional and motivational in nature and therefore definitive of the direction and pattern of our stream of consciousness (i.e., of who we are). The conflict arises from the opposition between one's own survival as a conscious being and the hostility of the external world, whether material or interpersonal. Some tasks are more conflict related in this sense than others, but both physical and existential survival inevitably require the performance of some conflict-related tasks.

Paradoxically, then, consciousness, in order to maintain its intensity and authenticity, must engage in conflict-related tasks that reduce its intensity and authenticity. The two possible responses to this dilemma constitute what I have called the masculine and feminine styles of consciousness, in the sense that the one type of response occurs with less practice and effort for a body dominated by female hormones and structural patterns, and the other type of response occurs with less practice and effort for a body dominated by male hormones and structural patterns. Both styles are possible to develop (and in fact are *necessary* to develop) for both biological genders, but to do so requires different amounts and kinds of practice and effort as influenced by the gender differences of the bodily organism that must serve as the substratum for the corresponding forms of consciousness. The 'masculine' attitude (i.e., the attitude developed with less practice and effort by the biological male, though it is also developed, with greater practice and effort, by the female) gives priority to accomplishing the conflict-related task at hand, even if at the risk of eroding the intensity and authenticity of consciousness. It determines itself to win the battle even if this sometimes entails the risk that we may harden ourselves into insensitive machines or brutes in order to accomplish this task. Far from entailing complete sacrifice of conscious interiority, this attitude requires the suppression only of ideas and feelings incompatible with the conflict-related tasks in question. The rigor of this self-discipline then helps compensate for the necessary repression by facilitating an epistemological scrupulosity that helps prevent the lazy self-deception to which we would all be prone if not challenged to overcome it. At the same time, the repression and denial of forms of consciousness that interfere with 'steeling oneself for combat' obviously create a tendency toward certain predominantly 'masculine' forms of inauthenticity and self-deception.

The feminine attitude, on the other hand, gives priority to maintaining a certain level of intensity and authentic feeling in consciousness, even if at the risk of neglecting important conflict-related tasks. It will forfeit a conflict situation if that is what is really necessary to prevent sensitivity from being hardened into feelingless brutality. But at the same time, to protect itself from the need for combat, this feminine style may become involved in its own forms of self-deception. Thus both masculine and feminine styles allow for their own particular forms of repression and denial, and each shows its own forms of courageous authenticity.

As I have stressed from the beginning, any normal person uses both these attitudes at different times; but, since character development depends largely on habit formation, and since certain patterns will be easier to enact using a masculine or a feminine body as substratum for the process, each individual eventually develops a fairly consistent pattern of allowing priority to one or the other of these conflicting concerns. This leads to a predominant development of one sexual polarity and to a relative neglect of the opposite one. It is also worth noting that, neurophysiologically speaking, the female brain contains a richer system of connections across the *corpus callosum* linking the left and right brains, suggesting that it is more likely that the male brain will be a little more geared to disconnect the analytical, problem-solving functions from the imaginative and more emotion-oriented ones. Also, the *corpus callosum* begins developing earlier in girls, and the brains of many homosexual men are more similar to women's brains in these respects than to other men's (for example, see Panksepp 1998, and also Lawrence Miller 1990). Again, this does not mean that women cannot disconnect intellectual activities from imaginative and emotional ones (as many outstanding female logicians and mathematicians show), or that men cannot connect them (consider, for example, what must occur in the brain of any great musician at work), but only that the corresponding cognitive skills, all else being equal, will tend to be developed with greater or lesser ease or practice. Thus, in terms of priority, there is a tendency for each of us to emphasize either the masculine or the feminine style of orienting ourselves toward the inevitable conflict between our feelings and the world of brutal alienation, hostility, and crass material survival in a world where living beings stay alive by eating each other, and in which famine, pestilence, war, and death define the conditions for existence. In the face of these conditions, the masculine style prioritizes a steeling for combat, while the feminine prioritizes maintenance of a full emotional interiority.

Yet it is also true that the two polarities must function together, in cooperation with each other. When the feelingless warrior realizes that he has lost his femininity, not only does he sense that something valuable has been lost; he also senses that the loss of a well-functioning feminine component has caused his entire consciousness to malfunction. Repressed feelings come back to haunt him by distorting his thought processes, facilitating self-deception, and undermining his stoic virtue. The result is thus weakness of character rather than strength. Thus, without the participation of the feminine style, he is also unable to be a 'real man.' He must enact feminine as well as masculine forms of consciousness, even though doing so requires greater effort and practice than it would for a person with a more feminine body and hormonal balance, hence a different learning history.

It is important to explore not only the ways in which the sexual polarities in consciousness are different, but also the ways they interact with each other. This also will help us to understand why the interaction of opposite predominant polarities in people tends so often to be such an important element in primary spiritual partnership, and thus why the need for spiritual partnership historically has taken the course of sexualizing the religious function by making 'romance' serve as the be-all and end-all of spiritual consolation for so many people.

1. The Interdependence of Polarized Forms of Consciousness

To *very intensely* exist a feminine form of consciousness without the support of a masculine style would seem impossible by definition. In the first place, to do so would place a person in a dangerously weakened condition that, if unchecked, would lead to self-pity, weakness of character, and erosion of stoic virtue to the extent that self-truthfulness (which requires stoic virtue) could not be maintained. Thus a completely feminized and utterly non-masculine consciousness would be unimaginable; it would defeat itself by eroding self-awareness and ultimately constricting consciousness per se. We are able to experience the interiority of consciousness with complete freedom and abandon only if we do so in a context of relative safety from any unmanageable conflicts they might precipitate, and this in turn requires self-confidence in performing conflict-related tasks.

In the second place, in the case of many feelings, intuitions, and interpretations of emotionally significant situations, to openly and defenselessly own or admit these feelings and interpretations *even to ourselves* without self-deceptive defenses requires a great deal of courage in the face of *what we may find* in the unknown into which we are thrust by these self-admissions. To face the potential threats posed by this unknown with courage and fortitude requires a confidence in the ability to defend ourselves against the ensuing threats. And this confidence in the face of possible combat is a function primarily of the 'masculine' form of consciousness, in the sense I have been using. It is the masculine form (in both men and women) that has trained itself to remain cool and composed in the face of combat, through the childhood rituals of fistfighting, the threat of condemnation by the society if one is not a career success, and so forth—all situations demanding the suppression of the emotions that normally get in the way of doing battle in the world of brutal combat where physical, social, or existential survival is at stake. It is the masculine style that must know how to forge ahead aggressively in the face of opposition, and whose motto is 'survival first; *then* worry about spirituality.'

The combination of a fully actualized feminine consciousness with a fully actualized masculine consciousness thus produces the effect of allowing feelings to be expressed with full feminine intensity and self-disclosure of one's own intense consciousness. The *threatening* aspect of self-disclosure requires the masculine form of stoic courage to protect its inherent vulnerability. Many women develop this masculine kind of courage to a great extent, and many to a lesser extent. Correlatively, many men develop the ability to expose their vulnerabilities defenselessly to a greater extent than others. These differences seem fairly obviously to be determined culturally (i.e., environmentally) and not just biologically, but it is also true that the forms of consciousness must be enacted in a *bodily* way, and the female body will lend itself more easily to the feminine form of consciousness.

This complementarity of sexual styles implies an important point for our purposes here: What is admired by the masculine subject in the space of empathy with a feminine subject is not her feminine consciousness per se. What is admired is the rare view of a fully actualized personality completely enacting *both polarities* of her consciousness *at the same time*, in effective support of each other's functioning, thus with maximum intensity and with maximum visibility to the observer who is in the space of empathy with her. One reason this occurs so completely within a full space of empathy is that she is simultaneously in the process of empathizing with the masculine consciousness of the masculine subject, which therefore brings out the masculine potential of her own consciousness. And the intense consciousness that she thus discloses is at a level of depth that even a well-balanced and relatively actualized person would not normally disclose with complete openness and vulnerability to another person; thus the vision of it in full activity through empathy is a rare thing.

A similar point can be made from the reverse perspective. The masculine subject is able to express his own ideas and feelings in a more feminine way, because he is encouraged by his partner's femininity to drop his usual masculine defenses enough to do so. Normally, a masculine subject (especially in an extremely competitive form of culture, such as ours) must clarify an idea or feeling in his own mind before expressing it to another person; that way, he is prepared to defend himself against possible attacks, opposition, objections, and generally to defend the vulnerable position into which such revelations may trap him. But, in the presence of the feminine subject in a space of empathy, the masculine consciousness is able to express ideas and feelings *before* they are fully worked out, when he is still groping for a way to understand them. Because the love of a spiritual partner bypasses masks, the feminine partner has no concern with whether his ideas are logically defensible at the point when he expresses them, or whether his feelings make any sense, or whether he can clearly say what they are about. In fact, she feels privileged that he is willing to show this much of his vulnerability to her. He is therefore able to exist more fully because his consciousness is concretely symbolized *while in the process of unfolding*, rather than waiting until afterward to be expressed. It is precisely at the time when we are working out ideas and feelings that we experience them most intensely; to express them afterward is simply to report facts about our biographical history. Also, if we symbolize experiences *while in the process* of working them out, the symbolization is able to contribute to a more authentic interpretation of *what* they mean, thus intensifying them (as the entire concept of psychotherapy through verbalization of feelings presupposes); thus it also contributes to a more authentically motivated *direction* in their unfolding into the future. We are therefore catapulted by this symbolization process into a more authentic future, which we then experience with greater intensity. At the same time, committing ourselves to the risk of unfolding in this uncontrolled and unforeseen direction forces us to mobilize conflict-related stoic virtue to protect ourselves from the corresponding threats, so that we also actualize our masculine potential more fully to just the extent that we have actualized our feminine potential more fully.

It is easy to see, then, that a person cannot really develop his or her feminine style without developing the masculine style virtually in proportion to it, and vice versa. One or the other style will of course tend to predominate, as explained earlier, but the further development of the dominant style will depend on further development of the subordinate one and vice versa. The reason for this is that we cannot intensely experience feminine sensitivity without the protection of the masculine type of stoic courage in the face of the resulting conflicts (i.e., the conflicts that result from self-disclosure). I am speaking here of a masculine type of stoic virtue—stoicism in a fight or conflict—and will also discuss a more feminine type of stoic virtue later. The point for now is that we cannot develop real stoic virtue unless we are honestly in touch with our genuine feelings and interpretations of situations. Without self-honesty, the prospective stoic ends up creating only a superficial appearance of self-control. The father who makes a show of sacrificing for his family, for example, often uses self-deceptive defenses to exact the price from them in other ways, demanding that they cater to his utterly non-stoic preferences and whims, while hiding this moral weakness underneath the flamboyant machismo of the padrone. Underneath this facade, his consciousness lacks masculinity because it is self-indulgent and undisciplined.

Spiritual partnership with an oppositely polarized subject therefore does not merely enable a person to develop his or her opposite sexual polarity. It enables us to experience and express our own predominant polarity much more completely, precisely because it becomes *possible* to do so when the oppositely polarized subject helps us to enact our own opposite polarity at the same time that we enact our predominant polarity. Each pole is intensified all the more in our own consciousness because its functioning is facilitated by cooperation with its opposite in the ways just indicated.

But, again, the fact that we may become more whole or more fully functional, as valuable as this outcome is, is not the most important result of spiritual partnership. The most important result is that we get to behold through empathy the exposed being of a consciousness *other than ourselves* who is intensely conscious, and whose value we can appreciate incomparably more vividly than we can our own. Only a being other than ourselves can be experienced in quasi-aesthetic awe through focusing on the being's finitude, uniqueness, and irreplaceability, so as to fulfill the need for a positive enough value experience to counterbalance the obnoxiousness of the cruel cosmic joke that constitutes the ontological conditions for the existence of conscious beings in a universe such as ours. Contrary to what Einstein hoped on his deathbed, the universe is not 'friendly.' It is up to us, in the existential condition of being 'without appeal' to any grandiose metaphysical fantasy (as Camus puts it), to compensate for this lack of friendliness by creating the positive intrinsic value experience of spiritual partnership through a space of empathy in which we are able to feel concretely toward a real being. This is not to suggest, of course, that feelings toward a primary spiritual partner by themselves can provide the entire positive meaning of life; the positive value experience must then unfold through still further dialectical stages, as discussed in chapter 4 above.

In a relationship between a predominantly masculine and a predominantly feminine consciousness within a space of empathy, the predominantly masculine person expands his feminine consciousness, but without abandoning the experience of his masculine consciousness in order to do so. Initially, he may be primarily an active creator of masculine content, and primarily a passive receiver of the feminine content with which he empathizes in the other, thus bringing out further his own feminine potential. She in turn may at first be the active creator of this feminine content with which he empathizes, while she passively receives masculine content from him by empathizing with it, thus enhancing her own masculine side. But in the final analysis, the being that he then admires is not the feminized subject per se, but the feminized subject *with her masculine potential simultaneously actualized*. Because her masculine potential is actualized, she feels safe in experiencing the full vulnerability of her feminine side (somewhat like a woman who is a judo or karate expert), and at the same time the creative energy to sustain the masculine style is not deflected from the full experiencing of the vulnerability, so that as a result she is able to exist her unique form of being more intensely than she normally could. This intensity allows the other person a full and clear view of her authentic and fully enacted being, and the intensity of this full consciousness is what he admires quasi-aesthetically as intrinsically valuable.

2. Critique of Jungian Formulations of Sexual Polarity

There is no feminine form of consciousness that cannot be fully and successfully enacted by a male organism, and vice versa, given the right kind and amount of practice and effort. The difficulty of accounting for this fact, as I suggested above, is the source of Jung's problems in conceptualizing masculine and feminine forms of consciousness in a clear way. Rather than formulating the differences in terms of the amount and types of practice and effort required, Jungians seem to search for patterns of consciousness that are peculiarly 'masculine' or 'feminine' in some sense whose relation to biological gender or to the balance of physical hormones is unclear. For instance, many Jungians seem to attribute exclusively to the masculine consciousness the ability to make distinctions and to precisely conceptualize information. The Jungian psychologist Sukie Colegrove, for example, refers to the "masculine discriminating principle" (96) and states that "an awakening of the masculine principle is necessary to give the person a sense of self, of independence, and the ability to discriminate, essential for understanding" (97). In a similar vein, Irene Claremont de Castillejo, in *Knowing Woman*, says that "overawareness of diffuse feminine values may paralyze us and make action impossible in the outer world. On the other hand a too-focused consciousness may render the wisdom from the feminine layer of our psyche invisible, and burn it up with too bright a flame" (16). Castillejo assumes throughout that focused, discriminating thought is a function of the masculine side of consciousness. But if these kinds of assumptions were true, then it would follow that men, who are more inclined to develop their masculine consciousness, would have higher IQs, since the ability to discriminate, make fine distinctions, and focus are essential to the kinds of cognitive functions measured by IQ tests. But the fact is that women's IQs on average are the same as men's. Thus, if men in our culture tend to develop their masculine form of consciousness even *slightly* more fully than women do, then the fact that women have developed their ability to discriminate just as fully as men have (as measured by IQ scores) would completely refute the notion that ability to discriminate, make distinctions, or use precise logic is any more associated with a masculine style of consciousness than with a feminine style.

Even if we confine the kind of 'discrimination' in question to the realm of distinguishing one's own individuality from the social and interpersonal environment, we still find that even this particular kind of discriminating function does not correlate with gender differences. If it did, then scores on authoritarianism, extraversion, and outer-directedness would be significantly higher for women than for men. But they are not. (See Adorno et al. 1964; Spence and Spence 1964; Eysenck 1957.)

What we do find is that overemphasis on right-brain functions and underdevelopment of left brain functions, together with a failure to coordinate and integrate the two halves of the brain—for example, through *corpus callosum* connections—lead to different symptoms in men and women. The same neurophysiological imbalance that in women leads to hysteria hardly ever does so in men. Instead, it leads to psychopathy in men (Eysenck 1957; Lawrence Miller 1990). Following Eysenck, I use the term 'psychopath' rather than the more general term 'sociopath' because the latter is often applied to anyone who shuns social norms, whereas 'psychopathy' connotes a more specific psychological dynamic, in which empathy is lacking and conflict is created for its own sake. The thought processes of hysterics and psychopaths are actually very similar: Both are high-anxious, extreme extraverts and score very similarly on the Manifest Anxiety Scale and the Eysenck Personality Inventory (for example, see Eysenck's *Dynamics of Anxiety and Hysteria*.) The difference is in the ways that their dysfunction expresses itself behaviorally. The hysteric uses an emphasis on histrionic expression of certain emotions to block out certain realities—especially realities involving interpersonal conflict. The psychopath, by contrast, uses an acting out through unmitigated interpersonal conflict as a way to avoid the internal experiencing of the emotions that for a normal person would arise from such conflict. Simply put, the hysteric escapes from external conflict by hiding in her emotional interiority, whereas the psychopath escapes from his emotional interiority by losing himself in external conflict.

This difference between the interpersonal behavior of the (usually male) psychopath and the (usually female) hysteric—so similar to each other in other respects—perfectly illustrates the difference between the feminized and masculinized forms of consciousness as I have conceived them. The masculine form responds to conflict by aggressively trying to repel the force against which the person experiences himself as in conflict. The hysteric responds by manipulating her inner emotions in such a way that the real conflict is not even seen by her. Both types of patients are masters *par excellence* of the art of self-deception, but they accomplish this self-deception in very different ways—the one essentially masculine, by trying to repel the adversary; the other feminine, by preserving the intensity of her emotion at all cost, even if this means dissociating the emotion from its real interpersonal connectedness. Notice also that both psychopathy and hysteria, which emphasize one sexual polarity almost to the exclusion of the other, are *dysfunctional* ways of being. Functionality requires balance, even though this balance in turn requires practice and effort.

Sexual polarization is determined not only biologically, but also culturally. Part of the reason why the designation of the masculine form of consciousness in terms of the way we orient ourselves toward *conflict* seems terminologically appropriate, in spite of the fact that both masculine and feminine exist in both sexes, is that men in almost all cultures have been the ones required to learn how to steel themselves *for combat* against both interpersonal and natural forces in an active way that involves immediately present danger. Women also must steel themselves, but they have not been so much required to do so *in the moment of action to repel a foe*—that is, in a context of active conflict. They may choose to engage in this type of conflict, but traditionally have not been negatively judged by their culture if they do not. Thus the steeling of oneself that has been essential for them has been predominantly a stoic resolution to endure adversity, and usually not a stoic determination to confront and end it once and for all.

It is true that there have been female warriors and athletes, as represented in the mythic archetype of Artimus. These women are not all the same, and actually can be divided into at least three types. First, there is the *ideal* Artimus type, in whom a fairly even balance exists between masculine and feminine—by contrast to women whose masculine side is considerably less developed than the feminine. Then there is the type of woman who has developed her masculine side *at the expense* of her feminine side, just as many men do. And third, there is the kind of woman whose body is female, but whose brain naturally develops in a predominantly masculine form, and whose personality simply resembles that of most men in that she neglects her feminine side. This third type need not concern us here, since these women can be counted simply as normal 'men' as far as the predominant polarization of their consciousness and personality is concerned.

The 'ideal' Artimus type is naturally admired. She is motivated to work at developing her masculine side out of an intense love for the masculine that comes naturally to a consciousness that is still rooted in a basic femininity by no means underdeveloped. In the same way, Chopin strongly developed the feminine side of his being—as is obvious from his music—not because of a lack of overall masculinity on his part, but out of an intense love for the feminine style (and indeed for women generally, as his biographies show), which arose precisely from his masculinity.

It is the second kind of reverse polarity—the one that works by *underdeveloping* one's predominant polarity—that does not elicit admiration, but neither does it present any problem for my characterization of the masculine and feminine polarities. A woman who develops her masculine style *at the expense* of her feminine side resembles psychologically the classic 'homophobic' type of male—that is, the one who develops stereotyped machismo and deprecates the development of the feminine in men. Such a person is not powerful, but merely abrasive. As every musician knows, a slow *pianissimo* is usually more physically challenging than a brisk *forte*, because gentleness requires strength. The one-sidedly masculine woman, like the one-sidedly masculine man, has overdeveloped an artificial and inferior form of 'masculinity' to the exclusion of all femininity. Both are too quick to attack because of a fundamental insecurity in their ability to defend against a possible attack, and often also because of a sadomasochistic dynamic resulting from physical or emotional power struggles with abusive parents (as very well discussed, for example, by Lynn Chancer). The hallmark of such artificially masculine people is a perceptible lack of the 'strength to be gentle' that is evident in both the Artimus-like female and the well-balanced male secure in his masculinity.

The third possible type of masculine woman, the one who does not merely *affect* to be, but *really is* predominantly masculine, has no special need to suppress her subordinate feminine polarity, although she may, like many men, somewhat neglect to develop it. But this type of case presents no particular conflict against the definitions of 'masculine' and 'feminine' we are using here.

Thus neither the Artimus-type female, nor the artificially 'masculine' woman, nor the one whose predominant style really is masculine (with greater or lesser development of her feminine side)—none of these is inconsistent with the concept of feminine consciousness as developed here. The Artimus is no less feminine than other women, but rather has developed a woman's usual love of the masculine in a certain way, and is a well-balanced and complete person. The overcompensatory 'masculine' woman, on the other hand, is not genuinely masculine at all, but artificially effects a false machismo as camouflage precisely for a lack of well-practiced masculine virtues; the hallmark of this falseness is that, like the classic homophobe, she must detest and suppress her femininity in order to achieve an awkward, stereotyped, and cartoonish *appearance* of masculinity.

Again, we see that the further development of a masculine personality is not facilitated by neglecting the development of the opposite polarity, as many Jungians seem to imply (e.g., Johnson, Colegrove 1979, and Castillejo 1990). Instead, the further development of one's own predominant polarity comes to a halt precisely at the point when one refuses to develop the opposite polarity.

Another problem with the Jungian approach (as noted for example by Hall and Lindzey 1957/1978) is that Jung's analysis seems logically more consistent for men than for women. Jungians assume that if we develop the masculine polarity too much, we do so at the expense of the feminine and vice versa. They then argue that, in our overly masculinized culture, men develop their masculine side too far, until a certain point is reached (usually around mid-life) when they sense their loss and feel an emptiness that can be filled only by developing the repressed *anima* or feminine side. The problem is that it is not clear why *women*, who also must overdevelop their masculine side during the early adult years in our competitive and work-oriented culture, would not also suddenly feel a need to develop the repressed feminine side and thus fall in love with other women, on whom they would project the repressed femininity. Instead, what does seem to happen is that women at this point regret the underdevelopment of their *masculine* side, and therefore fall in love with men, on whom they project the repressed masculinity or *animus*.

According to the analysis we have developed here, it may be true that men in our culture tend to underdevelop their femininity and women tend to underdevelop their masculinity. But, as each gender progresses through life, it can develop its predominant polarity still further only to the extent that it also develops its subordinate polarity as well. Men who pretend to develop their masculinity at the expense of the feminine polarity are in reality developing only an artificial, masculine-*appearing* mask of shrill hostility and false bravado in order to cover over a deficit of genuine masculine virtue, as is evident from their weakness of character, lack of self-discipline, and inability to show the gentleness that requires strength wherever this would be appropriate. Of course there may be imbalances along the way, and Jung may very well be correct that these imbalances must be corrected before further development can take place. But the person who grossly neglects his feminine virtue is likely to neglect his masculine virtue as well, as we have seen repeatedly throughout. Similarly, a woman who does not develop the courage to face the unknown into which experiencing of authentic emotions would catapult her also cannot experience those emotions freely and therefore must repress them, thus repressing her authentic femininity.

It is not the man who has most severely neglected his feminine side who feels the most urgent need to develop it later on. It is the one with the more balanced makeup, in which he has developed general self-awareness and authenticity—which require the *interaction* of both masculine and feminine styles—who finally is able to appreciate the beauty of the opposite polarity that he still has not developed as fully as he needs to. And it is this better-balanced subject who is *able* to execute the necessary skills to develop and understand the opposite polarity. The homophobic man of false machismo is really too riddled with self-deceptive defenses and chauvinistic belittlement of feminine virtue to understand its true value, let alone learn how to develop it.

3. Sexuality as a Catalyst for Self-Transcendence

There seems to be nothing about the concept of spiritual partnership per se that would essentially require that it can occur only in people whose predominant sexual polarities are opposite. The reason why it *does* appear to occur more easily under these conditions, especially in its fullest form, has to do with the inability for people in most circumstances to be completely overcome and swept away in an intensely positive and selfless appreciation of each other's value. There are many kinds of relationships in which many of the elements of spiritual partnership are present, yet the experience is not overwhelming enough either to overcome our egocentricity or to compensate adequately for the ontological dilemma of inevitable finitude (death, alienation, powerlessness, and insignificance).

The best way to understand how a full spiritual partnership may fail to occur even though many of the elements of spiritual partnership are present is to consider why it is that, occasionally, a relationship may appear to have the promise of developing into a spiritual partnership, yet something goes wrong to short-circuit the process because of a tendency toward mere *symbiosis* of two people's opposite polarities. In this case, all the initial ingredients for spiritual partnership seem to be present, but something crucial is missing in the way the people's sexual polarities interact as the relationship begins to develop.

Once the possibility of a spiritual partnership presents itself in a context involving complementary interaction of the sexual polarities of two people within a space of empathy, two strong natural tendencies must be avoided if the just-emerging spiritual partnership is not to abort itself. The first tendency is that the predominantly feminine person becomes wiltingly dependent on the masculine one as a sort of 'protector.' By this I mean that she fails to use his masculine form of consciousness as a catalyst for the development and enactment of *her own* masculine virtues, which if developed would lead to an integration of her own masculine style with her predominantly feminine style. The danger is that she fails in this case to actually *experience* his form of consciousness, and thus loses the vicarious appreciation of its value through empathy; instead, she may use him simply as a crutch to *avoid* developing her own masculinized stoic virtue. She says to him, in effect, 'I am too sensitive and vulnerable to protect myself against the cruel world; you be my protector.' The masculine partner is thus faced with two alternatives: Either (1) he plays the role of this indulgent 'protector'—which he senses would undermine her stoic virtue and promote weakness of character and selfishness, as well as destroying the authenticity of the interaction—or (2) he withdraws from the intimate relationship and restores a more normal distance, as exists in ordinary friendships, in order to avoid this harmful outcome. In either case, spiritual partnership is blocked.

The other natural but destructive tendency comes from the masculine partner's perspective. The danger is that, rather than allowing her to help him learn to actualize his own feminine consciousness, through vicarious participation in hers, he instead tries to use her feminine component as a *substitute* for his own. In effect, he proposes to her a Devil's pact: 'You do the feeling, and I'll calculate how to act on those feelings in the practical realm. Let me be your protector so that I can vicariously live your feelings to avoid coming to terms with my own. That way, I can avoid exposing my true vulnerability to anyone—even to you.' On these terms, the *mutual* space of empathy needed for spiritual partnership obviously cannot occur. She cannot empathize with his deepest feelings and philosophical problems because he never expresses them. A variation on this scenario is that the masculine subject, unable or unwilling to empathize with the philosophically important aspects of femininity we have been discussing, attempts to cover up this unwillingness or inability by cultivating only frivolous, superficial trappings of femininity, such as an interest in flowers or fancy china dishes. Women often experience such men as surreptitiously patronizing, because such attitudes reflect an essentially deprecatory attitude toward the feminine dimension—a view of it as trivial.

Either of these pitfalls leads to a *symbiosis* between two incomplete, deficient beings rather than to a mutual admiration between two fully functioning consciousnesses who face the ontological dilemma authentically and courageously, yet without becoming insensitive brutes (and thus suppressing consciousness) in order to do so. In such a deficiency-relationship or symbiosis, there may be a certain amount of genuine compassion, but admiration is destroyed. Also, each person senses the harmfulness of the symbiosis, withdraws from intimacy, and in doing so reduces even the intensity of compassion for the other. If an intense love is to be felt, both admiration and compassion for the other's embattled authenticity must be present, leading to a sharp focus on the person's positive value as finite and irreplaceable. Admiration and compassion in a true spiritual partnership feed each other in a vicious circle; admiration leads to gratitude that the other is willing to expose vulnerability, and the resulting further empathy with this vulnerability increases admiration for the other's courageous authenticity. If either part of this circle is deleted, the process is short circuited, and the positively valuing feelings cannot be felt so strongly as to provide the positive value experience needed to override the circle of egocentricity and the negativity of the ontological predicament.

I am speaking here of spiritual partnership 'in the primary sense,' as opposed to spiritual partnership 'in the derivative sense.' This distinction implies that, before we are able to focus on the finitude and embattled authenticity of *all* people in such a way as to pull an intense admiration-through-compassion, and hence a very strong *direct experience* (not intellectual acknowledgment) of the extreme positive value of the being of *all* people, we must first be taught *how* to do this. The way we learn this lesson is by being pulled into a relationship with one particular person such that we experience the other's value in a more intensely positive way than we can our own *in spite of* the egocentric perspective in which it is natural to care more about our own concerns and problems than about the concerns and problems of others. The relationship that is so overpowering as to initially tear down this egocentric perspective is what I call a spiritual partnership 'in the primary sense.' Subsequently, a somewhat similar quasi-aesthetic appreciation for the intrinsic value of other conscious beings is also able to occur in a non-egocentric way (although we may reach this point only through a painful series of developments, as discussed in chapter 4); these are 'spiritual partnerships' only in a 'derivative' sense. So, while it is true that many friends, colleagues, or family members may be spiritual partners in the derivative sense, I am speaking in this section of what seems to be required in order that a spiritual partnership in the primary sense can occur—namely, a relationship powerful enough to jolt us out of an egocentric perspective at a point when no other relationship has already adequately accomplished this task.

To be sure, a good friend in the ordinary sense may see positive value in a friend's unique form of being, and empathize with it, and interact with it in a helpful way. But, as far as spiritual partnership in the primary sense is concerned, it usually seems to be the case—at least in our form of culture—that he is not pulled out of himself in quasi-aesthetic and worshipful awe, nor does he endure every hardship with the thought that 'this little stroke of bad luck is infinitely compensated for by the mere existence of my wonderful friend'—which is precisely what a complete spiritual partnership in the primary sense *would* enable us to tell ourselves. The presence or absence of just such overwhelmingly positive feelings clearly highlights the difference between ordinary friendship and spiritual partnership. These feelings initially are almost always called into existence by admiration for a form of consciousness whose lack we sense in ourselves, which we envy and desire, and therefore desperately and sometimes recklessly crave to participate in, if only vicariously, even if this means giving up our natural egocentricity and fear of the unknown. We crave this participation because in a sense we feel that without it the fullness of our being is denied existence; it therefore seems necessary to the life of our soul. Or, in Bollas's terms, there is an important dimension of our being that needs this particular other person in relation to whom it can actualize itself and have the opportunity to exist. We are thus overwhelmed with gratitude when this craving is actually fulfilled by the other's willingness to engage in primary spiritual partnership.

Sometimes, of course, this kind of intense need is not felt, and thus we are not in the 'condition of readiness' discussed in chapter 3 above. But that is just to say that there may be certain developmental stages, or periods in the life cycle, when the need for spiritual partnership is not felt and is hardly present—just as there are certain ages at which a person feels little need for the consolation of any religion or way of dealing with the ontological dilemma. The need is felt most strongly when existential rather than pragmatic issues are at the forefront of our awareness—for example, in adolescence, when we must define ourselves, and in later life, when the concept of finitude ceases to be a mere abstraction because we have closed off so many options and burned so many bridges with regard to the existential potentialities available to us. But, since existential issues are always pressing to a greater or lesser extent, there is no age at which spiritual partnership may not be desperately needed and fully enacted.

We can see, then, that it is theoretically possible for close friends of the *same* sexual polarity to experience spiritual partnership to a certain extent and up to a certain point, yet for the most part this experience by itself falls short of pulling them out of the fundamentally egocentric position. They can interact in most of the ways described in our earlier discussions of the ways spiritual partners relate. But what is usually missing between similarly polarized friends—friends in the ordinary sense—is the urgent, driven quality that we experience when confronted with the vicarious experience (within a space of empathy) of someone whose entire character has been courageously constructed so as to emphasize and highlight the polarity that has been *neglected* in ourselves. This urgent, driven quality of our feeling toward the *oppositely* polarized spiritual partner—along with the initial pain of being deprived of the person's empathy and contact—puts the sharp edge on our experience of the other's value; it is this sharp edge that intensifies the entire experience and motivates us to abandon egocentricity well enough to view the spiritual partner, not merely as equal in value and importance to ourselves, but as unquestionably more important and more valuable. Only then can we fully appreciate the person's positive value in a way that is more intense than any possible appreciation of our own value. (Again, remember that we cannot directly experience our own value in this intensely positive a way because to take compassion on our own finitude would be to wallow in self-pity, which is a negative rather than a positive experience.)

This is why it is true that at certain times of extreme self-doubt, ego-fragility, threat from the external world, or rapid personality change or development (as in early adolescence, and in war), a same-sex friend *may* be seen as an exalted, larger-than-life, quasi-religious and awe-inspiring creature whom one almost worships as more valuable than oneself. The friend is almost worshipped because the person seems to embody certain patterns of consciousness that we wish we could integrate into our own way of being, but we are still very far from doing so. In such a case, there is nothing insurmountable about the essential structure of our being (such as different sexual polarity) that would prevent us from learning to enact the friend's pattern of consciousness; it is just that we have *not yet* learned this style of being, and wish we could. At such times, our gratitude for this person's friendship may be so intense that the experience seems very much like the experience of spiritual partnership, and we may even say to ourselves—much as in spiritual partnership—'Now that this wonderful person has entered my life, all possible misfortunes are more than compensated for.' But, as we develop further, we notice that the sharp edge of the urgent craving for a *complementary* form of consciousness within a complete space of empathy is still essentially missing in this relationship. So even these partial spiritual partnerships with same-sex friends during adolescence or war-like circumstances usually are not intensely positive enough to ultimately resolve the ontological predicament in the way that a complete spiritual partnership with an oppositely polarized person does. Even during the most enthusiastic budding of a new adolescent same-sex friendship, a nameless longing still exists for some as-yet-unthematized kind of relationship, which at that point we vaguely realize must have something to do with the opposite gender (or, in the case of homosexuals, with someone in relation to whom the realm of sexual attraction and expression of sexualized feelings would be available for symbolization purposes).

Again, it is not that same-sex friends cannot help each other develop their opposite polarities. Indeed, they do. But in most cases, neither friend can *urgently and irrepressibly crave* vicarious participation with the other's opposite polarity, which is just as awkward and effortful as her own. Thus neither can very *intensely* appreciate the other's embattled authenticity as being much more important and valuable than her own. This seems to be the main reason why the fully worshipful feelings of spiritual partnership are mostly missing in same-sex friendships.

Nonetheless, same-sex friendships in certain cases function in ways very analogous to primary spiritual partnerships, and in some instances may make a certain contribution to an overall positive value experience which at least to some extent may compensate for the harshness of the ontological abyss. This may be especially true after the occurrence of the 'ultimate spreading effect' discussed earlier. This effect causes our positive valuation of a spiritual partner as such to spread to an appreciation of the irreplaceability, uniqueness and finitude of all conscious beings regardless of sexual polarity—especially those with whom we are most intimate, and therefore whose value we can view most unobstructedly. But this occurs for the most part only after a certain sequence has occurred in the unfolding of a full spiritual partnership in the primary sense.

People sometimes wonder why strong opposite-sex friendships do not automatically turn into romantic relationships, since sexual attractiveness and intimacy are both present. A similar question for our purposes is why such relationships do not automatically produce spiritual partnership, since opposite polarization is usually such an important catalyst for it. What we observe is that most opposite-sex friendships function like same-sex friendships as far as the interaction of sexual polarities is concerned. Sometimes the woman relates to the man as if she were 'just one of the boys,' so that he does not get too complete a vicarious experience of her feminine side, and the space of empathy therefore does not develop too far. At other times, the man relates to the woman as if both were women. In these ways, men and women protect themselves from being drawn too close to each other, for many reasons. Sometimes we need to protect our privacy from being invaded by too many people. Sometimes we fear intimacy per se. Sometimes a person's character does not inspire trust for some reason, and we rightly fear intimacy with that particular person. Sometimes we avoid too much intimacy for fear that an unwanted romantic relationship will develop. According to Carlfred Broderick, a respected psychologist and relationship counselor, it is usually wise to avoid too much intimacy with a person with whom it is conceivable that an unwanted romantic relationship might develop. Broderick believes (rightly, in my view) that most adulterous relationships are caused not by sexual attraction or sexual need, but by compassion for the unmet emotional needs of a respected person with whom we empathize. From Boderick's perspective, it is therefore often appropriate and beneficial that oppositely polarized people should maintain a certain social distance from each other.

Part of what the concept of spiritual partnership suggests, however, is that an intimate emotional relationship between opposite-sexed people need not lead to sexual involvement, provided that we make room in our category system for the phenomenon of nonromantic spiritual partnership, at least in the secondary or derivative sense. It is precisely when we *fail* to make room for this category that we are most likely to be tempted by adultery, because the need for spiritual partnership is a fundamental religious need that is being met less and less adequately by traditional religions. Again, this aspect of the historical trend toward the 'sexualization of religious experience,' as a predominantly *inadequate* attempt to achieve the increasingly needed spiritual partnership, is consistent with empirical findings: As the power of traditional religions to meet existential needs declines, adultery increases among those who have no concept of non-romantic spiritual partnership. But for those who do possess some such concept, the temptation to adultery is less likely to be a factor.

For example, Maslow's 'self-actualizing' subjects in *Toward a Psychology of Being* describe their experiences of love in just the kind of all-consuming, transforming terms I have applied to spiritual partnership. "It is possible in . . . the love experience to become so absorbed and 'poured into' the object that the self, in a very real sense, disappears" (79). "It is reacted to with awe, wonder, amazement, humility and even reverence, exaltation and piety" (81). And "to perceive a person concretely, in his intrinsic uniqueness, is to perceive him aesthetically" (89). Yet, despite such intense appreciation, Maslow also reports in *Motivation and Personality* that his 'self-actualizing' subjects tend to be less interested than most people in the prospect of adultery, and that they tend to idealize their spouses. "These people are relatively less driven to love affairs outside the marriage. . . . There tends to be a rather easy relationship with the opposite sex, along with casual acceptance of the phenomenon of being attracted to other people, at the same time that these individuals do rather less about this attraction than other people" (188–89). And, at the same time, "hostility between the sexes, this suspicion of the opposite sex, this tendency to identify with one's own sex [as] an alliance against the other sex . . . is found often enough in neurotic people and even in average citizens in our society, but it is definitely not found in self-actualizing people, at least with the resources for investigation that I had at my disposal" (184). These facts taken together seem to imply that such people are able to form strongly loving relationships with members of the opposite sex regardless of whether the relationship involves sex and romance, and therefore that they operate from a frame of reference that includes a category for non-erotic love for members of the opposite sex. Similarly, psychologist Thomas Oden speaks of subjects' reported feelings toward "intimates" of both sexes in terms of "awe," "reverence" and a "giftlike quality" which made them "sense the fragility and finitude of human relationships this side of death" (9). Obviously, there must be room in such people's category systems for a feeling of intense but non-erotic love toward members of the opposite sex, at least in the sense that admiration-through-compassion for a primary partner has spread to others of both sexes.

The danger that an opposite-sex friendship *might* erupt into a romantic relationship (or spiritual partnership) is, in essence, probably one of the main reasons people fear and avoid such friendships. To a great extent, a fear of the opposite sex seems to be a primitive and basic feature of human consciousness, and it can be observed both culturally and in the etiology of individual personality. The complex rules, rituals, and taboos that governed almost every aspect of opposite-sex relationships in primitive cultures, as Rank and other anthropologists report, served in effect to keep men and women as separate as possible. Similarly, most of us can remember a period in early adolescence or prepubescence when we were inexplicably terrified of even talking to a certain person of the opposite sex, sometimes going so far as to rehearse our lines in advance for fear that we might not get them right, and rigidly unable to allow ourselves to be spontaneous in the person's presence. Yet we could not understand why we should be so afraid of these harmless creatures with whom, perhaps a year earlier, we had felt fully at ease and conversed as freely as with brothers or sisters.

It may be that part of the reason for this phenomenon is that, as consciousness develops in a sexually polarized way in the early adolescent boy, for example, the increasingly powerful urge to indulge in the oppositely polarized patterns which he is missing, combined with the difficulty of controlling the choice of a sexual love object, threatens his newly emerging ego-integrity and terrifies him that he will be robbed of control over his own destiny. Any approaching meeting with the person with whom he is 'infatuated' fills him with a dread comparable to that inspired by an approaching waterfall to a white-water rafter. It literally threatens his very being. To allow himself to submit to the absolute power of the enchantment of the other would be to give up control of the structure of his own consciousness and the ability to direct his own future; he feels that he would be absolutely within her power. And this would annihilate the just-emerging and difficult project of defining himself as adequately *competent* in executing the skills of his own gender, which requires much further practice before he is ready to engage in complementary interactions that could give him a taste of the opposite polarity, but without thereby submerging his autonomy. The dread he feels is a realistic assessment of the *power* of the pull to primary spiritual partnership, since this pull is stronger than any individual's will. His suffering at this stage is further complicated by the fact that, lacking the interpersonal skills necessary to *symbolize* his positive feelings in any other way than through physical sexualization (i.e., lacking the much more complex pattern of symbolization which we saw in chapter 2 is appropriate to spiritual partnership per se), he cannot separate the need for spiritual partnership from the need for sexual adventure and fulfillment. The pull of an opportunity for spiritual partnership is thus immediately felt as dooming him to an irresistible sexual infatuation that will destroy his feeling of self-control just as his ego integrity is beginning to be consolidated.

As people mature and stabilize ego structure, they normally do remain acutely aware that these are very real threats which are justly feared, and they do proceed with all necessary caution in their relations with the opposite sex. They know that eros per se threatens to pull us out of our stable ego structure into radical transformation, and to give the other person considerable power over us (and vice versa; hence the importance of ethical considerations). But the more secure personality does not close off all possibility of intimacy so completely as to preclude the possibility of spiritual partnership. Such a person has developed interpersonal and communicative skills well enough to know that there is another way to symbolize feelings toward a spiritual or romantic partner besides doing so in terms of erotic and romantic physicalization. The patterns of empathic communication described in chapter 2 above are indispensable to the concretion of positive feeling toward a spiritual partner, regardless of whether the spiritual partnership also happens to be a romantic one or not. The well-integrated and autonomous person thus tends to develop romantic relationships in such a way that they also involve spiritual partnership. Paradoxically, this same attitude allows access to authentic and meaningful interactions with the opposite polarity *without* mistakenly construing the real need for such interactions as equivalent with or inseparably bound up with erotic feelings. Spiritual partnership may then be combined with eros, or it may be purely non-romantic. But, either way, the need for spiritual partnership must express itself. Repression of such a basic existential need does not simply force it to disappear; it only causes it to manifest itself in confused and destructive ways.

Spiritual partnership is by no means inseparable or indistinguishable from the realm of romance and eroticism. We only tend to associate it with these realms because the possibility of symbolization by means of sexual feelings and behavior tends at least initially to intensify the feeling of love, and also because of an inherited nervousness about intersexual interactions from a historical period (both culturally and psychogenetically) when we lacked ways to symbolize important positive feelings *other than* by means of physically sexualizing them. Thus, as I have already stressed, neither sexual attraction nor opposite polarization is essential to the development of spiritual partnership; they serve only as catalysts for it.

That spiritual partnership without romance rarely occurs in our culture is hardly surprising. Given the almost unique power of sexual symbolization and opposite sexual polarity to tear down a very well entrenched egocentricity, most people prefer to make spiritual partnership exist only within their romantic relationships, even if such relationships as we typically practice them increasingly fall far short of bearing the entire burden to resolve the ontological predicament. But to take any kind of spiritual partnership seriously and be prepared to make the necessary sacrifices can lead to transformation, to a non-egocentric feeling of reverence that eventually spreads to other people and events, and thus to resolution of the ontological dilemma.

References

Adler, Alfred. 1927. *Practice and Theory of Individual Psychology.* Harcourt, Brace & World.
Adorno, Theodor, Else Frenkel-Brunswik, Daniel Levinson, and R. Nevitt Sanford. 1964. *The Authoritarian Personality.* New York: Wiley.
Augustine. 1964. *On Free Choice of the Will.* New York: Bobbs-Merrill.
Auxier, Randall. 1990. "Dewey on Religion and History." *Southwest Philosophy Review* 6: 45–58.
Beauvoir, Simone de. 1952. *The Second Sex.* New York: Vintage.
Binswanger, Ludwig. 1968. *Being in the World: Selected Papers of Ludwig Binswanger.* Edited by Jacob Needleman. New York: Harper.
Bollas, Christopher. 1989. *Forces of Destiny: Psychoanalysis and Human Idiom.* London: Free Association Books.
Branden, Nathaniel. 1980. *The Psychology of Romantic Love.* Toronto: Bantam.
Broderick, Carlfred. 1979. *Couples.* New York: Simon & Schuster.
Campbell, Joseph. 1972. *Myths to Live By.* New York: Bantam.
Camus, Albert. 1955. "Absurd Freedom." In *The Myth of Sisyphus and Other Essays.* New York: A. Knopf.
Carr, David. 1986. *Time, Narrative, and History.* Bloomington: Indiana University Press.
Cassirer, Ernst. 1946/1953. *Language and Myth.* New York: Dover.
———. 1969. *An Essay on Man.* New Haven: Yale University Press.
Castillejo, Irene Claremont de. 1990. *Knowing Woman.* Boston: Shambhala.
Chancer, Lynn. 1992. *Sadomasochism in Everyday Life.* New Brunswick, NJ: Rutgers University Press.
Chodorow, Mary. 1993. *The Reproduction of Mothering.* Berkeley: UCLA Press.
Chopin, Kate. 1984. *The Awakening and Selected Stories.* London: Penguin.
Colegrove, Sukie. 1979. *Uniting Heaven and Earth.* Los Angeles: Jeremy Tarcher.
Damasio, Antonio. 1994. *Descartes' Error.* New York: Putnam.
———. 1999. *The Feeling of What Happens.* New York: Harcourt Brace.
Dewey, John. 1934. *A Common Faith.* New Haven: Yale University Press.
Dostoievsky, Fyoder. 1956. *Notes from Underground.* New York: Macmillan.
Duncker, Karl. 1939. "Ethical Relativity? (An Enquiry into the Psychology of Ethics)." *Mind* 48: 39–57.

Durkheim, Emile. 1947. *The Division of Labor in Society.* Glencoe: Free Press.
Edelwich, Jerry, and Archie Brodsky. 1991. *Sexual Dilemmas for the Helping Professional.* New York: Brunner/Mazel.
Ellis, Ralph D. 1983. "Phenomenological Psychology and the Empirical Observation of Consciousness." *International Philosophical Quarterly* 90: 191–204.
———. 1986. *An Ontology of Consciousness.* Dordrecht: Martinus Nijhoff/Kluwer.
———. 1989. *Theories of Criminal Justice: A Critical Reappraisal.* Wolfeboro, NH: Longwood Academic.
———. 1992a. *Coherence and Verification in Ethics.* Washington, DC: University Press of America.
———. 1992b. "Moral Pluralism Reconsidered: Is There an Intrinsic-Extrinsic Value Distinction?" *Philosophical Papers* 21: 45–64.
———. 1992c. "A Thought Experiment Concerning Universal Expansion." *Philosophia* 21: 257–75.
———. 1995. *Questioning Consciousness: The Interplay of Imagery, Cognition and Emotion in the Human Brain.* Amsterdam: John Benjamins.
———. 1996. *Eros in a Narcissistic Culture.* Dordrecht: Kluwer.
———. 1998. *Just Results.* Washington, DC: Georgetown University Press.
———. 1999. "Why Isn't Consciousness Empirically Observable?: Emotion, Self-Organization, and Nonreductive Physicalism." *Journal of Mind and Behavior* 20: 391–402.
———. Forthcoming a. *Curious Emotions: Roots of Consciousness and Personality in Motivated Action.* Amsterdam: John Benjamins.
———. Forthcoming b. "Love, Religion, and the Psychology of Inspiration." Target article for *Philosophy in the Contemporary World.*
———. Forthcoming c. "Spiritual Partnership and the Affirmation of the Value of Being." Target article for special issue of *The Pluralist.*
Ellis, Ralph D., and Natika Newton. 2000. "The Interdependence of Consciousness and Emotion." *Consciousness & Emotion* 1: 1–11.
Eysenck, Hans J. 1957. *The Dynamics of Anxiety and Hysteria.* New York: Praeger.
Feuerbach, Ludwig. 1966. *Principles of the Philosophy of the Future.* Indianapolis: Bobbs-Merrill.
Foucault, Michel. 1972. *The Archaeology of Knowledge.* New York: Harper Colophon.
———. 1980. *The History of Sexuality.* Vol. 1, *An Introduction.* New York: Vintage.
Frank, Thomas. 2004. *What's the Matter with Kansas?* New York: Metropolitan Books.
Freud, Sigmund. 1959. *Beyond the Pleasure Principle.* New York: Bantam.
Fromm, Eric. 1941. *Escape from Freedom.* New York: Holt, Rinehart & Winston.
Gedo, Mary. 1980. *Picasso: Art as Autobiography.* Chicago: University of Chicago Press.

Gendlin, Eugene. 1962. *Experiencing and the Creation of Meaning.* Toronto: Collier-Macmillan.
———. 1971. "A Theory of Personality Change." In *Creative Developments*, edited by Alvin Mahrer. Cleveland: Case Western Reserve University Press.
———. 1973. "Experiential Phenomenology." In *Phenomenology and the Social Sciences*, edited by Maurice Natanson. Evanston, IL: Northwestern University Press.
———. 1980. *Focusing.* Toronto: Bantam.
———. 1992a. "The Primacy of the Body, Not the Primacy of Perception." *Man and World* 25: 341–53.
———. 1992b. "Thinking Beyond Patterns: Body, Language, and Situations." In *The Presence of Feeling in Thought*, edited by B. den Ouden and M. Moen. New York: Peter Lang.
Giorgi, Amadeo. 1971. "Phenomenology and Experimental Psychology." In *Duquesne Studies in Phenomenological Psychology*, edited by Amadeo Giorgi, I, 6–29. Pittsburgh, PA: Duquesne University Press.
Hall, Calvin, and Gardner Lindzey. 1957/1978. *Theories of Personality.* 4th ed. New York: John Wiley & Sons. See esp. chapter 4, "Jung's Analytic Theory."
Haule, John. 1992. *Pilgrimage of the Heart.* Boston: Shambhala.
Hemingway, Ernest. 1956. *A Farewell to Arms.* New York: Bantam.
Heidegger, Martin. 1962. *Being and Time.* New York: Harper & Row.
Horney, Karen. 1937. *The Neurotic Personality of Our Time.* New York: W.W. Norton.
———. 1950/1991. *Neurosis and Human Growth.* New York: W.W. Norton.
Husserl, Edmund. 1969. *Ideas.* London: Collier, 1969.
———. 1962. *Phenomenologische Psychologie.* The Hague: Martinus Nijhoff.
Ibn Hazm. 1953. *The Ring of the Dove.* London: Luzac.
Ibn Khaldoun. 1969. *The Muqaddimah.* Princeton: Princeton University Press.
Johnson, Robert A. 1977. *She: Understanding Feminine Psychology.* New York: Harper & Row.
———. 1986. *Inner Work.* San Francisco: Harper & Row.
———. 1987. *We: Understanding the Psychology of Romantic Love.* San Francisco: Harper & Row.
———. 1991. *Transformation: Understanding the Three Levels of Masculine Consciousness.* San Francisco: Harper.
Jones, Ernest. 1953. *The Life and Work of Sigmund Freud.* New York: Basic Books.
Jung, Carl G. 1961. *Memories, Dreams, Reflections.* New York: Pantheon.
Kauffman, Stuart. 1993. *The Origins of Order.* Oxford: Oxford University Press.
Klein, Melanie. 1975. *Envy and Gratitude.* London: Hogarth Press, English Institute of Psycho-Analysis.
Kohut, Heinz. 1985. *Self Psychology and the Humanities.* New York: W.W. Norton.
Kuhn, Thomas. 1962. *The Structure of Scientific Revolutions.* Chicago: University of Chicago Press.

Lacan, Jacques. 1973. *The Four Fundamental Concepts of Psycho-Analysis.* New York: W.W. Norton.

Langer, Suzanne. 1967/1982. *Mind: An Essay in Human Feeling.* Baltimore: Johns Hopkins University Press.

Lasch, Christopher. 1979. *The Culture of Narcissism.* New York: Warner.

Laudan, Larry. 1990. *Science and Relativism.* Minneapolis: University of Minnesota Press.

Lauer, Quentin. 1958. *Phenomenology: Its Genesis and Prospect.* New York: Harper.

Levinas, Emanuel. 1969. *Totality and Infinity.* Pittsburgh: Duquesne University Press.

Linton, Ralph. 1954. "The Problem of Universal Values." In *Method and Perspective in Anthropology*, edited by R. F. Spencer, 145–68. Minneapolis: University of Minnesota Press.

Marcel, Gabriel. 1965. "Sketch of a Phenomenology and a Metaphysic of Hope." In *Reality, Man and Existence: Essential Works of Existentialism*, edited by H. J. Blackham, 169–205. New York: Bantam.

Maslow, Abraham. 1954. *Motivation and Personality.* New York: Harper & Row.

———. 1968. *Toward a Psychology of Being.* New York: Van Nostrand.

May, Rollo. 1969. *Love and Will.* New York: W.W. Norton.

———. 1975. *The Courage to Create.* New York: Bantam.

Mayer, Nancy. 1978. *The Male Mid-life Crisis.* New York: Doubleday.

Merleau-Ponty, Maurice. 1962. *Phenomenology of Perception.* New York: Humanities Press International.

Miller, Arthur. 1951. *Death of a Salesman.* New York: Bantam.

Miller, Alice. 1981. *The Drama of the Gifted Child.* New York: Basic Books.

Miller, Lawrence. 1990. *Inner Natures: Brain, Self and Personality.* New York: Ballantine.

Monod, Jacques. 1971. *Chance and Necessity.* New York: Random House.

Muller, René. 1991. *The Marginal Self.* Atlantic Highlands, NJ: Humanities Press International.

Nature. Public Broadcasting System, October 29, 1989.

Needham, Joseph. 1956. *Science and Civilization in China.* Vol. 2. Cambridge: Cambridge University Press.

Neihardt, John. 1932/1988. *Black Elk Speaks.* Lincoln: University of Nebraska Press.

Newton, Natika. 1996. *Foundations of Understanding.* Amsterdam: John Benjamins.

Oden, Thomas. 1974. *Game Free: A Guide to the Meaning of Intimacy.* New York: Harper & Row.

Ornstein, Paul. 1991. "Why Self Psychology Is Not an Object Relations Theory: Clinical and Theoretical Considerations." In *The Evolution of Self Psychology*, edited by Arnold Goldberg, 17–30. Progress in Self Psychology, vol. 7. Hillsdale, NJ: Analytic Press.

Ortega y Gasset, José. 1961. *History as a System and Other Essays Toward a Philosophy of History.* New York: W.W. Norton.

Panksepp, Jaak. 1998. *Affective Neuroscience.* New York: Oxford University Press.
Person, Ethel. 1989. *Dreams of Love and Fateful Encounters.* New York: Penguin.
Rank, Otto. 1941. *Psychology and the Soul.* New York: A. S. Barnes.
———. 1950. *Beyond Psychology.* New York: Dover.
Rawls, John. 1971. *A Theory of Justice.* Cambridge: Harvard University Press.
Reik, Theodore. 1945. *Psychology of Sex Relations.* New York: Rinehart.
———. 1963. *Of Love and Lust.* New York: Noonday Press.
Rorty, Richard. 1979. *Philosophy and the Mirror of Nature.* Princeton, NJ: Princeton University Press.
Rougemont, Denis de. 1949. *Passion and Society.* London: Faber & Faber.
Sartre, Jean-Paul. 1969. *The Transcendence of the Ego.* New York: Noonday.
Satir, Virginia. 1967. *Conjoint Family Therapy.* Palo Alto, CA: Science and Behavior Books.
Scheler, Max. 1973. *Formalism in Ethics and Non-formal Ethics of Values.* Evanston, IL: Northwestern University Press.
Searle, John. 1984. *Minds, Brains, and Science.* Cambridge, MA: Harvard University Press.
Sheehy, Gail. 1976/1989. *Passages.* New York: Bantam.
Spence, Janet Taylor, and Kenneth W. Spence. 1964. "Relation of Eyelid Conditioning to Manifest Anxiety, Extraversion and Rigidity." *Journal of Abnormal and Social Psychology* 68: 144–49.
Spitz, R. A., and K. M. Wolf. 1946. "Anaclitic Depression: An Inquiry into the Genesis of Psychiatric Conditions in Early Childhood." In *P.A. Study of the Child II.* New York: International University Press.
Stendhal, Robert. 1947. *On Love.* New York: Liveright.
Trotsky, Leon. 1964. *The Age of Permanent Revolution.* New York: Dell.
Tucker, Robert. 1971. *Philosophy and Myth in Karl Marx.* Cambridge: Cambridge University Press.
Unamuno, Miguel de. 1972. *The Tragic Sense of Life.* Princeton: Princeton University Press.
Von Gulik, Robert Hans. 1974. *Sexual Life in Ancient China.* Atlantic Highlands, NJ: Humanities Press.
Watts, Alan. 1958. *Nature, Man, and Woman.* New York: Vintage.
Westfall, Richard. 1994. *The Life of Isaac Newton.* Cambridge: Cambridge University Press.
Williams, Tennessee. 1947. *A Streetcar Named Desire.* New York: New Directions.
Wilson, Edward O. 1969. *On Human Nature.* Cambridge, MA: Harvard University Press.
Zachar, Peter. 2000. "Child Development and the Regulation of Affect and Cognition in Consciousness: A View from Object Relations Theory." In *The Caldron of Consciousness: Motivation, Affect, and Self-organization,* edited by R. Ellis and N. Newton, 205–22. Amsterdam: John Benjamins.

Index

abstraction of value feelings, 187ff
agape, 32, 197–200, 227–28
alienation, 8
anthropology, 40–42
anxiety, 63–66, 245
Aquinas, Thomas, 22
art, 10, 88–89, 130
Artimus, 147–48
atomistic individualism, 8
Augustine, 208–11, 219ff
authenticity, 9, 31ff
authoritarianism, 81–82, 245
autonomy, 8, 161–63, 175, 227
Averroes (Ibn Rusd), 22

blame, 11, 49, 81, 122, 205, 227ff
Buddhism, 67–68, 76–77

Campbell, Joseph, 22, 117
Camus, Albert, 6, 63
Catharism (see also courtly love), 27, 119–20, 175
Chopin, Kate, 26
Christianity, 115–16, 199–200, 203ff, 227–28
circle of egocentricity, 6–8, 10, 12, 14, 19ff, 126
communitarianism, 212ff
compassion, 2–4, 8, 10–12, 14, 23, 55, 130, 160, 201ff, 227–29
continuous creation, 22

corpus callosum, 238, 245–46
courage, 201ff
courtly love, 113–14, 119–20, 174–75
cults of personality, 158

death, 6, 9, 14, 21, 57, 63ff, 81, 124, 201, 207
deconstruction, 49, 136, 166
depression, 8
derivative transcendent object, 12–13, 128, 180, 182–88, 200, 252
determinism, 195–96, 214–19, 221–22
Dewey, John, 20ff
dualism, 81, 120

ego ideal, 183ff
egoism, 7, 12–14, 165ff, 168–74
embodiment, 40, 45ff, 92–93, 235
erotic love, 3, 6, 9, 19, 26, 29, 51, 78–79, 83–84, 87, 102, 124–25, 127, 137ff, 158
evil, problem of, 81, 202–3, 206–12
evolution, 73
existential condition, 3ff, 16, 63ff, 127, 130
existential crisis, 131–33
extrinsic value. *See* instrumental value
extraversion, 245

feminism, 27, 231ff
fertility religions, 120–21
Feuerbach, Ludwig, 20, 23
free will, 49, 81, 195–96, 201–29
Freud, Sigmund, 3, 34, 57ff
friendship, 151–58
focusing, 43ff
fundamentalism, 10, 17, 21, 37, 73ff, 80ff

Gendlin, Eugene, 43ff, 53–54, 86, 150
Gestalt shift, 46
grasping, 188–97
gratitude, 188–97, 203

hedonism, 95ff, 134, 181, 188ff
Heidegger, Martin, 35, 43, 63ff, 166
hermeneutics, 33ff
hero worship, 158
hope, 68ff
hormones, 237–38
Horney, Karen, 34, 59, 63–65, 74
hubris, 4, 197
humility, 194, 203
Husserl, Edmund, 35, 46, 65ff
hysteria, 245

idealized object image, 183ff
imaginative variation, 37, 46
immanent god, 22
immortality, 9, 14, 24, 49, 68–69, 205
inspiration, 15–16, 50ff
instrumental value, 1–3, 5, 7, 10, 41, 194, 207, 211
intrinsic value, 1–3, 8, 10, 16, 41, 127, 225
introspection, 33ff
introversion, 245
Islam, 211–12

Johnson, Robert, 3, 27ff, 51, 113–14, 123, 125
judgmentalism, 11, 30, 77, 81, 122, 227–28
Jung, Carl, 3, 27ff, 47–48, 91–92, 104–5, 111, 117, 231ff, 244–50
justice, 14, 187–88, 211–12

Klein, Melanie, 194
Kohut, Heinz, 5, 34ff, 50ff, 76, 86, 149, 159–60, 184

Lasch, Christopher, 2–3, 5
Levinas, Emanuel, 4, 9, 63, 105, 198
Lewis, Sinclair, 6

marasmus, 15
Marcel, Gabriel, 64, 68ff
Marcuse, Herbert, 3
Marx, Karl, 20
masks, 144–47, 194
May, Rollo, 51, 63, 117
Merleau-Ponty, Maurice, 35, 65, 86, 233
Miller, Alice, 5, 50ff, 64
myth, 21–22, 73

narcissism, 1–6, 11, 13, 16, 19ff, 78–79, 122–23, 183ff
narcissism, unsuccessful, 1, 2
narcissistic self, 183ff
neurophysiology, 15, 58, 234ff

object relations theory, 4–5, 50–61
Ortega y Gasset, José, 42

phenomenology, 19, 36
postmodern culture, 1–5, 31. *See also* postmodernism
postmodernism, 33ff. *See also* deconstruction, poststructuralism

Index

poststructuralism, 38ff
primary transcendent object, 11–14, 32, 50ff, 85ff, 117ff, 252
psychopathy, 245
psychotherapeutic relationships, 149ff

Rank, Otto, 21, 57, 63, 89–90, 117, 121
realm of the sublime, 29, 93, 181
Reik, Theodore, 3, 4
relativism, 39ff
resentment, 194
Rougemont, Denis de, 3, 27ff, 38, 113–14, 117, 120

Sartre, Jean Paul, 3, 6
secondary transcendent object. *See* derivative transcendent object
self psychology. *See* object relations theory
self-deception, 10, 13–16, 19, 22–24, 31, 57, 74ff, 82, 127, 130, 201, 206, 240
self-organization, 15
self-pity, 9
serial monogamy, 172
sexualization of religious experience, 83–5, 94, 100ff, 119–28, 135, 158
sexual polarity, 32, 47, 91–92, 100–115, 167–68, 231–61

space of empathy, 11, 23, 77ff, 83, 85ff, 122, 136, 137–39, 143, 162, 176
spiritual partnership, 13ff, 32, 85ff, 250–61. *See also* transcendent value experience
spreading effect, 10, 12, 14, 19, 29, 61, 99, 165–200
Stendahl, Robert, 3
stoicism, 109–10, 242
symbiosis, 13, 78, 114, 127, 135, 167–68, 191
symbolization, 10, 29, 40, 57, 79ff, 84, 85–95, 102, 130–31, 147, 190

Tillich, Paul, 22
transcendent value experience, 5–8, 10–14, 15, 50ff, 96–99, 117ff
transformation of consciousness, 131–33, 135, 177, 250–60
Tristan myth, 174–75, 177

Unamuno, Miguel de, 8, 25, 75–76, 133
urban-industrial culture, 4, 82
utilitarianism, 169, 188, 225

victim persona, 4